Retail Depositor and Retail Investor Protection under EU Law

Retail Depositor and Retail Investor Protection under EU Law offers an original perspective on EU financial law in the area of retail investor protection, examining the status of protection awarded by EU law to retail depositors and retail investors in the event of financial institution failure. The analysis of relevant EU law is on the basis of effectiveness and has been elaborated in two levels of comparison. The first comparative approach examines relevant EU law both externally and internally: externally, vis-à-vis relevant international initiatives and developments in the area of financial law, as the latter affect the features and evolution of EU law, and internally by examining relevant instruments of EU law with regard to each other as to their normative structure and content. The second comparative approach also examines the status of retail depositors in relation to that of retail investors under EU law, in the event of financial institution failure, and the relevant legal consequences thereof.

Constantinos Tokatlides is an Attorney at Law based in Athens, Greece. He is also Lecturer in Commercial Law, University of London International LL.B. programme.

Routledge Research in EU Law

Available titles in this series include:

The Governance of the European Union and the Internal-External Nexus
Paul James Cardwell

Towards a System of European Criminal Justice
The Problem of Admissibility of Evidence
Andrea Ryan

The Legal Order of the European Union
The Institutional Role of the European Court of Justice
Timothy Moorhead

The Greening of European Business under EU Law
Taking Article 11 TFEU Seriously
Beate Sjåfjell & Anja Wiesbrock

The Habitats Directive in its EU Environmental Context
European Nature's Best Hope?
Charles-Hubert Born, An Cliquet, Hendrik Schoukens, Delphine Misonne, and Geert Van Hoorick

Global Data Protection in the Field of Law Enforcement
An EU Perspective
Cristina Blasi Casagran

Kadi on Trial
A Multifaceted Analysis of the Kadi Trial
Matej Avbelj, Filippo Fontanelli and Giuseppe Martinico

The Judge and the Proportionate Use of Discretion
A Comparative Administrative Law Study
Sofia Ranchordás & Boudewijn de Waard

European Agencies and Risk Governance in EU Financial Market Law
Paul Weismann

EU Health Systems and Distributive Justice
Towards New Paradigms for the Provision of Health Care Services?
Danielle Da Costa Leite Borges

EU Criminal Law and Policy
Values, Principles and Methods
Joanna Beata Banach-Gutierrez and Christopher Harding

The European Union as an Area of Freedom, Security and Justice
Maria Fletcher, Ester Herlin-Karnell and Claudio Matera

Retail Depositor and Retail Investor Protection under EU Law

In the Event of Financial Institution Failure

Constantinos Tokatlides

Routledge
Taylor & Francis Group
LONDON AND NEW YORK

First published 2017 by Routledge

2 Park Square, Milton Park, Abingdon, Oxfordshire OX14 4RN
52 Vanderbilt Avenue, New York, NY 10017

Routledge is an imprint of the Taylor & Francis Group, an informa business

First issued in paperback 2018

British Library Cataloguing in Publication Data
A catalogue record for this book is available from the British Library

Library of Congress Cataloging-in-Publication Data
Names: Tokatlides, Constantinos, author.
Title: Retail depositor and retail investor protection under EU law : in the event of financial institution failure / Constantinos Tokatlides.
Description: New York : Routledge, 2016. | Series: Routledge Research in EU Law | Includes bibliographical references and index.
Identifiers: LCCN 2016034554| ISBN 9781138655010 (hbk) | ISBN 9781315622835 (ebk)
Subjects: LCSH: Financial institutions--Law and legislation--European Union countries. | Financial services industry--Law and legislation--European Union countries. | Individual investors--Legal status, laws, etc.--European Union countries. | Consumer protection--Law and legislation--European Union countries. | Risk management--Law and legislation--European Union countries.
Classification: LCC KJE2188 .T65 2016 | DDC 346.24/092--dc23
LC record available at https://lccn.loc.gov/2016034554

ISBN: 978-1-138-65501-0 (hbk)
ISBN: 978-0-367-07558-3 (pbk)

Typeset in 10/12 Baskerville MT by
Servis Filmsetting Ltd, Stockport, Cheshire

Contents

Foreword

European Union law has had an extensive, and indeed pervasive, influence in the commercial and consumer laws of the Member States. Its impact, in particular, in the area of financial regulation has been transformative. Since the Commission presented its Financial Services Action Plan in 1998, capital markets and financial services law has become the fastest-growing area of EU law. A host of EU instruments has not only introduced normative standards in virtually every area of financial regulation, but also provided fruitful ground for regulatory experimentation by implementing new supervisory and governance structures. This Europeanisation of financial markets regulation has been one of the key developments in EU and commercial law in the last 20 years.

In the 1998–2008 decade, the harmonisation of capital markets law became a policy priority in recognition of the role of financial markets in job growth and consumer welfare. The coordination of national laws and enhanced EU presence sought to provide a solid legal framework within which a pan-European capital market could develop and thrive. The global financial crisis of 2008 and the ensuing Eurozone crisis led to a shift in policy priorities and new waves of EU measures which broadly fell into two categories: crisis management and law reform initiatives. An array of measures sought to strengthen the regulation of financial institutions and address systemic risk. A further set of instruments pursued the aim of bolstering budgetary discipline and sustaining public finances at government level. In short, EU law has come to regulate extensively both market participants and sovereigns in an intricate, often interwoven, set of rules which spread across the broad area of financial regulation and raise challenges of governance and a plethora of issues in, among others, the fields of constitutional, administrative, banking, and securities law.

Dr Tokatlides's book provides an excellent analysis of some key developments in the changing regulatory landscape. It examines the EU legal framework governing the protection of retail depositors and investors in the event of financial institution failure. In fact, its remit is much broader. In the first part, the book places EU law in the light of international initiatives for more effective financial markets regulation and navigates the reader through the multitude of post-crisis EU measures governing financial institutions and EU agencies. The second part provides an exposition of EU measures governing depositor and investor protection. It examines, among others, the Deposit Guarantee Schemes Directive, the Investor Compensation Schemes Directive, the proposal for a European Deposit Insurance Scheme, the Bank Recovery and Resolution Directive, and the Single Resolution Mechanism. It also addresses the issue of supervisory liability under EU law.

The perspective is ambitious and the analysis systematic and comprehensive. The book traces the development of EU law and the gradual shift in policy objectives from investor protection to the avoidance and management of systemic risk. It discusses the statutory landscape and the case law of the Court of Justice addressing one of the most vexed areas in financial regulation. The parallel analysis of investor and depositor rights adds a breath of fresh air to the bibliography, enlightening theoretical issues and inviting reflection whilst providing a comprehensive guide to the practising lawyer.

One might identify, perhaps, three issues that emerge from the analysis. First, we are witnessing the gradual federalisation of banking law. Banking Union, which is the most complex and far-reaching of the post-crisis initiatives, marks a qualitative difference. It focuses not on substantive harmonisation but on establishing a common supervisory and resolution framework, thus leading to the emergence of a post-internal market governance model. Second, despite its many imperfections, there is, for the first time, a cogent effort to establish a comprehensive framework for the resolution of banking institutions at supranational level. This is accompanied by a realignment of property rights. The common resolution framework, with a view to breaking the vicious circle between banks and sovereigns, changes the default position by providing for depositor bail-in. Whilst depositor participation in bank failure is subject to many safeguards and caveats, the new regime suggests a realignment of the taxpayer–depositor dynamic in the event of a systemic bank failure. Third, the book poignantly places at the centre of analysis the citizen *qua* depositor/investor and, perhaps, displays the relative lack of remedies at their disposal. Whilst the new edifice seeks to bolster financial stability and provide for a more robust financial framework, investor remedies at EU level remain limited. Preventive intervention and public agency action rather than depositor/investor rights are the central pillars.

This book addresses one of the most difficult and complex areas of contemporary EU banking law, and one which gives rise to a host of theoretical and practical issues. It makes a very valuable addition to the bibliography and will be of interest both to practising lawyers and students interested in financial services and bank resolution.

Takis Tridimas
Professor of European Law
King's College London
London 12 September 2016

Preface and acknowledgements

The purpose of this book is to examine the status of protection awarded by EU law to retail depositors and retail investors in the event of financial institution failure. The analysis of relevant EU law is on the basis of effectiveness and has been elaborated in two levels of comparison. The first comparative approach examines relevant EU law both externally and internally: externally, vis-à-vis relevant international initiatives and developments in the area of financial law, as the latter affect the features and evolution of EU law, and internally by examining relevant instruments of EU law with regard to each other as to their normative structure and content. The second comparative approach also examines the status of retail depositors vis-à-vis that of retail investors under EU law, in the event of financial institution failure, and the relevant legal consequences thereof.

This book would not have been completed had I not the continuous support of many people along the way. In particular, I would like to express my gratitude to Professor Takis Tridimas, for his continuous interest and support.

I would also like to thank Professor Rosa Maria Lastra, Professor Andrea Biondi and Professor Mads Andenas for reviewing earlier drafts of parts of this study and for their useful comments.

I would also like to thank the people at Routledge, especially Siobhán Poole, Veronica Morgan and Laura Muir. Also, Rob Gibson and Heather Jones.

My most profound thanks go to my wife, Anna Spertou, for her understanding and encouragement through years of research and writing.

Acronyms and abbreviations

AG	Advocate General
All ER	All England Law Reports
APA	Approved Publication Arrangement
ARM	Approved Reporting Mechanism
BCBS	Basle Committee on Banking Supervision
BIICL	British Institute of International and Comparative Law
BIS	Bank for International Settlements
BoD	Board of Directors
BRR	Bank Recovery and Resolution
BRRD	Bank Recovery and Resolution Directive: Directive 2014/59/EU
CAD	Capital Adequacy Directive
CBD	Consolidation Banking Directive: Directive 2000/12/EC
CCP	Central Counterparty
CDE	*Cahiers de Droit Européen*
CEBS	Committee of European Banking Supervisors
CEIOPS	Committee of European Insurance and Occupational Pensions Supervisors
CESR	Committee of European Securities Regulation
CGFS	Committee on the Global Financial System (BIS)
CJEL	*Columbia Journal of European Law*
CLJ	*Cambridge Law Journal*
CLP	*Current Legal Problems*
CMLRev.	*Common Market Law Review*
CoB	Conduct of Business
CoR	Committee of the Regions (EU)
CPMI	Committee on Payments and Market Infrastructures (BIS)
CRD IV	Capital Requirements Directive IV: Directive 2013/36/EU

CRD IV/CRR	Capital Requirements Directive IV/Capital Requirements Regulation
CRR	Capital Requirements Regulation: Regulation (EU) No 575/2013
CSD	Central Security Depositary
DGS	Deposit Guarantee Scheme
DGSD	Deposit Guarantee Schemes Directive: Directive 94/19/EC
DGSD (Recast)	Deposit Guarantee Schemes Directive (Recast): Directive 2014/49/EU
DIF	Deposit Insurance Fund
DIS	Deposit Insurance System
EBA	European Banking Authority
EBA Regulation	Regulation (EU) No. 1093/2010
EBLR	*European Business Law Review*
ECLR	*European Competition Law Review*
ECU	European Currency Unit
EDIS	European Deposit Insurance Scheme
EEA	European Economic Area
EEC	European Economic Community
EC	European Community/Communities
ECB	European Central Bank
ECHR	European Convention on Human Rights and Fundamental Freedoms
ECtHR	European Court of Human Rights
ECR	European Court Reports
EESC	European Economic and Social Committee
EFTA	European Free Trade Area
ELRev	*European Law Review*
EMI	European Monetary Institute
EMS	European Monetary System
EMU	Economic and Monetary Union
EFSF	European Financial Stability Facility
EIOPA	European Insurance and Occupational Pensions Authority
EP	European Parliament
ESA	European Supervisory Authority
ESCB	European System of Central Banks
ESFS	European System of Financial Supervision
ESFS Regulation	Regulation (EU) No. 1092/2010
ESM	European Stability Mechanism
ESMA	European Securities and Markets Authority
ESMA Regulation	Regulation (EU) No. 1095/2010
ESRB	European Systemic Risk Board
EU	European Union

FCA	Financial Conduct Authority (UK)
FDIC	Federal Deposit Insurance Corporation (US)
FI	Financial Institution
FMI	Financial Market Infrastructure
FSA	Financial Services Authority (UK)
FSAP	Financial Services Action Plan
FSB	Financial Stability Board
FSF	Financial Stability Forum
FSMA	Financial Services and Markets Act 2000 (UK)
FSN	Financial Safety Net
G-7	Group of Seven
G-10	Group of Ten
G-20	Group of Twenty
GATT	General Agreement on Tariffs and Trade
GDP	Gross Domestic Product
G-SIFI	Global Systemically Important Financial Institution
IADI	International Association of Deposit Insurers
IBRD	International Bank for Reconstruction and Development
ICLQ	*International and Comparative Law Quarterly*
ICS	Investor Compensation Scheme
ICSD	Investor Compensation Schemes Directive: Directive 97/9/EC
IFLR	*International Financial Law Review*
IMF	International Monetary Fund
IOSCO	International Organization of Securities Commissions
IPS	Institutional Protection Scheme
ISD	Investment Services Directive: Directive 93/22/EEC
JIBL	*Journal of International Banking Law*
JIBLR	*Journal of International Banking Law and Regulation*
JIBR	*Journal of International Banking Regulation*
JIEL	*Journal of International Economic Law*
JIFM	*Journal of International Financial Markets*
JIFRC	*Journal of International Financial Law and Compliance*
LIBOR	London Interbank Offered Rate
LoLR	Lender of Last Resort
MiFID	Markets in Financial Instruments Directive: Directive 2004/39/EC
MiFID II	Markets in Financial Instruments Directive: Directive 2014/65/EU
MiFIR	Markets in Financial Instruments Regulation: Regulation (EU) No. 600/2014

MJ	*Maastricht Journal*
MLR	*Modern Law Review*
MREL	Minimum Required Eligible Liabilities
MTF	Multilateral Trading Facility
NATO	North Atlantic Treaty Organization
nyr	not yet reported
OEEC	Organisation for European Economic Cooperation
OECD	Organisation for Economic Cooperation and Development
OJ	Official Journal of the E(E)C / EU
OUP	Oxford University Press
OTC	Over The Counter
OTF	Organised Trading Facility
PRA	Prudential Regulation Authority (UK)
RA	Resolution Authority
RRP	Recovery and Resolution Plan
SA	*Société Anonyme*
SEA	Single European Act
SEC	Securities and Exchange Commission (US)
SIFI	Systemically Important Financial Institution
SGP	Stability and Growth Pact
SME	Small and Medium-sized Enterprise
SRB	Single Resolution Board
SRF	Single Resolution Fund
SRM	Single Resolution Mechanism
SRM Regulation	Regulation (EU) No. 806/2014
SRDI Board	Single Resolution and Deposit Insurance Board
SSB	Single Supervisory Board
SSM	Single Supervisory Mechanism
SSM Framework Regulation	Regulation (EU) No. 468/2014
SSM Regulation	Regulation (EU) No. 1024/2013
THDB	Temporary High Deposit Balances
TFEU	Treaty for the Functioning of the European Union
TLAC	Total Loss Absorbing Capacity
US	United States (of America)
WTO	World Trade Organization
YEEL	*Yearbook of European Environmental Law*
YEL	*Yearbook of European Law*

Table of legislation

Directives

Commission communications

Commission recommendations (relevant legislation in brackets)

Commission proposals (relevant legislation in brackets)

Council decisions (relevant legislation in brackets)

European Parliament decisions (relevant legislation in brackets)

European Parliament opinions (relevant legislation in brackets)

INTERNATIONAL

Treaties and other instruments

Basel Committee on Banking Supervision (BCBS)

Financial Stability Board (FSB)

Financial Stability Forum (FSF)

International Association of Insurance Supervisors (IAIS)

International Association of Deposit Insurers (IADI)

Table of cases

ECJ and General Court

EFTA Court

United Kingdom

To my father, Haralampos Tokatlides

1 Introduction

What is the status of protection awarded by EU law to retail depositors and retail investors in the event of financial institution (FI) failure? Who is a considered to be a protected retail depositor or retail investor (financial consumer) in such a case? What is the difference in the protection awarded by EU law to retail depositors vis-à-vis retail investors, and how is it justified? Does EU law in this area provide coherent, predictable and flexible enough rules to allow for the protection of financial consumers? In other words, is it effective? Should it be effective in protecting financial consumers in the event of FI failure – or is its aim only or primarily to protect financial market stability and integrity? If its aim is (also) to protect financial consumers, does EU law confer upon them justiciable rights?

These are the main questions addressed in this study, which can be summarised under the general question: how effective is retail depositor and retail investor protection under the light of EU law in the event of FI failure? To start examining these issues, it would be best to begin from a general survey of the basic underlying concepts of the operation of financial markets.

1.1 The real economy and the financial market – the issue of promises and trust

While there can be a real economy without a financial market, as happened for many centuries, the opposite does not stand. The financial market depends on – and is, or should be, secondary to – the real economy.

The development of complicated forms of exchange in the context of the real economy, forms more complicated than bilateral barter and exchange, has led to the invention on the one hand of currencies, representing or incorporating value, and on the other hand to the provision of services by persons intermediating in the transactions.

Thus, two fundamental forms of promises could be said to have emerged from the growth and refinement of transactions through the ages: the first relates to the medium used as payment in a transaction (concerning the value represented or incorporated in the currency used), and the second to the behaviour of the contracting parties to each other (concerning the execution of the obligations undertaken by the main and any third parties).

The acceptance of such fundamental promises by interested parties is understood as trust – which is thus at the foundation of any transaction.

The complication of the structure of transactions, in terms of media and persons involved, has an exponential effect on the promises provided and thus to the trust required for the transactions to be successfully completed.

In this context, trust in the media used in the transaction, i.e. in the value of the currency or currencies used, is relevant to monetary policy considerations, whereas trust in the execution of obligations by the transacting parties is relevant to market and counterparty considerations. Both have many aspects, including legal, economic and financial, social and behavioural.

Where obligations undertaken have the form of financial instruments, then trust in the financial market, its stability and integrity, is essential not only for transactions to be successfully completed, but also for agreements on transactions to be concluded in the first place.

Financial consumers, i.e. persons not sophisticated in financial transactions, may participate in the financial market in many ways; mainly, financial consumers participate in financial markets as depositors or as investors trusting their money with FIs – and this will be the focus of this study.

Financial consumers participating in the financial market may realise or accept a degree of risk because of the very nature of financial operations, especially in the context of investment services. In this sense, market risk (the risk associated with fluctuation of values, so that profit expectations cannot be guaranteed) under usual market conditions is intrinsic to financial markets.

However, it is possible that the trust expressed by a financial consumer to an FI, or more generally to the financial market, may be disproved in situations where the consumer incurs financial loss for reasons not directly connected to market risk, but because of failure of the FI which is the counterparty of the consumer.

A first issue that emerges then, in particular in relation to the protection awarded to financial consumers in the event of FI failure, is how financial market supervision and regulation is connected to financial consumer protection.

1.2 The reason to regulate and supervise the financial market, and financial consumer protection

Many theories have been advanced for the reason to regulate (in a wide sense) and supervise the financial markets.[1]

1 For an overview, see generally BAMFORD, C. (2015) Principles of International Financial Law, 2nd edition, Oxford: OUP; FERRAN, E. MOLONEY, N., and PAYNE, J. (eds) (2015) *The Oxford Handbook of Financial Regulation*, Oxford: OUP; WYMEERSCH, E., HOPT, K. J. and FERRANINI, G. (eds) (2015) *Financial Regulation and Supervision: A Post-crisis Analysis*, Oxford: Oxford University Press; BRUNNERMEIER, M., CROCKETT, A., GOODHART, C., PERSAUD, A. D., and SONG SHIN, H. (2009) The Fundamental Principles of Financial Regulation, International Center for Monetary and Banking Studies: Geneva; DAVIES, H. and GREEN, D. (2008) *Global Financial Regulation*, Cambridge: Polity Press; WALKER, G. A. (2007) *European Banking Law – Policy and Programme Construction*, Sir Joseph Gold Memorial Series, International

Often, reference is made to the need to achieve market stability (protecting the market from systemic dangers), and individual participant protection, as the *ratio* of financial law.

Regulation of financial markets through state intervention has thus been connected to 'public interest' considerations. Intervention in the public interest has been criticised by 'public choice' theory, which has in turn influenced the development of new theories in favour of the need for state intervention (relevant to 'public interest' notions). According to these 'revised' public interest arguments, the main reasons for regulating financial markets, investment firms and transactions, relate to controlling systemic risk, providing financial stability to the market, and to correcting information asymmetries in the market.[2]

Information asymmetry is regarded as inherent in the financial system, in that certain participants in the financial market will possess less or less important information on certain factors affecting the market than other participants – in particular, financial consumers will be less informed than professionals of the financial markets, and issues arising from information asymmetry may have serious consequences for financial consumers.

Several objectives of financial law and regulation may be identified, including economic development, market competition, integrity and efficiency and combating financial crime.

However, in general it appears valid to support that regulation and supervision of financial markets is primarily connected to 'systemic risk' considerations.

The notion of 'systemic risk' refers to the threat arguably presented to the financial system at large, in the event of a FI collapse, which may have serious repercussions to the whole market, as has happened many times through the centuries.[3]

Thus, traditionally, banks have been regarded as the main source of systemic risk.

They are, in general, understood as inherently unstable, largely due to liquidity risks relevant to maturity transformation, i.e. owing to the fact that banks borrow

Financial and Economic Law, vol. 6, London: British Institute for International and Comparative Law, LASTRA, R. M. (2006) *Legal Foundations of International Monetary Stability*, Oxford: OUP; LLEWELLYN, D. (1999) 'The Economic Rationale for Financial Regulation', *FSA Occasional Papers in Financial Regulation*; *idem* (6–7 July 2006) 'Institutional Structure of Financial Regulation and Supervision: The Basic Issues', World Bank Seminar – Aligning Supervisory Structures with Country Needs, Washington, D.C.; GOODHART, C., HARTMANN, P., LLEWELLYN, D., ROJAS-SUAREZ, L. and WEISBROD, S. (1998) *Financial Regulation – Why, How and Where Now?*, London: Routledge; LASTRA, R. M. (1996) *Central Banking and Banking Regulation*, London: LSE, Financial Markets Group; KAHN, A. E. (1989) *The Economics of Regulation – Principles and Institutions*, 2nd edition, New York: John Wiley; LLEWELLYN, D. (1986) *The Regulation and Supervision of Financial Institutions*, London: Institute of Bankers; STIGLER, G. (1975) *The Citizen and the State: Essays on Regulation*, Chicago and London: University of Chicago Press; POSNER, R. A. (1974) 'Theories of Economic Regulation', *Journal of Economics and Management Science*, vol. 5, no. 2, pp. 335–58.

2 See DAVIES, H. and GREEN, D. (2008) *Global Financial Regulation*, (n. 1), p. 15 *et seq.*; WALKER, G. A. (2007) *European Banking Law – Policy and Programme Construction*, (n. 1), p. 9, n. 22.

3 See, e.g., MUELLER, R. C. (1997) *The Venetian Money Market: Banks, Panics and the Public Debt, 1200–1500*, John Hopkins University Press: London.

short from depositors and lend on a medium- to long-term basis, so that massive deposit withdrawals in a short period may lead to exhaustion of reserves.[4]

In legal terms, at least in the EU legal order, no definition of 'systemic risk' had been issued until recently.[5]

Thus, systemic risk is perceived as a form of financial risk affecting the financial system as a whole, causing disruption to the functions of the financial system which are vital to the operation of the economy, and thus having the potential to cause 'serious negative consequences' for the real economy and, at the EU level, for the functioning of the internal market.

A particular source of systemic risk is a situation where the collapse of FIs affects or leads to the collapse of other FIs, in a chain of reactions. The so-called 'domino effect', in which the failure of one FI leads to the failure of another, until the banking and payments system is led to collapse, has been traditionally regarded as the fundamental reason for rescuing failing FIs – usually banks – by states, by bailing them out, through some form of public funding.

In particular, in relation to the banking sector, the loss of confidence by the public, i.e. by depositors who constitute the basis of retail banking, is strongly connected to the danger of bank collapses.

A wave of withdrawals by retail depositors (a 'bank run') for fear of instability of a bank may lead itself to its collapse, and at the same time cause further 'bank runs', eventually even causing risk to the banking system as a whole.[6]

In this sense, enhancing confidence of the public to the banking system, inter alia by deposit insurance, may be considered as a means to deal with an externality potentially threatening the stability of the system.[7]

The Global Financial Crisis (GFC)[8] has shown that systemic risk to the financial

4 The GFC has shown, as e.g. in the case of the Lehman Brothers collapse, that large investment firms may also cause systemic danger, especially when financial providers in the banking and investment services sectors are closely interconnected; see for analysis reports n. 8 below.

5 Systemic risk has only recently been defined in the EU legal order as 'a risk of disruption in the financial system with the potential to have serious negative consequences for the internal market and the real economy', with the statement that 'all types of financial intermediaries, markets and infrastructure may be potentially systemically important to some degree'. See ESFS Regulation, Article 2 point (c). Cf. CRD, Article 3 point 10.

6 A classic presentation of this argument is found in BAGEHOT, W. (1873) *Lombard Street*, London: Henry S. King & Co. See also THORTON, H. (1802) *An Enquiry into the Nature and Effects of the Paper Credit System of Great Britain*, Reprints of Economic Classics, August M. Kelley: New York, 1965.

7 The potential threat to financial stability presented by uncontrolled damage sustained by individual participants may be perceived as an 'externality' in economic terms to financial market stability, i.e. an external factor which could negatively affect the financial market and which thus has to be taken into account in the regulation of this system. For a definition of 'externality' or 'external diseconomy', see e.g. BANOCK, G., BAXTER, R. E. and DAVIS, E. (1987) *The Penguin Dictionary of Economics*, New York: Penguin.

8 The GFC will be understood, for the purposes of this study, as the banking, financial and economic crisis affecting mostly the US and the EU, commencing in 2007 and continuing until now. For an analysis of the causes and effects of the GFC, see inter alia FSA (March 2009) *The Turner Review. A Regulatory Response to the Global Banking Crisis*, FSA; US Department of the Treasury (2008) *Blueprint for a Modernized Financial Regulatory Structure*, available at www.treasury.

sector may be caused not only by a 'bank run' and deposit withdrawals, but also by lack of funds on interbank markets, withdrawal of credit on money markets, speculative attacks on bank share prices or other share price collapses; and that banking sector stability can be undermined by exposures in more volatile securities, derivatives and other financial instruments,[9] and by the operation of unofficial, unregulated and unsupervised 'shadow banking'.[10]

In the banking sector in particular, systemic risk has (at least until the GFC) been ultimately addressed by the 'Lender of Last Resort' (LoLR) function usually held by the central bank of a state. Operating as the LoLR, the central bank of a state has traditionally been expected to provide liquidity to a failing bank, so as to prevent its collapse and also the eventual systemic danger emanating from

gov/press-center/press-releases/Documents/Blueprint.pdf; US Department of the Treasury, 'Financial Regulatory Reform. A New Foundation: Rebuilding Financial Supervision and Regulation, 2009, available at www.treasury.gov/initiatives/Documents/FinalReport_web.pdf; the 2012 EU *Liikanen Report*, available at http://ec.europa.eu/internal_market/bank/docs/high-level_expert_group/report_en.pdf. According to the *Liikanen Report* analysis, the GFC evolved through five interlinked phases (or 'waves'), which can be summarised as follows: Wave 1: 'subprime crisis phase' (mid-2007 to September 2008), in which investment portfolios collapsed. Wave 2: 'systemic crisis phase' (as of September 2008), in which unprecedented state aid to the banking sector was required as liquidity evaporated. Wave 3: 'economic crisis phase' (as of 2009), in which automatic stabilisers were connected to the recession and fiscal sustainability was imperilled through fiscal stimulus and state aid. Wave 4: 'sovereign crisis phase' (as of 2010), in which bank–sovereign feedback loops raised significant challenges in the context of existing institutional EU framework. Wave 5: 'crisis of confidence in Europe phase' (current). Further on the *Liikanen Report*, Ch. 8 below. For a detailed historical analysis of the initial stages of the GFC, see LYBECK, J. (2011) *A Global History of the Financial Crash of 2007–2010*, Cambridge University Press: Cambridge. For data and policy analysis of the GFC see De HAAN, J., OOSTERLOO, S. and SCHOENMAKER, D. (2012) *Financial Markets and Institutions: A European Perspective*, 2nd edition, Cambridge University Press: Cambridge. See also, generally, KEELEY, B. and LOVE, P. (2010) *From Crisis to Recovery: The Causes, Course and Consequences of the Great Recession*, OECD Insights, OECD Publishing, Paris. See also BEALE, L. (2010) 'In the Wake of the Financial Crisis', *Wayne State University Law School Research Paper Series*, vol. 10-07, July, http://ssrn.com/abstract=1681577; COFFEE, J. (2009) 'What went wrong? An initial inquiry into the causes of the 2008 financial crisis', *Journal of Corporate Law Studies*, vol. 9, no. 1, April, pp. 1–22; WALKER, G. A. (2007) 'Credit crisis: regulatory and financial systems reform', *BJIBFL*, p. 568; *idem* (2009) 'Credit contraction, financial collapse and global recession: pt 1', *BJIBFL*, p. 5 (including a useful timeline of the first stages of the GFC at p. 10); *idem* (2009) 'Credit crisis, Bretton Woods II and a new global response: pt 2', *BJIBFL*, pp. 77–81; BRAITHWAITE, J. P. (2014) 'Law after Lehmans', *LSE Legal Studies Working Papers*, vol. 11, available at http://ssrn.com/abstract=2391148.

9 See WALKER, G. A. (2009) 'Credit crisis, Bretton Woods II and a new global response: pt 2', n. 8, at p. 81. For a discussion on interconnectedness risk and high leverage of derivative transactions, see BLUNDELL-WIGNALL, A. and ATKINSON, P. (2011) 'Global SIFIs, Derivatives and Financial Stability', *OECD Journal: Financial Market Trends*, vol. 2011/1, pp. 167–200.

10 Further, it has been considered that 'shadow banking' (entities and activities involved in credit intermediation outside the regular banking system) may also represent a threat to market stability, depending on the size of relevant transactions: see FSB Report of 27.10.2011 'Shadow Banking: Strengthening Oversight and Regulation, available at www.financialstabilityboard.org/publications/r_111027a.pdf; see also Commission Communication *Shadow Banking – Addressing New Sources of Risk in the Financial Sector*, COM(2013) 614 final, 09.04.2013.

wavering of public confidence to the banking system as a whole, as a result of a not avoided bank collapse.[11]

State intervention to save a bank in distress, using public funds, has thus been used as a last resort mechanism to avoid collapse of the financial sector.

At least until the GFC, the so-called 'too-big-to-fail' approach entailed an understanding that certain FIs were too large in financial volume or too important to fail, or at any extent that owing to their size or importance they would not be allowed to fail, even if state intervention were necessary to save them from collapse. So, the 'too-big-to-fail' concern has been linked to the size of a FI (usually a bank), which has been traditionally considered as a factor for the state not to allow it to fail, since repercussions to market stability have been perceived, at least until the GFC, as analogous to market share of the failing FI. In practice, however, foreseeing whether the failure of one FI, of systemic importance, may lead to distortion of the whole market has proven to be quite difficult.

While the bailing-out of a failing FI protects the institution itself and its clients, and arguably the financial market at large especially when the FI is systemically important, it is an ultimate measure, applied when all else has practically failed. It is a measure to protect depositors and thus ultimately confidence in the financial market, promoting financial stability.[12]

Thus, the existence of a 'financial safety net' (FSN) for financial consumers participating in the financial market has been considered essential, in particular in the direction of enhancing their trust in the financial system, and more specifically in the banking sector.

Such an FSN in the banking sector is considered to include prudential regulation and supervision, LoLR and deposit insurance functions.

Financial consumer protection may take various forms in the context of participation in the financial market, when the consumer is receiving services provided by financial intermediaries, on the basis of available information and by concluding financial contracts.[13]

11 According to the general understanding of the function of the LoLR; this concept has been affected by new proposals and legislation on the bank recovery and resolution regime: see Chs. 3.1, 5, 8 below.

12 See OSTERLOO, S. and De HAAN, J. (2004) 'Central Banks and Financial Stability: A Survey', *Journal of Financial Stability*, vol. 1, pp. 257–73. It has been noted that defining financial stability is difficult: see GOODHART, C. (2004) 'Some New Directions for Financial Stability?', BIS, Per Jacobsson Foundation, Zurich.

13 Such protection relates in particular to the stages of the formation of the decision of financial consumers to participate in the financial market, the selection of appropriate financial contracts taking into account their nature and needs, the conclusion and execution of such contracts, and in general issues relating to the conduct of business by financial intermediaries. Such protection focusing mainly on pre-contractual and contractual issues arising from the participation of consumers in the financial market, and financial intermediation, relates mainly to the problematic of 'information asymmetry' connected to the vulnerability of financial consumers as non-professional financial market participant. Thus it relates in general to consumer protection and to market integrity and efficiency (as in relation to the regulation of prospectus requirements for the public offering of securities by issuers, the regulation of distance marketing and conclusion

A FI may fail either as a result of wider financial market reasons or for reasons more closely connected to its particular circumstances.

In cases of FI failure, financial law may include mechanisms to protect financial consumers in particular *ex post*, in the form of a minimum compensation payable by a third party, usually in the form of a guarantee fund or a compensation scheme managed or supervised by state authorities.[14]

Bailing out FIs by use of public funds has been the object of criticism on 'moral hazard' grounds, i.e. that if the persons in control of an FI or the public have the certainty that a bank will be saved by public funds then they are discouraged to act wisely: managers and shareholders may not take necessary measures to protect the FI from exposure to excessive risks, while financial consumers may not carefully review the financial condition of the FI to protect their position.[15]

With regard to financial consumer protection an important policy question is thus posed, as to the extent and depth of FSN protection.[16]

With regard to FI protection and in particular after the outbreak of the GFC, the same question is posed as to the degree and conditions of rescues.

Thus, systemic protection and moral hazard considerations, among other factors, have led to a reconsideration by financial law theory, international

of financial services contracts, the suitability requirements for the conclusion of certain financial contracts with financial consumers, and others), and ultimately to financial literacy and inclusion considerations.

14 For example, in the US, the Federal Deposit Insurance Corporation (FDIC) was established in 1933, with a view to protect depositors following the bank failures during the Great Depression. Since then, it has intervened in many bank failures; for a historical perspective in US deposit protection, see www.fdic.gov/bank/analytical/index.html. The US Federal Deposit Insurance Act (12 United States Code 1811 *et seq.*, P. L. 81–797) (FDI Act), which constitutes the main legal framework for the operation of the FDIC (see www.fdic.gov/regulations/laws/rules/1000-100.html), provides inter alia that the FDIC may accept applications by banks to be admitted to the Federal Deposit Insurance scheme, which thus become 'insured depository institutions' (FDI Act, Section 5). The FDIC has important powers to monitor insured banks, to impose regulation relevant to deposit insurance, and to withdraw insurance, on certain conditions; see FDI Act, Sections 8 and 18. The deposit insurance mechanism is activated when a bank is closed on account of inability to meet the demands of its depositors; according to FDI Act, Section 11(b), this is 'in any case in which it has been closed for the purpose of liquidation without adequate provision being made for payment of its depositors'. Payment of insured deposits by the FDIC is made 'as soon as possible' and either by cash or by making available to each depositor a transferred deposit in a new insured depository institution in an amount equal to the insured deposit; see FDI Act, Section 11(f)(1). The FDIC may, in its discretion, require proof of claims to be filed and may approve or reject such claims for insured deposits (FDI Act, Section 11(f)(2)). The FDIC is subject to important auditing and reporting obligations (FDI Act, Section 17). A Deposit Insurance Fund operates within the context of the FDIC. See also FDIC (2011) 'The orderly liquidation of Lehman Brothers Holdings Inc. under the Dodd-Frank Act', *FDIC Quarterly*, vol. 5, no. 2, pp. 31–49.

15 See for discussion WALKER, G. A. (2007) *European Banking Law – Policy and Programme Construction*, British Institute for International and Comparative Law (n. 1), Ch. 3, wherein there are further references.

16 See, generally, SCHICH, S. and KIM, B.-H. (2011) 'Guarantee Arrangements for Financial Promises: How Widely Should the Safety Net Be Cast?', *OECD Journal: Financial Market Trends*, vol. 2011/1, pp. 201–35; FSB (2010) 'Reducing the moral hazard posed by systemically important financial institutions', available at www.financialstabilityboard.org/publications/r_101111a.pdf.

organisations and *fora*, as well by states, of the regulatory and supervisory apparatus in case of FI failure.

The contingency where financial distress is transferred from one FI to the other, owing to the interconnectivity of institutions and markets, and to public finances (where bail-out is performed by the use of public funds) and the emerging dangers for systemic stability, have led to new initiatives, including initiatives to isolate distressed FI or markets (so as to control contagion) and also to achieve recovery or orderly resolution of distressed FIs, without affecting the financial market at large.[17]

Such considerations have led to important developments in advanced Western economies with developed financial markets sensitive to systemic risk, such as that of the US which was historically first hit by the GFC.[18]

17 See, e.g., SCHICH, S. and KIM, B.-H. (2013) 'Developments in the value of implicit guarantees for bank debt: The role of resolution regimes and practices', *OECD Journal: Financial Market Trends*, vol. 2012/2, pp. 35–65; HAENTJENS, M. (2014) 'Bank Recovery and Resolution: An Overview of International Initiatives', *International Insolvency Law Review*, (2014/3), pp. 255–70.

18 Although non-EU law is not within the scope of this study, a reference to developments in the USA in relation to the GFC is useful, owing to their importance in relation to overall evolution of financial law after the GFC. The US effort to respond to the GFC has been particularly important, as it has involved a fundamental review of its financial supervisory architecture and reform of its financial law. Among the critical features of the US reform were the enhancement of the deposit insurance regime (see n. 14 above), the introduction of restrictions on proprietary trading by depositary banks and the separation of retail and investment banking. See in general US Department of the Treasury (2008) *Blueprint for a Modernized Financial Regulatory Structure*; Troubled Asset Relief Program (TARP), enacted following the (US) Emergency Economic Stabilization Act of 2008 (EESA; P.L. 11 –343), also known as the *Paulson Plan*; see also, WEBEL, B. (2013) 'Troubled Asset Relief Program (TARP): Implementation and Status' Congressional Research Service, available at www.fas.org/sgp/crs/misc/R41427.pdf; US Department of the Treasury (2009) 'Financial Regulatory Reform. A New Foundation: Rebuilding Financial Supervision and Regulation' (also known as 'Obama Financial Reform Plan'). In relation to the separation of retail and investment banking activities, initially the US Banking Act of 1933 (48 Stat. 162, known as the Glass–Steagall Act, inter alia prohibited commercial banks from engaging in investment activities, and controlled affiliations between commercial banks and investment firms. The Glass–Steagall Act of 1933 was repealed by the Financial Services Modernization Act of 1999 (P. L. 106–102, 113 Stat. 1338, also known as 'The Gramm–Leach–Bliley Act'. Following the GFC, the main elements of the 'Obama Plan' were the consolidation of regulatory agencies and the creation of a new supervisory authority to control systemic risk, the comprehensive regulation of financial markets (including increased transparency of derivatives), consumer protection reforms (including a new consumer protection agency) and strengthened investor protection, tools for financial crises, including a resolution regime complementing the Federal Deposit Insurance Fund to allow for orderly winding down of failing institutions, and a series of measures to increase international standards and cooperation related to accounting issues and credit rating agencies. This was followed by the Dodd–Frank Wall Street Reform and Consumer Protection Act of 2010 (P. L. 101–203, H.R. 4173, available at www.sec.gov/about/laws/wallstreetreform-cpa.pdf). The 'Volcker Rule', as part of the Dodd-Frank Act (H.R. 4173, § 619), aims to control speculative investments by banks (insured depositary institutions, companies controlling them and such company's affiliates and subsidiaries), banks not being permitted to own more than small percentage of the total ownership interest in hedge funds or private equity funds, and being in such cases under disclosure obligations and conflict of interest tests. The 'Volcker Rule' prohibits proprietary trading by commercial

In Europe, EU Member States equally responded to the GFC through national initiatives, in particular in the initial stages of the crisis and as the EU did not have in place at the time the legal and financial apparatus to effectively defend the Euro area and Member States' economies and financial markets.

Measures taken at Member State level in certain cases involved the separation of banking from securities sectors of banks and the 'ring-fencing' of the banking sector.[19]

At the EU level, efforts to combat the GFC which after its initial financial crisis characteristics perceived sovereign debt characteristics necessarily involved close EU and Member State cooperation, and also the conclusion of new intergovernmental agreements.[20]

Among other measures, initiatives to control systemic risk in case of failing FIs have introduced new regulatory and supervisory mechanisms which transfer, to an extent and under certain conditions, the burden of financial rescue of a distressed FI not only to its shareholders, but also to its creditors, and in particular to depositors.

In this context, the traditional 'bailing-out' of banks and generally FIs by the

banks and opts for a different approach to 'ring-fencing' than the *Vickers Report* in the UK; for the latter, see n. 19 below. See also IMF, 'Making banks safer: Can Volcker and Vickers do it?', IMF Working Paper, November 2011.

19 During this period, in the UK an Independent Commission on Banking chaired by Sir J. Vickers was mandated to investigate the causes of the GFC and to propose measures for a reform of the regulation and supervision of the financial sector in the UK. In September 2010, the Vickers Commission issued a paper outlining its preliminary views. In April 2011 it published its Interim Report, and in September 2011 its final report *(Vickers Report)*, available at http://webarchive.nationalarchives.gov.uk/+/bankingcommission.independent.gov.uk. The *Vickers Report* recommended the 'ring-fencing' of retail banking activities, differentiating between 'mandated services' (services that only authorised banks would be allowed to provide, owing to their systemic importance, such as deposit taking from, and the provision of overdrafts to, individuals and SMEs), 'prohibited services' (services that retail, 'ring-fenced' credit institutions should be prohibited to provide, such as any service that would result in a requirement to hold regulatory capital against market risk, or the purchase or origination of derivatives or other contracts which would result in a requirement to hold regulatory capital against counterparty credit risk), and 'ancillary activities' (relating to non-prohibited services provided by a 'ring-fenced' credit institution in order for its efficient operation, such as employing staff or procuring operational infrastructure). Many of the recommendations of the *Vickers Report* were endorsed in the (UK) Financial Services (Banking Reform) Act 2013. On the new financial supervision system in the UK, see WALKER, G. and PURVES, R. (eds) (2014) *Financial Services Law*, 3rd edition, Oxford: OUP; HUDSON, A (2013) *The Law of Finance*, 2nd edition, Sweet & Maxwell: London. For the reaction of EU Member States to the GFC, see KATTEL, R., KREGEL, J. and TONVERONACHI, M. (2015) *Financial Regulation in the European Union*, Abingdon: Routledge, Routledge Critical Studies in Finance and Stability. For France see also FERNANDEZ-BOLLO, E. (2013) 'Structural Reform and Supervision of the Banking Sector in France', *OECD Journal: Financial Market Trends*, vol. 2013/1, pp. 31–38.

20 See Treaty Establishing the European Stability Mechanism (ESM) OJ L91/1, 06.04.2011. The ESM took over responsibilities of the European Financial Stability Facility (EFSF) and the European Financial Stabilisation Mechanism (EFSM). See, generally, OLIVARES-CAMINAL, R. (2012) 'The EU Architecture to Avert a Sovereign Debt Crisis', *OECD Journal: Financial Market Trends*, vol. 2011/2, pp. 167–97.

use of public funds is opposed to this new 'bail-in' approach, which demands strong private sector participation (including to an extent by depositors, as creditors) in the financial loss sustained to allow for the orderly resolution of a failing FI and, arguably, the minimisation of damage to the financial market and to public funds.[21]

While this new resolution mechanism, and the eventuality of bail-in, may be considered as enhancing market discipline and minimising moral hazard and transfer of damage to the public finances, it also appears reasonable to assume that it protects financial consumers who are clients of a failing FI *a priori* less than a bail-out, while it is not clear how it may affect public confidence in the financial system.

Indeed, the *animus contrahendi* of financial consumers to trust banks with their money appears to have been formed on this premise – i.e. that they will not be left financially unprotected by the state or public authorities in general, in case there is risk of the bank failing. Whether this premise is based on a (explicit or implicit) promise is secondary to the understanding of financial consumers.

Moreover, traditionally the financial market has been understood as consisting of three main areas of activity, differentiated in their nature and essential features according to the idiosyncrasy of the institutions participating in them: the banking sector, the investment services sector, and the insurance sector.[22] Each of these sectors has, in turn, also been traditionally understood as consisting of several subsectors. The distinction of categories of financial consumers, into retail depositors and retail investors (and policy-holders), reflects this distinction of financial markets in sectors.

In general, retail investors have been the subject of a lesser degree of protection by financial law in the event of FI failure, apparently because of the perceived lesser importance of investment firms for the stability of the financial market, in terms of systemic risk, as well as perhaps in view of the acceptance of (market) risk by retail investors, who are understood to prefer to enter into more complex and risky transactions than just to trust their money with a bank.[23] This applies also vice versa: retail depositors have not been considered – at least until the GFC and the emergence of the new resolution and bail-in regime – as making an investment decision when selecting which bank to trust their money with.

The interconnection of FIs in the modern nexus of financial transactions at a global level, the emergence of universal banking and of new financial instruments of a complex or hybrid nature have questioned the lines of distinction of the financial market.[24] As the experience of the GFC has proven, this interconnection of the banking and other sectors of the financial market renders contagion possible – and

21 See Chs. 3.1, 5.2, 8.1 below.

22 The two first sectors are more closely related to each other than with the insurance sector.

23 In this sense, both the perception and the nature of (retail) investors appears to have been defined by reference to the notion of what a bank, and respectively a depositor, is traditionally understood to be.

24 E.g. financial consumers investing in highly-rated government bonds may in terms of intention be considered as savers, rather than as investors; on the other hand, as will be discussed, under the

perhaps unpredictable – as systemic risk may be caused also by investment firms or other non-bank FIs.

In consequence, the distinction of the level and conditions of financial consumers' protection in the event of FI failure according to a sector-based analysis is also questioned.

Thus, the developments in financial law as a result of the GFC brings to the fore questions as to whether financial consumer protection may be considered to be an autonomous aim of financial law, and as to the distinction of the legal status of retail depositors vis-à-vis retail investors.

In the context of EU law more specifically, a central question posed relates to the effectiveness of the protection awarded to financial consumers in the event of FI failure.

1.3 The question addressed

The question addressed by this study is on the effectiveness of financial consumer (retail depositor and retail investor) protection under EU law in the event of FI failure. It involves addressing the *ratio* of EU financial law in relation to financial consumer protection and the delineation of retail depositor vis-à-vis retail investor protection.

This question will not be dealt with *in abstracto*, when no specific difficulties have occurred, or on a purely theoretical level, but in a situation where regulation and supervision have already failed, at least in relation to the financial consumer incurring financial loss as a result of FI failure (and not as a result of market risk connected to investment services).

So, it is an *a posteriori* analysis. Indeed, evaluating the effectiveness of protection *in abstracto* and *a priori* appears difficult and inconclusive, as the question then becomes unavoidably large and vague.

The evaluation of the rules under examination will necessitate the exclusion of any presumptions as to their *ratio* and effectiveness, in order to avoid fallacies of presumption – otherwise the present exercise might amount to a *petitio principii*.[25]

Therefore, the question addressed, as presented, will entail not only the examination of the consistency of legal rules provided by an instrument in relation to legal rules provided by other instruments in a hierarchical system,[26] as in the EU legal order, but also the examination of the inner consistency of legal instruments, as well as the interrelation of rules classified horizontally in different

new resolution regime in case of bail-in a retail depositor may be functionally treated as an investor (at least for the amount of deposit beyond the level of coverage by deposit insurance).

25 Aristotle, *Prior Analytics II* xvi 64b28–65a26: see COOK, H. C., TREDENNICK, H. (trans.) (2009) *Aristotle: Categories. On interpretation. Prior Analytics*, Loeb Classical Library No. 325, Harvard University Press: Cambridge, MA.

26 See KELSEN, H. (1960) *Pure Theory of Law*, 2nd edition (translation KNIGHT M., 2009) The Lawbook Exchange: Clark, New Jersey.

areas of EU law, but which are in practice interconnected in the event of FI failure.[27]

Furthermore, the EU legal order, as a system of rules of a supranational organisation, needs in certain aspects to be examined in relation both to work at the international level as well as to the institutional structure of the EU legal order per se and in relation to national legal orders.[28]

Secondary EU legislation produced in the form of Directives (which has been the norm in the case of financial law harmonisation instruments until the GFC) intrinsically takes (or has to take) into account the disparity of national legal orders. The conformity of national transposing measures is relevant to the effectiveness – to the *effet utile* achieved by their application.[29]

Such problematic is further linked to the effectiveness potentially achieved by acting at the EU level in comparison to that potentially achieved by acting at the national level.[30]

The wide context of financial law and the series of issues related directly or indirectly to the question addressed necessitate defining the main terms used in this study, and at the same time delimitating its scope.

27 Indeed, a rule (whether of legislative, administrative or judicial origin) is not produced in vacuum and does not produce its effects in vacuum. It belongs to a group (if not a *corpus*) of rules, the interrelation and interoperability of which has to be examined, in order to evaluate the *ratio* and effectiveness of the legal protection available to retail investors by the legal system *in toto*.

28 See, in general, SCHÜTZE, R. (2015) *European Union Law*, Cambridge: Cambridge University Press; WEATHERILL, S. and BEAUMONT, P. (1999) *EU Law*, 3rd edition, London: Penguin; HARTLEY, T. C. (1998) *The Foundations of European Community Law*, 4th edition, Oxford: OUP; Van RAEPENBUSCH, S. (1998) *Droit institutionnel de l'Union et des Communautés européennes*, 2nd edition, Paris: De Boeck Université; DRUESNE, G. (1996) *Droit et Politiques de la Communauté et de l'Union européennes*, 5th edition, Paris: Presses Universitaires de France; BOULOUIS, B. J. (1993) *Droit institutionnel des Communautés Européennes*, 4th edition, Paris: Montchrestien. See also, generally, ECJ decision of 05.02.1963 in Case 26/62, *NV Algemene Transport- en Expeditie Onderneming van Gend & Loos v Netherlands Inland Revenue Administration* [1963] ECR 1; ECJ decision of 15.07.1964 in Case 6/64, *Flaminio Costa v E.N.E.L.* [1964] ECR 347.

29 Apart from cases where non-conformity may be established in an unambiguous manner (as e.g. in case of the non-transfer of a Directive within the relevant time limit), the determination of non-compliance by a Member State owing to the ineffective transposition of a Directive may be a complex issue. Especially in the case of Directive conform interpretation, an in-depth analysis of the rules of the national order is necessary in order to establish what form the Directive conform interpretation may take and whether and which *a priori* applicable national rules may have to not be applied. See generally ECJ decision of 10.04.1984 in Case 14/83, *Sabine von Colson and Elisabeth Kamann v Land Nordrhein-Westfalen* [1984] ECR 1891; ECJ decision of 14.07.1994 in Case C-91/92, *Faccini Dori* [1994] ECR I-3325, para. 26; ECJ decision of 16.12.1993 in Case C-334/92, *Wagner Miret* [1993] ECR I-6911, para. 20; ECJ decision of 18.12.1997 in Case C-129/96, *Inter-Environnement Wallonie ASBL v Région wallonne* [1997] ECR I-07411; ECJ decision of 27.06.2000 in Joined Cases C-240/98 to C-244/98, *Océano Grupo Editorial and Salvat Editores* [2000] ECR I-4941, para. 30. Also, for discussion of relevant issues, CRAIG, P. (2009) 'The legal effect of Directives: policy, rules and exceptions', *ELR*, vol. 34, no. 3, pp. 349–77; TRIDIMAS, T. (1994) 'Horizontal effect of directives: a missed opportunity', *ELR*, vol. 19, no. 6, pp. 621–36; *idem* (2002) 'Black, white, and shades of grey: horizontality of Directives revisited', *YEL*, vol. 21, pp. 327–54.

30 See e.g. relevant considerations in ECJ decision of 13.05.1997 in Case C-233/94, *Federal Republic of Germany v European Parliament and Council of the European Union* [1997] ECR I-2441.

Defining and delimiting the question addressed

The following definitions and delimitations will apply (except if otherwise noted):
'Bank': the same as 'credit institution'.
'Competent authority': competent Member State financial market regulatory and/or supervisory authority.
'Credit institution': as defined by applicable EU law.
'European law': law issued by the EEC, the EC, or the EU, as a general term. [31]
'EU law': law issued by the EEC, the EC, or the EU.
'Financial Consumer': a retail depositor or a retail investor.
'Financial Institution': a credit institution or an investment firm.
'Financial Institution failure': the situation in which an FI is unable to return money and/or instruments belonging to financial consumers in a definite way. For the purposes of this study, such a situation will be considered to include the situation of a FI when in recovery or resolution process as concerns the position of financial consumers.
'Financial law': the law relating to the activities of credit institutions and investment firms and the relevant sectors.[32]
'Financial market': the banking and investment services sectors.
'Financial services': banking and investment services.
'Fraud': used in a wide sense, as the behaviour of consciously misrepresenting reality to another person with a view to obtaining some form of profit or benefit through such misrepresentation.[33]
'Investment firm': as defined by applicable EU law.
'Misappropriation of funds': used in a wide sense, usurpation of third party's assets.
'Regulation': used in a wide sense to denote rule-making, either by the legislature (in the EU, Council and EP, or Commission following legislative delegation) or by the administration (including agencies and competent authorities) following legislative delegation.
'Securities': the same as investment (services) titles, instruments.
'Tort': in the general meaning of unlawful, delictuous behaviour.[34]

While it is necessary to choose a term to define, for the purposes of this study, the person who participates in the financial market as consumer without having special knowledge and/or experience in financial markets and of financial market transactions, this task becomes complicated by the relevant and in some cases interchangeable terms that have been used by EU and national legislation (in the English language).

31 It does not refer to the legal order of the ECHR.
32 Insurance law does not fall within the scope of this research; insurance firm failures and the relevant issues regarding policyholders' protection will not be examined.
33 Not to be understood as the equivalent legal term and offence described by any national legal order, except if specifically noted otherwise.
34 Does not refer to the identical English law legal term.

Such relevant definitions used by legislation include:

- 'Retail client': used in the MiFID, the term 'retail client', as opposed to 'professional client'.[35]
- 'Professional investor' and 'institutional investors' were used in the ISD.[36]
- 'Small investor': while not defined in EU law, it appears in the ICSD, and rather implies the non-professional and non-specialist investor.[37]

Other relevant terms may be used in various jurisdictions using the English language.

Thus, the terms 'retail depositor' and 'retail investor', or more generally 'financial consumer' will be defined in a functional way: they will signify an individual (natural or legal person) with no professional capacity for participating in the financial market, and no relevant knowledge or experience in participating in the financial market as a (retail) depositor or (retail) investor (with a view to investing his own money or other assets for gain). Such a financial consumer may have either deposited money with an FI (retail depositor) or entered into investment transactions in the financial market ('*stricto sensu* investor'), or may have deposited money or instruments with an FI with a view to entering into such transactions having concluded relevant contracts mandating FIs, even if transactions in financial instruments have not taken place ('*lato sensu* investor').[38]

Legal protection awarded to the financial consumer by EU law in the event of FI failure will be understood to comprise protection provided by legislative, administrative instruments and judicial decisions of the EU legal order.[39]

The focus will be on issues related to the *ex lege* obligation to provide protection, mainly in the form of compensation, to financial consumers in the event of FI failure, taking also into account the problematic relating to competent authorities' non-contractual liability from an EU law perspective.

35 MiFID, Preamble, recital 31 points 11 and 12; Annex II.

36 References to the 'professional nature' of the investor, to 'professional investor' and to 'institutional investor' appeared in the ISD, although no definition of these terms was provided by it; see ISD, Preamble, recital 31; Article 11 (1) and (3), and Article 14(4).

37 See ICSD, Preamble, recitals 4, 5 and 11.

38 The *lato sensu* investor is further to be distinguished from the prospective investor or prospective client, who are persons intending to enter into transactions in the financial market but who have not necessarily proceeded to a relevant act (such as depositing money and/or instruments with an FI with a view to entering into transactions in the financial market).

39 Protection offered in the context of extrajudicial procedures, whether compulsory or not, or in the context of mediation and alternative dispute resolution procedures will not be examined, and any relevant references will be in the margin of the analysis of other issues. The same applies to protection offered in the context of law of obligations, including rules on pre-contractual or contractual obligations and relevant contractual clauses, and case law. Also, financial consumer protection against the failing FI, the persons directing it, and relevant matters and claims, do not fall within the scope of this study. In the same direction, issues relating in general to financial consumer protection which are connected to financial damage incurred by the consumer but not as a result of FI failure (such as e.g. issues connected to market risk or bad or wrong execution of orders, bad financial advice, breach of CoB rules by the intermediary, etc.) will not be examined.

In this direction, research will take into account developments at the wider international and EU levels, attempting to understand their *ratio* and assess their dynamic, as they relate to the subject under investigation.

Analysis will follow a deductive approach, commencing with the general *ratio* and features of initiatives at the international level, and then proceeding to the examination of relevant EU law.

Criteria and methodology

Protection awarded under EU law will be examined and assessed on the basis of the effectiveness of the available legal system as a whole. The notion of effectiveness is widely used and understood at various levels and in various contexts by jurisdictions, while it also constitutes a general principle of EU law.[40]

The European law general principle of effectiveness is connected to the rules of primacy and direct effect of European law, in that European law has to produce a useful effect *(effet utile)*.[41]

The notion of effectiveness has progressed as the European legal order has evolved, the case law of the ECJ having an important role in its development;[42] it refers not only to the effective protection of rights emanating from the EU legal order, but more specifically to the effective invoking and enforcement of EU law in national courts, thus relating also to the fundamental right of judicial protection as also protected under the ECHR.[43]

40 See, among many, TRIDIMAS, T. (2007) *The General Principles of EU Law*, 3rd edition, Oxford: OUP; BERNITZ, U. and NERGELIUS, J. (eds) (2005) *General Principles of European Community Law*, Lund: Lund University Press; GROUSSOT, X. (2005) *Creation, Development and Impact of the General Principles of Community Law: Towards a Jus Commune Europium*, Lund: Lund University Press; USHER, J. A. (1998) *General Principles of EC Law*, European Law Series, Edinburgh: Longman; PAPADOPOULOU, R. E. (1996) *Principes Généraux du Droit et Droit Communautaire*, Bruxelles: Bruylant; BOULOUIS, B. J. (1993) *Droit institutionnel des Communautés Européennes*, 4th edition, Paris: Montchrestien; ARNULL, A. (1990) *The General Principles of EEC Law and the Individual*, Leicester: Leicester University Press. Various classification systems of general principles of EU law have been suggested by theory. According to Professor Tridimas, 'the term general principles may be reserved for fundamental propositions of law which underlie a legal system and from which concrete rules or outcomes may be derived'; (above), p. 1. Further, Professor Tridimas proposes a classification of principles as (a) principles which derive from the rule of law, and (b) systemic principles which underlie the constitutional structure of the Community and define the Community legal edifice; ibid., p. 4 *et seq*. Professor Boulouis classifies principles as (a) general principles common to the law of Member States, (b) principles inherent in every organised legal system, and (c) principles deriving from the nature of the Communities; (above), p. 208 *et seq*.

41 See e.g. ECJ decision of 05.03.1996 in Joined Cases C-46/93 and C-48/93, *Brasserie du Pêcheur SA v Bundesrepublik Deutschland and The Queen v Secretary of State for Transport, ex parte Factortame Ltd and Others* [1996] ECR I-1029, at para. 95.

42 For a presentation of the historical evolution of the principle of effectiveness in EU law, see TRIDIMAS, T. (2007) (n. 40), p. 420 *et seq*.

43 For a discussion on effective protection of rights in the EU legal order and of the interrelation between effective protection of rights and the general principles of EU law, see, generally, SCHÜTZE, R. (2015) European Union Law, (n. 28), pp. 343–469; WARD, A. (2007) *Judicial Review and the Rights of Private Parties in EU Law*, 2nd edition, Oxford: OUP; Van GERVEN, W.

The principle of effectiveness is further connected to the principle of equivalence (or non-discrimination), which demands that rights emanating from EU law are equally protected in the national legal order as domestic rights. The two principles are interrelated, as EU law is integrated into the national law of remedies.[44] It is the obligation of 'Community loyalty'[45] that has been considered by the ECJ as posing an obligation to national authorities, including national Courts, to provide full and effective protection of EU rights;[46] this involves not only substantive rules but may also include national rules of procedure.[47]

This study does not intend to explore in depth the complicated issues arising from the notion of effectiveness, as it has evolved through the case law of the ECJ, and as it may be relevant to individual protection in the area of financial services.

Instead, for the purposes of this study the criterion of effectiveness will be understood in a wide sense as the condition of providing for the useful effect of EU law in practice.[48]

In this approach, effectiveness is linked as an emanation of supremacy in practice to all applicable rules and principles of EU law, as a legal system; in this sense, specific issues relating to other general principles, such as legal certainty or proportionality, may be identified in the course of the examination of the subject matter of this study, but they will be understood as ultimately relating to the useful interpretation and application of EU law.

In order to proceed to this examination, it will first be necessary to identify the *ratio* and aim of applicable EU law, first investigating its inner consistency, so as to

(2000) 'Of rights, remedies, and procedures', *CMLRev*, vol. 37, Issue 3, pp. 501–36; RUFFET, M. (1997) 'Rights and remedies in European Community law: a comparative view', *CMLRev*, vol. 34, Issue 2, pp. 307–36; SZYSZCZAK, E. (1996) 'Making Europe more relevant to its citizens: effective judicial process', *ELR*, vol. 21, pp. 351–64.

44 For discussion, see TRIDIMAS, T. (2007) *The General Principles of EU Law*, (n. 40), p. 423.

45 TEU, Article 4(3).

46 See e.g. ECJ decision of 19.11.1991 in Joined Cases C-6/90 and 9/90, *Andrea Francovich and Danila Bonifaci and Others v Italian Republic* [1991] ECR I-5357, at para. 36.

47 See e.g. ECJ decision of 25.07.1991 in Case C-208/90, *Theresa Emmott v Minister for Social Welfare and Attorney General* [1991] ECR I-; ECJ decision of 14.12.1995 in Case C-312/93, *Peterbroeck, Van Campenhout & Cie SCS v Belgian State* [1995] ECR I-4599; ECJ decision of 02.12.1997 in Case C-188/95, *Fantask A/S and Others v Industriministeriet (Erhvervsministeriet)* [1997] ECR I-06783; ECJ decision of 14.12.1995 in Case C-430/93, *Jeroen van Schijndel and Johannes Nicolaas Cornelis van Veen v Stichting Pensioenfonds voor Fysiotherapeuten* [1995] ECR I-04705; ECJ decision of 16.05.2000 in Case C-78/98, *Shirley Preston and Others v Wolverhampton Healthcare NHS Trust and Others and Dorothy Fletcher and Others v Midland Bank plc* [2000] ECR I-3201; ECJ decision of 01.12.1998 in Case C-326/96, *B.S. Levez v T.H. Jennings (Harlow Pools) Ltd* [1998] ECR I-07835. For discussion see SCHÜTZE, R. (2015) European Union Law, (n. 28), pp. 394–426; LENAERTS, K. (2007) 'The rule of law and the coherence of the judicial system of the European Union', *CMLRev*, vol. 44, issue 6, pp. 1625–59; STEINER, J., WOODS, L. and TWIGG-FLESNER, C. (2006) *EU Law*, 9th edition, Oxford: Oxford University Press, pp. 170–82; Van GERVEN, W. (2000) 'Of rights, remedies, and procedures', (n. 43). KAKOURIS, K. (1997) 'Do the Member States possess judicial procedural autonomy?', *CMLRev*, vol. 34, pp. 1389–412.

48 Cf. ECJ decision of 30.09.2003 in Case C-224/01, *Gerhard Köbler v Republik Österreich* [2003] ECR I-10239, at para. 33.

consider in turn how the structure and content of relevant rules may be assessed in terms of effectiveness.

The application of effectiveness as a criterion for the evaluation of the question of research further relates to the methodology applied to treat it. The determination of research methods suitable for a specific research project depends not only on the nature of the research question, but also on the nature of the available data, which ultimately determine the structuring of the research. Thus, this study attempts to analyse its subject matter at a normative level, from a doctrinal point of view. It does not aspire to provide any definitive understanding of its subject matter, but only to make a contribution in the examination of the relevant issues raised.[49]

It is structured in two main parts: in the first, the question of the aim of financial law is addressed, in relation to financial consumer protection in the event of FI failure. The perceptions as to the need to protect financial consumers prior to the GFC and its effect on this matter are examined first at the international level, and then at the EU level.

In the second part of the study, the protection of financial consumers is examined in the context of the particular mechanism to provide compensation in the event of FI failure, also taking into account the question of judicial protection on the ground of rights conferred to financial consumers by EU law.

This study refers to law as stated on 31 December 2015. The factual background refers to the same period.

49 The bibliography is not comprehensive, but general, taking into account the nature of the subject treated. Electronic sources referred to were last accessed on 26 March 2016. The pronouns 'he/him' are used throughout this study for practical reasons as equivalent to 'she/her'.

Part I

The double aim of protecting financial consumers and the stability of the markets in the context of financial institution failure

2 International initiatives on financial law and financial consumer protection prior to the GFC

From economic externalities to legal rules

Introductory note

International financial law is connected to the circulation of capital, as well as of services, on an international scale.[1]

Many important developments in international financial law have occurred following international financial crises, such as the Great Depression (1928),[2] the destruction of European economies as a result of the Second World War,[3] the collapse of the Bretton Woods agreement (1973),[4] or the current financial crisis (since 2007).

1 The term 'international financial law' strictly interpreted refers to legally binding provisions, as emanating from international, bilateral or multilateral treaties. However, for the purposes of this study, developments on the international level which do not have legally binding effect are important, i.e. the work, proposals and recommendations of international organisations which are not legally binding ('soft law') but have been very influential to the development of EU and national laws. These are as a whole referred to as international initiatives. For a general review of international financial regulation and the role of international soft law in its formation before the GFC, see ALEXANDER, K., DHUMALE, R. and EATWELL J. (2006) *Global Governance of Financial Systems: The International Regulation of Systemic Risk*, Oxford: OUP. For an overview of international financial regulation before the GFC, see BRUNNERMEIER, M., CROCKETT, A., GOODHART, C., PERSAUD, A. D. and SONG SHIN, H. (2009) *The Fundamental Principles of Financial Regulation*, International Center for Monetary and Banking Studies: Geneva; WOOD, P. R. (2007) *Regulation of International Finance*, London: Sweet & Maxwell.

2 The Bank for International Settlements (BIS) was established in 1930 under Swiss law; see www.bis.org.

3 The Organisation for European Economic Co-operation (OEEC) was established in 1948 in order to organise the economic revival of Europe on the basis of the US-financed Marshall Plan. In 1961 the Organisation for Economic Co-operation and Development (OECD) replaced the OEEC. See www.oecd.org.

4 For a discussion of the Bretton Woods Agreement of 1944, and of the world financial system that it organised, providing for the establishment of capital controls and fixed (and adjustable) currency exchange rates, and establishing the IMF, the IBRD and the GATT, see LASTRA, R. M. (2015) *International Financial and Monetary Law*, 2nd edition, Oxford: OUP; FRASER, R. and LONG, C. (1992) *The World Financial System*, Harlow: Longman; HOOKE, A. W. (1982) 'The International Monetary Fund – Its Evolution, Organization and Activities', Washington, D.C., IMF Pamphlet Series No. 37; WILLIAMSON, J. (1977) *The Failure of World Monetary Reform 1971–1974*, New York: New York University Press.

It will be useful, then, to first examine certain selected, important international initiatives on banking law, and then to proceed to the examination of relevant initiatives on investment services law, prior to the global financial crisis (GFC), under the scope of this study, as they affect financial consumer protection, in particular in the event of financial institution (FI) failure.

2.1 International initiatives on banking law

Modern banking, international finance and regulation have always been strongly interconnected.[5]

The Basel Committee on Banking Supervision (BCBS) has been established as one of the most important financial *fora* for banking regulation.[6] One of its main aims of is the protection from systemic risk. In this respect, the BCBS has proposed a series of rules on bank prudential regulation and supervision, in particular with regard to capital adequacy.

In 1975, the BCBS issued a Concordat which related to the responsibilities of home- and host-state supervisors.[7] In 1988, it issued the First Basel Accord on capital adequacy (referred to as Basel I). This Accord was amended in 1996 by the Amendment to the Basel Capital Accord (referred to as the Market Risk Amendment), which related to capital adequacy in case of certain market risks arising from banks' trading in certain financial instruments. These amendments proposed a capital adequacy methodology to be used by FIs (banks, investment firms and others). The First Basel Accord was revised in 2004, after long consultations, by the Second Basel Accord (referred to as Basel II).[8] Following the GFC, the BCBS proposed in December 2010 the Third Basel Accord (Basel III), regarding capital requirements, which was revised in June 2011; with regard to liquidity

5 For a historical and political economy discussion of financial markets development, see VALDEZ, S. and MOLYNEUX, P. (2013) *An Introduction to Global Financial Markets*, 7th edition, Basingstoke: Palgrave MacMillan. For a discussion of international financial law, with focus on money and payment functions, see BAMFORD, C. (2015) *Principles of International Financial Law*, 2nd edition, Oxford: OUP; LASTRA, R. M. (2015) *International Financial and Monetary Law*, 2nd edition, (n. 4); See also GORTSOS, C. (2012) *Fundamentals of Public International Financial Law: International Banking Law within the System of Public International Financial Law*, Baden-Baden: Nomos Verlag; PROCTOR, C. (2010) *The Law and Practice of International Banking*, Oxford: OUP; SCOTT, H. S. (2010) *International Finance*, 17th edition, New York: Foundation Press; WOOD, P. R. (2008) *The Law and Practice of International Finance*, London: Thomson/Sweet & Maxwell; *idem* (2007) *Regulation of International Finance*, (n. 1).

6 The BCBS was established in 1974 by the G-10 as a Committee on Banking Regulations and Supervisory Practices (later renamed as the BCBS) operating within the framework of the BIS. Its establishment is connected to questions relating to the responsibility for banking supervision especially in cross-border transactions, following the collapse in 1974 of the Bankhaus Herstatt Bank; for an analysis, see BCBS (2004) 'Bank Failures in Mature Economies', BCBS Working Paper No. 13, available at www.bis.org/publ/bcbs_wp13.pdf. See also GOODHART, C. (2011) *The Basel Committee on Banking Supervision: a history of the early years, 1974–1997*, Cambridge: Cambridge University Press.

7 Available at www.bis.org/publ/bcbs00a.htm.

8 See www.bis.org/bcbs/basel3.htm.

requirements, reform measures were proposed in 2013 and 2014 by Basel III seeking to strengthen the regulation, supervision and risk management of the banking sector, mainly by proposing measures to enhance capital adequacy and to control excessive leveraging.

In relation to supervisory standards of worldwide application, the Basel Committee has elaborated the *Core Principles of Banking Supervision*, adopted in 1997, revised in 2006,[9] and further revised in 2012.[10]

Further, the BCBS published in 1999 a report on *Core Principles Methodology*, which was also updated in 2006, as part of the *Core Principles for Effective Banking Supervision* review.[11]

Although the BCBS initiatives have legally non-binding character, they have exercised great influence on the formation and development of international financial law and regulation, and further to European financial law and regulation.

As noted in the Introduction, the main form of *ex post* protection of financial consumers in the event of FI failure which dates back to the Great Depression is that of payment of compensation by relevant funds, providing deposit insurance.

In relation to the protection of financial consumers in the form of deposit insurance, the BCBS has noted the importance of deposit guarantee systems for the protection of market stability. BCBS proposals, especially regarding the form of depositor protection in case of bank collapses, are relevant in particular to systemic risk control.

The BCBS has noted in relation to depositor insurance systems, that '[p]rovided such a system is carefully designed to limit moral hazard, it can contribute to public confidence in the system and thus limit contagion from banks in distress'.[12]

In the area of deposit insurance, a relevant Study Group was set up in 1999 by the Financial Stability Forum (FSF).[13]

The findings of this study were the basis of the research undertaken by the Working Group on Deposit Insurance established next by the FSF in 2000.

The efforts of this Working Group, which took the form of international guidance,[14] led to the issuing of guidance on deposit insurance systems by the FSF in 2001, and to the creation of the International Association of Deposit Insurers (IADI) in 2002.[15]

It is useful to take note of the main findings of this guidance.

9 Available at www.bis.org/publ/bcbs129.htm.

10 Available at www.bis.org/publ/bcbs230.pdf.

11 Available at www.bis.org/publ/bcbs130.htm. Now part of the 2012 *Core Principles for Effective Banking Supervision*.

12 See the 2006 BCSB *Core Principles for Effective Banking Supervision* at para. 15. Cf the 2012 BCBS *Core Principles for Effective Banking Supervision* at para. 52.

13 The FSF was established in 1999 by the G-7 with a view to promote reform of international financial regulation. It was succeeded by the FSB: see Ch 3 (n. 12).

14 See FSF (2000) *International Guidance on Deposit Insurance – A Consultative Process*, available at www.fsb.org/wp-content/uploads/r_0006.pdf.

15 The IADI was established under Swiss law as a non-profit organisation and is based in Basel. See www.iadi.org.

The 2000 FSF Guidance for developing effective deposit insurance systems

By its 2000 Guidance,[16] the FSF provided directions to states interested in the introduction of effective explicit limited-coverage insurance systems.

According to the FSF, '[t]he principal objectives of a deposit insurance system are to contribute to the stability of a country's financial system and to protect less-financially-sophisticated depositors from the loss of their deposits when banks fail'.[17]

In discussing policy issues relevant to deposit insurance, the FSF Guidance noted the implicit versus explicit deposit protection dilemma and suggested that the latter is preferable, 'if it clarifies the authorities' obligations to depositors and limits the scope for discretionary decisions that may result in arbitrary actions'.[18]

Further, it noted that moral hazard, linked to excessive risk taking either by banks or by those receiving the benefit of protection from failure, can be mitigated inter alia 'by market discipline exercised by shareholders as well as by larger creditors and depositors who are exposed to the risk of loss from the failure of a bank'.[19]

However, the FSF Guidance noted that for market discipline to be effective, information must be accessible and understandable by the public, for assessment of risks to be possible.[20]

Observing that an effective deposit insurance system contributes to the stability of a financial market, by strengthening depositors' confidence, the FSF Guidance clearly stated that deposit insurance 'is not designed to protect banks from failing'.[21]

Instead, the FSF noted, '[t]he provision of deposit insurances relieves insured depositors of the difficult task of monitoring and assessing the conditions of banks and their asset quality'.[22]

Indeed, it appears reasonable to assume – as well as difficult to confirm in practice – that where deposit insurance mechanisms are in place and are considered effective by depositors, depositors holding covered deposits (i.e. deposits for which

16 Available at www.fsb.org/wp-content/uploads/r_0109b.pdf.

17 Ibid., pp. 4, 12.

18 Ibid., p. 9.

19 Ibid., p. 9. The ways to mitigate moral hazard include, according to the FSF Guidance, good corporate governance and sound risk management of banks, effective market discipline, strong prudential regulation and supervision, and laws. The design of deposit insurance systems can also mitigate moral hazard (by placing coverage limits, excluding certain categories of depositors, using co-insurance, using differential or risk-adjusted premium assessment systems, early intervention and early closure of distressed banks to minimise risk of loss, applying personal liability measures against responsible persons and others); ibid., pp. 9–11.

20 The FSF Guidance did not extend its analysis on this issue, but noted that in this direction 'sound accounting and disclosure regimes are required, as well as ongoing attention to a bank's soundness by rating agencies, market analysts, financial commentators and other professionals'; ibid., p. 10. See also ibid., pp. 14–15, 21.

21 Ibid., p. 12.

22 Ibid.

they may claim compensation in case of FI failure) will not be as vigilant on the status of the bank they have trusted their assets with since they will consider their deposits safe.

Thus, at least for the amount covered by deposit insurance (retail) depositors will not be incentivised to proceed to an in-depth survey and assessment of the status of the bank – even if relevant information was available, accurate and understandable by (retail) depositors.

The FSF Guidance noted that deposit insurers' mandates may range from narrow 'pay-box' functions (to provide payments to depositors after a bank failure) to broader 'risk-minimiser' functions (including controlling entry and exit from deposit insurance systems, conducting examinations of banks, providing financial assistance to resolve failing banks in order to minimise deposit insurer losses).[23]

Furthermore, the FSF Guidance noted that when FSN functions are assigned to different organisations, clarity of mandates and accountability issues may rise; thus information sharing, allocation of powers and responsibilities and coordination between different organisations need to be addressed in a clear and explicit manner by applicable law.[24]

On the crucial issue of what is defined as a covered (insured) deposit, the FSF Guidance notes that '[p]olicymakers should define clearly in law or by private contract what is an insurable deposit';[25] thus, according to the FSF, there are no such features of a deposit that, by their nature, render it insurable but such designation appears to be rather considered as a policy option.

Indeed, according to the FSF Guidance, policy options apply to deposit insurance both *ratione materiae* and *ratione personae*: the coverage of deposits 'or deposit-like products' offered by non-bank FIs depends on policy objectives regarding avoidance of competitive distortion among FIs offering similar products, and application of prudential and regulatory rules to all institutions offering such products enhancing the stability of the financial system. However, where stability of the financial market does not appear dependent on such non-bank institutions and they are subject to different regulatory and supervisory rules, they may be excluded from deposit insurance (and subject to special protection schemes for them).[26] Moreover, the persons protected by deposit insurance systems may not include depositors deemed capable of ascertaining the financial condition of a bank and exerting market discipline such as banks, government bodies and professional investors.[27]

Ultimately, the FSF Guidance observed the complicated issues arising out of the interconnection between depositor ranking, deposit insurance and liquidation, which are to be resolved by applicable law formulated according to national policies and priorities.[28]

23 Ibid., p. 18.
24 Ibid., p. 20.
25 Ibid., p. 24.
26 Ibid., p. 23.
27 Ibid., p. 24.
28 Ibid., p. 39.

The FSF Guidance included in total 20 guidance headings addressed to states, providing a concise and critical review of the status of deposit insurance in the majority of jurisdictions globally, as at the time of its issuance.

It emerges, in our view, that deposit insurance at a global level, and in effect the overall structure of the FSN at that time, reflected the status of the banking sector and the policy choices and practical arrangements of the time on the basis of a sector-based approach, according to which systemic risk was intrinsic to the banking sector.

2.2 International initiatives on investment services law

Important to the development of international investment services law has been the work of the International Organization of Securities Commissions (IOSCO),[29] issuing proposals with a view inter alia to develop, implement and promote 'internationally recognized and consistent standards of regulation, oversight and enforcement in order to protect investors, maintain fair, efficient and transparent markets, and seek to address systemic risks'.[30]

In relation to the complicated issue of client asset protection, prior to the GFC the IOSCO published in 1996 a Report of its Technical Committee, which explained the necessity for client asset protection and proposed certain recommendations, in the form of general principles and specific guidelines for the protection of client assets in insolvency, as well as in relation to particular types of client assets.[31]

The 1996 IOSCO Report on Client Asset Protection

In defining 'client assets', the IOSCO included both client money, as well as client securities and positions.[32]

Discussing the reason to protect client assets, the IOSCO proposed that '[t]he ultimate objective of client asset protection is to enhance investor protection and public confidence in financial markets'.[33]

Focusing on insolvency of investment firms, the IOSCO noted the danger of conflict arising between general creditors of the insolvent firm and investors, and the differentiation of the responses to this issue by national legal orders.[34]

The resulting variety of legal mechanisms to address the issue of client asset protection was interpreted by the IOSCO as resulting inter alia from public

29 IOSCO was established in 1983 as a 'global cooperative body' (see www.iosco.org).

30 See http://iosco.org/about. It is noted that investor protection aims do not appear in IOSCO members' objectives before the year 2009; see e.g. IOSCO (2009) *Annual Report 2009*, at www.iosco.org/annual_reports/annual_report_2009/; IOSCO (2008) *Annual Report 2008*, at www.iosco.org/annual_reports/annual_report_2008/.

31 Available at www.iosco.org/library/pubdocs/pdf/IOSCOPD57.pdf.

32 Ibid., p. 6.

33 Ibid., para. 5, p. 7.

34 Ibid., pp. 7–8.

policy underlying insolvency law, the importance given to the protection of individual investors or to overall market integrity, and to differing legal concepts and requirements.[35]

In particular, in relation to the issue of the dual aim of financial law (individual protection versus protection of the financial market), the IOSCO considered that this amounts to 'an aspect of public policy which may differ between jurisdictions', and while both are important in many jurisdictions, the balance of emphasis on them may differ per jurisdiction.[36]

In the mechanisms available to national legal orders in order to protect client assets, the IOSCO included the different legal treatment of client assets (preferential creditor status awarded to clients where their assets are not segregated from those of the firm, or mechanisms to segregate clients' assets from the firm), compensation of clients who sustain losses as a result of insolvency, and other measures (such as insurance).[37]

The IOSCO Report made brief reference to compensation, as a mechanism of client asset protection, noting the differentiation in various compensation regimes and including in the listed disadvantages of compensation schemes that '[t]hey impose a cost on firms which are not likely to fail, although proponents of compensation schemes contend that all firms benefit from the increased confidence which such schemes create in markets'.[38]

Importantly, the IOSCO Report referred to both the issue of client asset protection in the sector of investment services vis-à-vis the banking sector, and also in relation to the issue of the subject of (retail) investor protection.

In relation to the first issue, the IOSCO marked the importance of selection of custodians in terms of client asset protection, especially when a bank is selected as custodian by an investment firm.[39] Short reference was also made to the case where a bank acts as a broker, the IOSCO Report mentioning in this regard that, '[w]here a bank receives money from customers in the course of undertaking investment services business, it will usually hold these funds as deposits rather than as client money, and banking protections will apply to these funds',[40] without entering into a discussion of the two regimes, investment services vis-à-vis banking.

In relation to the second issue, relating to the subject of investor protection rules, the IOSCO Report appeared to be proposing that it depends on the aim of financial law; according to the Report, '[i]f client asset protection is deemed to be an important factor in overall market confidence and integrity and in facilitating the transition of funds from and the isolation of risk to a failing firm, some might argue that such protection should apply regardless of the status of the client'.[41]

However, the IOSCO Report did not discuss this issue further.

35 Ibid., para. 10, p. 8.
36 Ibid., para. 11, p. 8.
37 Ibid., pp. 13–16.
38 Ibid., para. 48, p. 17.
39 Ibid., paras 56–63, pp. 20–23.
40 Ibid., para. 67, p. 25.
41 Ibid., para. 65, p. 24.

The 1998 IOSCO Objectives and Principles of Securities Regulation

Later, in 1998, the IOSCO issued a document on the *Objectives and Principles of Securities Regulation*.[42]

In this, IOSCO categorised 30 principles of investment services law, on the basis of three objectives, stated to be the protection of investors; ensuring that markets are fair, efficient and transparent; and the reduction of systemic risk, maintaining that these objectives form a basis for an effective system of securities regulation.[43]

According to the IOSCO, '[i]nvestors should be protected from misleading, manipulative or fraudulent practices, including insider trading, front running or trading ahead of customers and the misuse of clients' assets'.[44]

Beyond these issues, investor protection was significantly linked by the IOSCO to market fairness, which is connected to disclosure and transparency issues.[45]

Investment services law should aim to control the danger of FI failure: the IOSCO recognised inter alia that '[m]arket intermediaries should be required to comply with standards for internal organization and operational conduct that aim to protect the interests of clients, ensure proper management of risk, and under which management of the intermediary accepts primary responsibility for these matters';[46] however, in case FI failure is unavoidable, '[t]here should be a procedure for dealing with the failure of a market intermediary in order to minimize damage and loss to investors and to contain systemic risk'.[47]

The IOSCO further recognised that '[t]he oversight of market intermediaries should primarily be directed to the areas where their capital, client money and public confidence may most be put at risk'.[48]

Regulation of intermediaries as proposed by the IOSCO covers entry criteria (licensing), capital and prudential requirements, ongoing supervision and discipline of intermediaries, and the consequences of failure, noting the importance of segregation and identification of assets in order inter alia to protect from defalcation, to facilitate transfer of positions in case of severe market disruption, to

42 Available at www.iosco.org/library/pubdocs/pdf/IOSCOPD82.pdf. Cf. IOSCO (2003) *Methodology for Assessing Implementation of the IOSCO Objectives and Principles of Securities Regulation*, available at www.ebrd.com/downloads/legal/securities/IOSCOPD155.pdf. With regard to investor protection before the GFC, see also IOSCO Technical Committee (1993) *Protecting the Small Investor: Combating Transnational Retail Securities and Futures Fraud*, available at www.iosco.org/library/pubdocs/pdf/IOSCOPD30.pdf; IOSCO Technical Committee (1996) *Measures Available on a Cross-Border Basis to Protect Interests and Assets of Defrauded Investors*, available at www.iosco.org/library/pubdocs/pdf/IOSCOPD55.pdf.

43 Ibid., p. 1.

44 Ibid., p. 6.

45 Ibid., p. 7. Cf. ibid., p. 24, with regard to regulation of issuers.

46 Ibid., 23rd Principle.

47 Ibid., 24th Principle.

48 Ibid., p. 33, and further references therein.

prevent the use of clients' assets for proprietary trading, and to assist in the orderly winding up if necessary.[49]

As far as investor protection *ex post facto* is concerned, i.e. when FI failure has occurred, the IOSCO *Objectives and Principles of Securities Regulation* are limited in stating that '[t]here must be effective and legally secure arrangements for default handling. This is a matter that extends beyond securities law to the insolvency provisions of a jurisdiction'.[50]

Further, regarding investor protection in case of FI failure, the IOSCO stated that '[i]nvestors should have access to a neutral mechanism (such as courts or other mechanisms of dispute resolution) or means of redress and compensation for improper behaviour'.[51] This reference does not appear to be excluding liability of competent authorities in tort.[52]

Thus, the IOSCO seems to have proposed investor redress and compensation for 'improper behaviour' on the one hand, and protection of competent authorities acting *bona fide* on the other hand, without entering into further discussion of these issues.

2.3 Cross-sectoral considerations on the status of financial consumers

Relevant to the issue addressed here is the object of research conducted by the Joint Forum[53] operating under the aegis of the BCBS, the IOSCO and the IAIS, on a cross-sectoral comparison of the Core Principles.

The first such study, conducted by the Joint Forum before the current international financial crisis erupted, was published in 2001 under the title *Core Principles – Cross-sectoral Comparison*.[54]

49 Ibid., pp. 33–39.

50 Ibid., p. 8. See also the IOSCO notes on appropriate domestic legal framework, ibid., Annexure 3.

51 Ibid., p. 7. The notion of 'improper behaviour' is not defined by the IOSCO; a question is raised as to whether 'improper behaviour' refers only to the defaulting intermediary, or may also be understood as referring to other entities, even supervisory and regulatory authorities. In this regard, it is interesting to note that the IOSCO refers to regulatory accountability (which is not equivalent to liability, though), stating inter alia that '[t]he regulator should be … accountable in the use of its powers and resources. … Accountability implies: a regulator that operates independently of sectoral interests; a system of public accountability of the regulator; a system permitting judicial review of decisions of the regulator'; ibid., p. 11.

52 This approach is supported by the position that '[t]he capacity of the regulator to act responsibly, fairly and effectively will be assisted by: … adequate legal protection for regulators and their staff acting in the bona fide discharge of their functions and powers'; ibid., p. 10.

53 www.bis.org/bcbs/jointforum.htm.

54 Available at www.bis.org/publ/joint03.pdf and www.iosco.org/library/pubdocs/pdf/IOSCOPD121.pdf. The second relevant study, *Review on the Differentiated Nature and Scope of Financial Regulation – Key Issues and Recommendations*, which builds on the first, was conducted in the wake of the GFC and was published in January 2010; see Ch. 3.2.

The 2001 Joint Forum Report, Core Principles – cross-sectoral comparison

In 1999 the Joint Forum was mandated by its parent organisations – BCBS, IOSCO and IADI – to compare core principles of financial law in the three sectors of banking, securities and insurance, 'identifying common principles and understanding differences where they arise'.[55]

Such comparative research was regarded as beneficial in the assessment and implementation of core principles; the focus was on the issue of consistency of the various core principles as had been developed by the relevant international organisations, with a view to facilitating their implementation.[56]

Thus, it appears that the issue of certainty, predictability and effectiveness in implementation was at the origins of this Joint Forum research. The Core Principles issued by the BCBS, the IOSCO and the IAIS were taken into account for the purposes of this Joint Forum survey.[57]

The Joint Forum took into account the historical background to the Core Principles, referring to the creation of the organisations that have issued the respective documents, and noted that despite the different backgrounds, the processes followed were similar in many respects,[58] and that following their issuing, the Core Principles have been followed by elaboration of compliance or self-assessment criteria issued by the relevant organisations.[59]

The Joint Forum noted that bank supervisors focus only on solvency issues, and thus on the supervised institutions (a factor which is reflected in the structure of the Core Principles for banks); while, on the other hand, securities supervisors supervise not only institutions (market intermediaries), but also collective investment schemes (both intermediaries and products), secondary markets and disclosure by issuers.[60]

The Joint Forum also noted that 'some of the similarities and differences among the core principles reflect, at least in part, intrinsic characteristics of the banking, insurance and securities sectors',[61] without, however, defining the notion of 'intrinsic characteristics'. It did, however, observe that the boundaries between banking, insurance and securities sectors have been blurred, due also to the growth of financial conglomerates.[62]

The Joint Forum observed that one of the areas where the three sectors differ

55 Ibid., p. 4, para. 13.
56 Ibid., p. 4, para. 12.
57 I.e. BCBS (1997) *Core Principles for Effective Banking Supervision*, and the relevant BCBS (1999) *Core Principles Methodology*; IAIS (2000) *Insurance Core Principles*, and the relevant IAIS (2000) *Core Principles Methodology*; and IOSCO (1998) *Objectives and Principles of Securities Regulation*. However, the methodologies were used only as a secondary source, and other documents fell out of its scope. See ibid., p. 5, paras 14–16.
58 Ibid., p. 5.
59 Ibid., p. 6.
60 Ibid., p. 7, paras 29–30.
61 Ibid., p. 8, para. 35.
62 Ibid., p. 8, para. 36.

is the form of financial intermediation and risk transfer,[63] and that perhaps the most difficult issue to compare is risk identification and risk management among the three sectors.[64]

Analysing the 'intrinsic differences' between banking, investment services and insurance sectors, the Joint Forum considered inter alia that while banking supervisors in many jurisdictions avoid or postpone public disclosure of banks' problems, in an effort to maintain public confidence in the banking system,[65] securities regulators, on the other hand, generally disclose enforcement actions, because 'in the securities sectors, supervisory transparency and accountability are linked to the maintenance of confidence in the markets'.[66]

Although no definition of supervisory transparency and accountability was provided by the Joint Forum, it was mentioned that transparency in the view of securities supervisors strengthens perceptions of supervisory predictability, and also that transparency contributes to supervisory accountability.[67]

In addition, the Joint Forum identified four features, which it considered unique to the investment services sector: the existence and role of Self-Regulatory Organisations (SROs), the importance of full and fair disclosure by issuers, the responsibility of market surveillance (including monitoring by supervisors of trading in listed securities), and enforcement.[68] The reasoning of the Joint Forum as to the broad enforcement powers of supervisors is important, if somewhat laconic: '[i]nvestors are vulnerable to misconduct by intermediaries. Securities violations also can occur both on and off the securities markets'.[69]

In attempting to explain this specificity, the perception of risk in the organisation of securities and banking regulation and supervision, as related to individual protection, comes to the fore. In this aspect, the Joint Forum was clear, it maintained that although 'all three sets of core principles mention both customer (i.e. depositor, policyholder, investor) and systemic stability as key objectives', the IOSCO has a third (additional) objective: ensuring that markets are fair, efficient and transparent.[70]

According to the Joint Forum, the IOSCO places equal weight on its three objectives. Further, the Joint Forum maintains that '[a]lthough all three sectors regard systemic stability as an objective, the Basel core principles place greater

63 Ibid., p. 9, para. 37.
64 Ibid., p. 8, para. 33.
65 Ibid., p. 9, para. 41.
66 Ibid., p. 11, para. 52.
67 Ibid. An indication as to how the notion of accountability is perceived by the *Joint Forum* is offered by its reference that 'the core principles in all three sectors mention the need for supervisors to be accountable to the public for their supervisory actions. This is achieved in part by issuing annual reports to the public'; ibid., p. 14, para. 62. It is submitted, however, that in our opinion publishing of reports does not achieve per se accountability, although it certainly enhances transparency and allows for public scrutiny.
68 Ibid., p. 12, para. 54.
69 Ibid.
70 Ibid., p. 13, para. 58.

emphasis on systemic stability and consider customer protection as a by-product of stability'.[71]

Moreover, on the central issue of customer protection, the Joint Forum noted that '[c]ustomer protection is not specifically addressed in the Basel core principles, except to the extent that depositor protection is cited as an objective of banking supervision'.[72] However, it is one of the three announced objectives of investment services law according to the IOSCO and, as the Joint Forum observed, it includes segregation and protection of client assets that are held separate from investment firm funds.[73]

The Joint Forum concluded that:

> [t]he comparison actually reveals a good deal more by way of similarity between the three sectors than initial appearances might suggest. On some important issues, the core principles have many common features, in respect of the supervisory system, the supervised entity, ongoing supervision and at least some aspects of prudential requirements … Only in the area of markets and customers does it become difficult to establish such high-level common ground, and that is primarily because of the difference in the traditional scope of supervisory responsibility between the three sectors.[74]

On the other hand, the Joint Forum also found that there are some significant differences, 'which emerge from the comparison of the core principles which are not readily explained either as differences of form or as intrinsic differences'.[75]

Importantly, it noted that while these differences were discussed at length, there was no agreement as to their reasons, which it considered perhaps attributable to differences of choice of supervisory approach, objectives or underlying philosophy.[76]

One of the areas where such difficult to explain differences appear is, according to the Joint Forum, safeguarding of client assets, as it mentioned, 'it is not clear what accounts for the differences in detail between Basel and IOSCO on this issue'.[77]

In the approach adopted before the GFC, this difference, beyond being described as attributable to the 'traditional' difference of supervisory responsibility between the banking and the investment sectors, was left essentially unexplained.

As the GFC set upon the economic order and financial architecture in particular in the US and the EU, the *ratio* of both banking and investment services law and their interrelation were reconsidered.

71 Ibid., p. 14, para. 59.
72 Ibid., p. 21, para. 112.
73 Ibid., p. 21, para. 114.
74 Ibid., p. 22, para. 121.
75 Ibid., p. 23, para. 129.
76 Ibid.
77 Ibid., p. 24, para. 129. The Joint Forum noted that the BCSB places greater emphasis on systemic stability and the IAIS on customer protection, while the IOSCO places equal emphasis on investor protection, fair, transparent and efficient markets, and reduction of systemic risk.

Interim concluding remarks

Financial consumer protection is understood, according to analysis elaborated by international financial organisations and *fora*, as part of the double aim of financial law, to protect non-professional financial market participants and (through also achieving their confidence in the financial system) the stability of the financial market.

Although relevant considerations and criteria have been expressed through economic and financial research and analysis, on the basis mainly of the criterion of risk understood to be connected to the 'intrinsic characteristics' of each sector and activity of the financial market (the banking sector considered vital to the economy and more prone to systemic risk), their expression in legal terms and rules has proven challenging.

Financial services (banking, investment and insurance) law has traditionally been differentiated per sector of financial activity on the basis of an unclearly defined criterion of risk, which has been further reflected in an uncertain differentiation in the legal status and the level of protection of retail depositors vis-à-vis retail investors.

In the area of banking, implicit or explicit state guarantee of deposits was considered to a great extent vital to the avoidance of bank runs and so to the control of systemic risk. On the other hand, in the area of investment services, a limited compensation payable to retail investors was linked mainly to confidence in the market considerations.

Thus, financial consumer protection was endorsed in financial regulation as an externality which potentially affected financial market stability and integrity and therefore need to be regulated, according to a sector-based approach and by differentiated means, which emerged from the historical evolution of financial markets.

As will be discussed, the GFC has led to a reassessment of perceptions as to the *ratio* and *modus operandi* of financial law, including the sources of systemic risk and the reasons as to the differentiation in the treatment of retail depositors vis-à-vis retail investors.

3 International initiatives on financial law after the GFC

Reconsidering systemic risk and the protection of financial consumers

Introductory note

The global financial crisis (GFC) has been a catalyst to financial law development at a global level, causing re-examination of the existing financial law perceptions from their foundations, reassessment and redesigning of normative structures, content and mechanisms.[1]

The major change brought about by the GFC is the need to bring the 'too-big-to-fail' concept concerning large financial institutions (FIs) to an end – and with it the implicit or explicit guarantee of deposits by states and thus public finances; in other words, to break the interconnection between banking systems and sovereigns (public finances and funds).[2]

To achieve this, the new resolution regime for FIs that has emerged as a result of the GFC affects not only the position of FIs in the system, but equally the position of financial consumers.

In this direction, important developments have initiated from the work of international *fora* and organisations, which led to further developments in the EU (and Member State) legal orders.

Initially, some of the fundamental issues raised by the GFC were addressed at the political level at international meetings held mainly by the G-20[3], the

1 See, generally, LASTRA, R. M. (2015) *International Financial and Monetary Law*, 2nd edition, Oxford: OUP; WYMEERSCH, E., HOPT, K. J. and FERRANINI, G. (eds) (2012) *Financial Regulation and Supervision: a Post-crisis Analysis*, Oxford: OUP; BLACK, J. (2010) 'Risk-based regulation: choices, practices and lessons learnt' in OECD *Risk and Regulatory Policy: Improving the Governance of Risk*, Paris: OECD, pp. 185–236; *idem* (2010) 'The role of risk in regulatory processes' in BALDWIN, R., CAVE, M. and LODGE, M. (eds) *The Oxford Handbook of Regulation*, New York: OUP, pp. 302–48.

2 See ESTRELLA, A. and SCHICH, S. (2012), 'Sovereign and Banking Sector Debt: Interconnections through Guarantees', *OECD Journal: Financial Market Trends*, vol. 2011/2, pp. 21–45.

3 The 'Group of Twenty' (G-20) is an international forum for cooperation on important economic and financial issues at a global level. It consists of 19 member states, as well as the EU. The first G-20 Leaders' Summit meeting took place on 14 and 15 November 2008, where its member states discussed the financial crisis and agreed to an action plan to control it. It aims at policy coordination between its members in order inter alia to promote financial regulation, to reduce risks and prevent future financial crises; see www.g20.org and www.imf.org/external/np/exr/facts/groups.htm#G20.

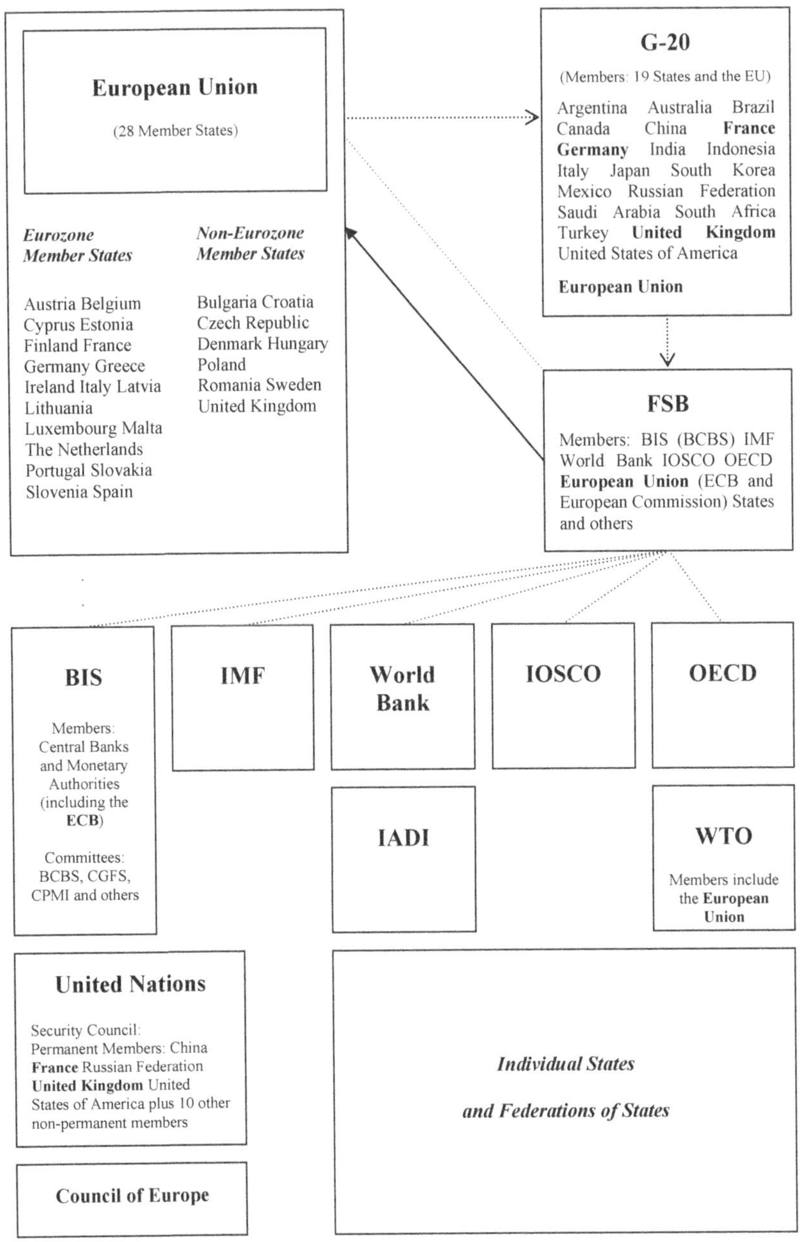

Figure 1 International organisations, *fora* and the EU (as the only supranational organisation) in a network producing legally binding or non-binding rules of financial supervision and regulation, and other rules (as in December 2015).

G-10 and the G-7.[4] The series of frequent meetings of the G-20 on the matter, especially in the first years of the financial crisis, have been accompanied by relevant statements, declarations and *communiqués*, aiming at important financial regulation reform with a view to enhancing the effectiveness of regulation and supervision.[5]

In their Declaration of 15 November 2008, following the Washington Summit, the G-20 referred to the root causes of the GFC, mentioning also the responsibility of policy-makers, regulators and supervisors.[6]

Referring to the common principles for reform of financial markets, the G-20 noted inter alia that intensified international cooperation among regulators and strengthening standards and implementation are necessary,[7] and announced their commitment to protect the integrity of the world's financial markets by the use of several measures, including 'bolstering investor and consumer protection'.[8]

Further, in 2008 the G-20 agreed at the Washington Summit to an *Action Plan to Implement Principles for Reform*.[9]

Regarding the principle of enhancing sound resolution, the G-20 called for a review of '[t]he differentiated nature of regulation on the banking, securities and insurance sectors and provide a report outlining the issue and making recommendations on needed improvements'.[10]

It further noted that national and regional authorities should review resolution regimes and bankruptcy laws, to ensure that they permit an orderly wind-down of large complex cross-border FIs.

Regarding the principle of promoting integrity of financial markets, the G-20 asked as an immediate action to be taken by 31 March 2009, for national and regional authorities to 'review business conduct rules to protect markets and investors, especially against market manipulation and fraud'.[11]

Similarly, regarding the principle of reinforcing international cooperation, the G-20 asked for the collection of information on the status of convergence in regulatory practices in various areas, including deposit insurance.

4 See www.imf.org/external/np/exr/facts/groups.htm#G7.

5 At the outbreak of the financial crisis, a G-7 finance ministers and central bankers' meeting was initially held on 11 and 12 October 2008; its discussions were continued in the G-20 summit held in Washington on 14 and 15 November 2008, called *New Bretton Woods* or *Bretton Woods II*, since the structure and operation of the international monetary and financial system were to be discussed again. Further G-20 summits were held in London on 2 April 2009 (see G-20 'Declaration on Strengthening the Financial System – London, 2 April 2009'; see also G-20 'The Global Plan for Recovery and Reform, 2 April 2009'), in Pittsburgh on 24 and 25 September 2009, in Toronto on 26 and 27 June 2010, in Seoul on 11 and 12 November 2010, in Cannes on 4 November 2011, in Los Cabos on 19 June 2012, in St Petersburg on 4–5 September 2013, in Brisbane, Queensland on 15–16 November 2014, and in Antalya on 15–16 November 2015.

6 Ibid., p. 1.

7 Ibid., p. 2.

8 Ibid., p. 3.

9 Annexed to the G-20 Declaration of 15 November 2008.

10 Ibid.

11 Ibid.

In the *Communiqué* of the London Summit of 2 April 2009, the G-20 stressed inter alia that '[r]egulators and supervisors must protect consumers and investors, support market discipline, avoid adverse impacts on other countries, reduce the scope of regulatory arbitrage, support competition and dynamism, and keep pace with innovation in the marketplace'.

In its respective Declaration of 2 April 2009, the G-20 decided that the FSF should be expanded by having its mandate broadened and its institutional basis and capacity enhanced, should be renamed as the Financial Stability Board (FSB), and should closely collaborate with the IMF, each complementing the other's role and mandate.[12]

On the basis of the above G-20 decision, the FSB published on 25 September 2009 a Report to the G-20 entitled *Improving Financial Regulation*.[13]

Among other issues, the FSB stressed the need for effective and consistent implementation of financial law reforms in the national legal orders, setting the bases for the new FI resolution regime and ending 'too-big-to-fail' approaches.

3.1 International initiatives on banking and investment services law: ending 'too-big-to-fail' – the new resolution regime and bail-in

The GFC and the ensuing questioning of the 'too-big-to-fail' perception in financial law, as well as the will to avoid saving failing FIs through the use of public funds at the expense of taxpayers and public finances, led to initiatives at the international level to seek ways to achieve the resolution of FIs, including those of systemic importance, without resorting to 'bail-out'.

In this direction, the G-20 sought to explore policies which could lead to such a result; already at the November 2010 Seoul Summit, the G-20 Leaders endorsed the 2010 FSB Report entitled *Reducing the moral hazard posed by systemically important financial institutions*,[14] which set out a policy framework for addressing this issue.

The policy framework that gradually emerged has at the centre the adoption of a resolution framework so that FIs can be resolved in an orderly manner, without causing systemic risk or exposing taxpayers to the risk of loss, the adoption of higher loss absorbency capacity for SIFIs and G-SIFIs, a more intensive supervision on SIFIs, and other requirements.

12 See FSB, 'Re-establishment of the FSF as the Financial Stability Board', available at www.fsb.org/wp-content/uploads/r_090402.pdf. See also Ch. 2 (n. 13).

13 Available at www.fsb.org/wp-content/uploads/r_090925b.pdf?page_moved=1.

14 Available at www.fsb.org/wp-content/uploads/r_101111a.pdf?page_moved=1.

The 2009 BCBS/IADI Core Principles for Effective Deposit Insurance

In 2009, the BCBS and the IADI published the *Core Principles for Effective Deposit Insurance Systems*.[15] Earlier research had been elaborated by IADI in the wake of the financial crisis.[16]

One of the positions advanced in the 2009 BCBS/IADI *Core Principles for Effective Deposit Insurance Systems (Core Principles)* is that:

> In order to be credible, and to avoid distortions that may result in moral hazard, a deposit insurance system needs to be part of a well-constructed financial system safety net, properly designed and well implemented. A [FSN] usually includes prudential regulation and supervision, a lender of last resort and deposit insurance. The distribution of powers and responsibilities between the financial safety-net participants is a matter of public policy choice and individual country circumstances.[17]

According to this BCBS/IADI report, depositor protection appears rather as a prerequisite of systemic stability than as an autonomous aim of financial regulation:[18] despite the disparity in the various depositor protection regimes in the world, there is a general implicit expectation of the public for banks to be rescued[19] (connected to the economic and political risk of bank runs), yet the expectation of using public funds to save banks causes moral hazard (in particular where there is total coverage, as in 'blanket guarantees').[20] The problematic on

15 Available at www.bis.org/publ/bcbs156.htm. The BCBS/IADI report took into account inter alia the BCBS (2006) *Core Principles for Effective Banking Supervision*, the FSF (2001) *Final Report of the Working Group on Deposit Insurance*, and the IADI (2005) *Key Conclusions of the APEC Policy Dialogue on Deposit Insurance and IADI Guidance Points*. See also BCBS and IADI (2010) *Core Principles for Effective Deposit Insurance Systems – Methodology and Compliance Assessment*, Basel.

16 In October 2007, IADI published a (draft) Guidance Paper on *General Guidance for an Effective Deposit Insurance Mandate*, available at www.iadi.org/docs/IADI%20Draft%20Discussion%20Paper%20on%20Effective%20Deposit%20Insurance%20Mandate_Basel_2007a.pdf. In this the IADI took into account previous research and in particular the 2001 FSF Guidance for Developing Effective Deposit Insurance Systems, and examined the status at the time of DISs. Its research revealed that most DISs had a pure pay-box function (i.e. to collect premiums, to manage funds and to reimburse depositors), and that pay-box DISs with extended powers could assume a significant role in bank resolution (having certain risk management and supervisory competences), while risk-minimising DISs could intervene directly and supervise member institutions and so to directly handle bank failures. Among other conclusions, IADI found that there existed some variations in alignment between the stated mandates of DISs and their associated powers; ibid., p. 24.

17 See BCBS and IADI (2009) *Core Principles*, (n. 15), at para. 4.

18 According to the BCBS/IADI report, '[t]he principal objectives for deposit insurance systems are to contribute to the stability of the financial system and protect depositors'; ibid., Principle 1 – Public Policy Objectives.

19 The BCBS/IADI state that '[i]mplicit deposit protection arises when the public, including depositors and perhaps other creditors, expect some form of protection in the event of a bank failure. This expectation usually arises because of the governments past behaviour or statements made by officials'; ibid., p. 6, n. 2.

20 Ibid.

resolution regimes was probably not central at the time, in the discussion concerning FSNs.

In November 2014 IADI published its revised *Core Principles for Effective Deposit Insurance Systems*,[21] placing greater emphasis inter alia to moral hazard issues, which it considered horizontally across the various Principles, and to the implication of DISs in resolution procedures.

The 2012 FSB Thematic Review on Deposit Insurance Systems

In its 2012 *Thematic Review on Deposit Insurance Systems*,[22] the FSB examined the response of its member jurisdictions to the GFC in relation to their deposit insurance regimes. The FSB found that important reforms had resulted from the reaction to the financial crisis, and noted that some of them reflected a change in the prevailing views as to the role of deposit insurance in the FSN, and that greater convergence and a consensus emerged from the GFC in certain areas. Developments included higher coverage levels, the elimination of co-insurance, and improvements in the payout process, in depositor awareness, in information sharing and coordination with other FSN participants and the involvement of deposit insurance in resolution of banks. Also, the FSB found that the responses of its members with explicit deposit insurance systems suggested consistency in general with the BCBS/IADI Core Principles for Effective Deposit Insurance (in particular in the areas of DGS mandates, membership and coverage), and proceeded to certain recommendations including the adoption of explicit deposit insurance systems by all its members and full implementation of the Core Principles for Effective Deposit Insurance.

The 2011 IOSCO Final Report for the protection of client assets

Furthermore, after the GFC had begun, the IOSCO published in 2011 a Final Report on the *Survey of Regimes for the Protection, Distribution and/or Transfer of Client Assets*,[23] in the wake of the collapse of *Lehman Brothers* and the ensuing legal and regulatory uncertainty. The report focused on analysing different client asset protection regimes, with a view to assist both regulators and market participants.

In its 2011 Report, the IOSCO defines 'client assets' in securities and derivative markets, as consisting of securities, positions and client money (with certain variations relating to each particular investment services sub-sector).[24]

FSB published in February 2012 a Peer Review Report on *Thematic Review on Deposit Insurance Systems*,[25] which examined the adaptation of jurisdictions to

21 Available at www.iadi.org/docs/cprevised2014nov.pdf.
22 Available at www.fsb.org/wp-content/uploads/r_120208.pdf?page_moved=1.
23 Available at www.iosco.org/library/pubdocs/pdf/IOSCOPD351.pdf.
24 Ibid., pp. 5–6.
25 Available at www.fsb.org/wp-content/uploads/r_120208.pdf?page_moved=1.

deposit insurance as necessitated by the GFC and puts forward certain proposals to achieve effective protection of market stability and depositors.

The 2011 FSB Key Attributes of Effective Resolution Regimes of FIs

Furthermore, in 2011 the FSB issued as an international guideline the *Key Attributes of Effective Resolution Regimes for Financial Institutions* (the *Key Attributes*),[26] which set out a number of essential features as part of a resolution framework for application by all jurisdictions.[27]

The 2011 *Key Attributes* provide general guidance, applicable horizontally across financial regulatory regimes, aiming to promote the adoption of effective resolution regimes at a global level.

According to the 2011 *Key Attributes*, a resolution regime should interact 'with applicable schemes and arrangements for the protection of depositors, insurance policy holders and retail investors',[28] and for it to be effective it should satisfy a number of conditions, including ensuring continuity of SIFIs, protecting 'such depositors, insurance policy holders and investors as are covered by such [insurance] schemes and arrangements',[29] allocating losses to shareholders and creditors in a manner respecting the hierarchy of claims, and not relying on public solvency support nor creating such an expectation.

Moreover, the FSB proposed that jurisdictions should empower the competent resolution authority to resolve non-viable firms, and that the resolution regime should include both stabilisation options (to achieve continuity of SIFIs, including sale or transfer of shares or business to a third party, and/or creditor-financed recapitalisation) as well as liquidation option in a way that protects insured depositors, policyholders and retail investors.[30]

In particular in relation to 'resolution powers' (Key Attribute 3), proposals were made to empower the resolution authorities to proceed to a 'bail-in' with the resolution procedure, by writing down equity (or other instruments of ownership) of the FI and creditor claims in conformity with the hierarchy of claims in liquidation, by converting claims (debt) into equity, also in a manner that respects the hierarchy of claims in liquidation, and by converting or writing down any contingent convertible or contractual bail-in instruments that had not been triggered prior to entry into resolution.[31]

26 Available at www.fsb.org/wp-content/uploads/r_111104cc.pdf?page_moved=1.

27 Such essential features include proposals on the scope of resolution, the resolution authority and its powers, issues relating to set-off, netting, collateralisation, and segregation of client assets, safeguards relating to the protection of creditors, funding of firms in resolution, legal framework conditions for cross-border cooperation, the establishment of crisis-management groups, resolvability assessments, recovery and resolution planning, and access to information and information sharing, and others.

28 *Key Attributes*, p. 3.

29 Ibid., point (ii).

30 Ibid., pp. 3–4.

31 Ibid., pp. 3–4.

More specifically, in relation to the respect of creditor hierarchy as recognised by them to be a safeguard in the context of resolution procedures, the *Key Attributes* also proposed a degree of flexibility, by departing 'from the general principle of equal (pari passu) treatment of creditors of the same class',[32] when that is deemed 'necessary to contain the potential systematic impact of a firm's failure or to maximise the value for the benefit of all creditors as a whole'.[33]

In this sense, the FSB proposed flexibility in the application of the credit hierarchy rules in the context of resolution, by the application of what is, in our view, an extra-legal criterion of financial risk analysis.

In this way, the FSB appears to have opted for flexibility rather than legal certainty and predictability.

In parallel, and perhaps as counterweight and limit to degree of proposed flexibility, the FSB also proposed a 'no creditor worse off than in liquidation' safeguard, according to which a creditor's right to compensation should be recognised when under the resolution regime they do not receive at a minimum what they would receive under the applicable insolvency regime.[34]

The FSB proposed inter alia measures to avoid relying on public or bail-out funds for the purposes of resolution, and such funds to be used only as a temporary measure and in combination with measures to recover losses incurred from shareholders and unsecured creditors (subject to the 'no creditor worse off than in liquidation' safeguard) and if necessary from the financial system.[35]

In providing temporary financing, the FSB further proposed that jurisdictions should use mechanisms of privately-financed deposit insurance or resolution funds or of *ex post* recovery from the industry, and also that mechanisms to minimise moral hazard risk during temporary funding should be in place, including resorting to temporary funding only when necessary.[36]

Placing a failing FI under temporary public ownership was considered by the FSB only as a last resort and only for the purpose of maintaining financial stability, again in combination with measures to recover losses incurred from shareholders and unsecured creditors and, if necessary, from the financial system.[37]

While the option of orderly resolution of FIs in danger of failing is in the focus of the *Key Attributes*, the option of attempting the recovery of a FI in distress was also taken into account. In this direction, the *Key Attributes* placed emphasis on reliable recovery and resolution plans (RRPs) which should be prepared in jurisdictions covering at minimum systemically significant FIs.[38]

The purpose of recovery plans is to identify options for FIs to withstand severe financial stress.[39]

32 Ibid., Key Attribute 5.1, p. 11.
33 Ibid.
34 Ibid., Key Attribute 5.2.
35 Ibid., Key Attributes 6.1 and 6.2, p. 12.
36 Ibid., Key Attribute 6.2.
37 Ibid., Key Attribute 6.3.
38 Ibid., Key Attribute 11.
39 Ibid., Key Attribute 11.5, p. 16.

The purpose of resolution plans is to facilitate resolution 'to protect systemically important functions, with the aim of making the resolution of any firm feasible without severe disruption and without exposing taxpayers to loss'.[40]

It emerges that protection of financial consumers is not the aim of the resolution mechanism, at least as proposed by the FSB; its aim is to protect systemic stability without burdening public finances and, in particular, taxpayers.

Although it could be argued that upholding systemic stability resolution procedures may, in general and indirectly, also protect the financial consumers who are clients of a failing FI, in the end, they may be called to bear part of the costs of resolution procedures, as though they were owners (shareholders) of such institutions.

Although a minimum protection regime is proposed by the FSB through the proposal of the 'no creditor worse off than in liquidation' principle, the *Key Attributes* do not, however, explain the interconnection of this principle with rules on deposit or retail investor compensation regimes.

The 2014 FSB Key Attributes of Effective Resolution Regimes of FIs

Further to the 2011 *Key Attributes*, in October 2014, the FSB adopted additional elements to the initial *Key Attributes*, providing in particular sector-specific guidance, in which a differentiated treatment is proposed in relation to the resolution of FMIs and insurance service providers.

In the 2014 *Key Attributes*,[41] new, more detailed guidance is provided inter alia on the protection of client assets in resolution.

According to the new entry on the Protection of Clients Assets in Resolution,[42] '[c]lient assets are held by different types of firms in the course of different financial activities and services, including safeguarding, administration and custody, investment services and brokerage, prime brokerage and collateral taking in connection with other financial transactions',[43] which are subject to different legal, regulatory and contractual characterisation and arrangements in different jurisdictions.

Making reference to the relevant work and conclusions reached by the IOSCO, the FSB proceeded to a number of interesting proposals inter alia on the objectives of resolution in relation the protection of client assets, the definition of client assets,[44] transfer powers in relation to client assets, identification, safeguard-

40 Ibid.

41 Available at www.fsb.org/wp-content/uploads/r_141015.pdf. The text of the 2011 *Key Attributes* was not modified in the 2014 edition, but a number of Annexes on general guidance as well as on sector-specific guidance were added.

42 Ibid., p. 85, Appendix II, Annex 3.

43 Ibid.

44 The FSB defines client assets broadly, for the purposes of its 2014 Key Attributes, noting that they typically include: '(i) money held on behalf of or owed to a client by a firm that is classified as "client money" under applicable national law; … (ii) financial instruments or other assets held for or on behalf of a client; (iii) client collateral …; and (iv) assets and other (contractual) rights arising from transactions entered into by a firm on behalf of a client'; ibid., Annex 3, para. 3.1, p. 87.

ing and segregation of client assets, shortfalls in client assets and use of protection funds, information requirements and record keeping, and other issues.[45]

Moreover, the 2014 *Key Attributes* exclude from their definition of client assets inter alia 'deposits held by banks …, unless the deposits held by a firm with a bank constitute customer funds under the applicable legal framework and are labelled as such';[46] notably, the FSB adds that deposits 'are defined for the purposes of the regulation of the activity of taking deposits under applicable law'.[47]

Thus, the 2014 *Key Attributes* refer to the national legal orders for the legal characterisation of the holding of client monetary assets by FIs – in relation both to the notion of client money held by an FI and also to deposits, being confined by the lack of cohesion in relevant definitions, i.e. legal characterisations by the various legal orders.[48]

In relation to the role and operation of compensation schemes, the 2014 *Key Attributes* again ask for clear rules[49] (as in relation to the definition of client assets), and in particular in relation to resolution planning, propose that resolution plans should consider inter alia 'the role of investor protection schemes or other guarantee schemes or funds to support transfers of client assets or to make advance payments of client funds and delivery of securities'.[50]

While the approach adopted by the FSB on the matter of client asset protection and the role of compensation schemes thereto is quite broad, it appears that the FSB, even if somewhat indirectly, recognises that the aims of achieving resolution of distressed financial firms and of protecting client assets (as defined by it) may not be easy to reconcile.[51]

In case of such antagonism between these aims, the *Key Attributes* do not provide any guidance. What is more, they identify client asset protection regimes as a

45 See 2014 *Key Attributes*, Appendix II, Annex 3, pp. 87–94.

46 Ibid., para. 3.2, point (i), p. 88. Other client assets excluded from the *Key Attributes* definition in relation to client asset protection include assets held by an insurer or policyholder and assets delivered in a full title transfer transaction; ibid., points (ii) and (iii).

47 Ibid.

48 As the matter transcends the problematic of soft-law proposals by international organisations, and touches upon the essence of the *ratio* and content of differentiated legal definitions in this area, it is reasonable that the FSB does not expand on it. In a way, the cyclicality in the effort to define client assets held by FIs and to elucidate the differentiation of various categories thereof is perhaps noticeable in the *Key Attributes* proposal that '[t]he legal framework should include clear and transparent rules on how: (i) client assets are defined …; and (ii) client assets are treated in the event of failure of the firm that holds the client assets either directly or indirectly'; ibid., para. 3.3, p. 88.

49 Ibid., paras 7.1 and 7.2, p. 90.

50 Indeed, in our view, the *Key Attributes* appear to imply that the use of investor compensation schemes in the context of resolution procedures may lead to excessive depletion of the schemes for the financing of resolution measures and not for the protection of client assets; ibid., para. 9.1, point (ix), p. 92.

51 Ibid., para. 7.3, p. 90.

potential impediment to the orderly resolution and the fast return or transfer of client assets.[52]

Thus, it appears, in our view, that in the context of resolution of FIs as examined by the FSB, systemic protection takes priority over the protection of client assets.

The latter may be regarded, as analysed in the *Key Attributes*, as constituting a parameter which has to be taken into account in case of resolution, forming what amounts to a limit of minimum protection (by application of the 'no creditor worse off than in liquidation' principle) and even a potential impediment to the effectiveness of the resolution process.

3.2 Cross-sectoral considerations on the status of financial consumers

Taking into account all the considerations in relation to the role and function of financial law, as such questions were reconsidered in the wake of the GFC, the rationale of differentiating the protection awarded to financial consumers according to a sector-based criterion was also reconsidered, even if briefly, at the international level.

The 2010 Joint Forum (BCBS, IOSCO, IAIS) Report on the Differentiated Nature and Scope of Financial Regulation

Mandated by the G-20, the Joint Forum of the BCBS, the IOSCO[53] and the IAIS, published in January 2010, a *Review on the Differentiated Nature and Scope of Financial Regulation – Key Issues and Recommendations*.[54] As the Joint Forum noted, the purpose of its Report was 'to help identify potential areas where systemic risks may not be fully captured in the current regulatory framework'[55] and to make relevant recommendations.

One of the main areas on which the research by the Joint Forum focused were the key regulatory differences across the banking, insurance, and securities sectors.

One of the 'Guiding Principles' used by the Joint Forum in its research is that '[s]imilar activities, products, and markets should be subject to similar minimum supervision and regulation'.[56]

Another such 'Guiding Principle' referred to by the Joint Forum in the same context is that '[c]onsistency in regulation across sectors is necessary; however, legitimate differences can exist across the three sectors'[57] – the question then in whether differentiation of the protection awarded in the case above is legitimate; and according to which criteria.

52 Ibid., para. 11.1, p. 94.

53 See also KARMEL, R. (2012) 'IOSCO's Response to the Financial Crisis', *Brooklyn Law School, Legal Studies Paper* No. 268, March, http://ssrn.com/abstract=2025115.

54 Available at www.bis.org/publ/joint24.pdf.

55 Ibid., p. 1.

56 Ibid., p. 4.

57 Ibid.

The Joint Forum accepted that international financial law is sector-specific (banking, investment services and insurance), which explains the development of sector-specific regulatory standards (core principles) in each of these sectors.[58]

This sector-specific approach entails dangers of regulatory gaps, which in turn may cause supervisory challenges and allow for regulatory arbitrage.[59]

The Joint Forum research built on the premise that '[t]he core principles reflect the main characteristics of the respective sector and the nature of the financial institutions supervised under each framework',[60] and focused on an update of its relevant work in 2001.[61]

According to the Joint Forum, despite the different format, content and language used, there are substantial commonalities across sectors – a fact which also reveals the converging nature of business in the three sectors.[62]

At the same time, there are differences among core principles, which always, according to the Joint Forum, 'reflect – at least in part – intrinsic characteristics of the banking, securities and insurance sectors'.[63]

One of the areas where regulatory differences are identified by the Joint Forum is 'the extent to which regulation of the different sectors deal with business conduct and consumer or investor protection'.[64]

Thus, although certain differences may be objectively justified, according to the Joint Forum research, as related to the nature of the persons or business regulated, it is concluded that certain differences cannot be objectively justified.[65]

The 2011 G-20/OECD High Level Principles on Financial Consumer Protection

Following a call by the G-20 in 2011, a G-20/OECD Task Force on Financial Consumer Protection, in cooperation with the FSB and other international organisations as well as consumer and industry organisations, prepared a set of *High Level Principles on Financial Consumer Protection*,[66] which were endorsed by the G-20

58 Ibid., p. 3.
59 Ibid.
60 Ibid., p. 5.
61 Ch. 2.3 (n. 54).
62 Joint Forum (2010) *Review on the Differentiated Nature and Scope of Financial Regulation – Key Issues and Recommendations*, (n. 54), p. 5.
63 Ibid., pp. 5, 25.
64 Ibid., p. 6.
65 Ibid.
66 The High Level Principles refer to: (1) the Legal, Regulatory and Supervisory Framework, (2) the Role of Oversight Bodies, (3) Equitable and Fair Treatment of Consumers, (4) Disclosure and Transparency, (5) Financial Education and Awareness, (6) Responsible Conduct of Financial Services Providers and Authorised Agents, (7) Protection of Consumer Assets against Fraud and Misuse, (8) Protection of Consumer Data and Privacy, (9) Complaints Handling and Redress, and (10) Competition. The High Principles are inter-connected in essence, since financial consumer protection requires effective measures in all these areas. The relevant High Level Principles were designed to assist states to enhance financial consumer protection, especially through financial

in 2011,[67] and which were further issued as a Recommendation by the OECD in 2012.[68]

In relation to the issue of the aim of financial regulation, it is noted that '[t]raditional regulatory and supervisory frameworks adopted by oversight bodies contribute to the protection of consumers – which is often and increasingly recognised as a major objective of these bodies together with financial stability'.[69]

The development of effective approaches to support the implementation of the High Principles was decided by the G-20 in 2012,[70] and in 2013 the G-20 stated its support to the first effective approaches prepared by the G-20/OECD Task Force.[71]

The G-20/OECD Task Force proposed in 2014 a set of *Effective Approaches to Support the Implementation of the Remaining G20/OECD High Level Principles on Financial Consumer Protection*,[72] which are of interest here particularly in relation to the seventh High Level Principle, relating to the protection of consumer assets against fraud and misuse.

In the underlying assumptions referring to this High Level Principle, the G-20/OECD consider inter alia that '[r]esolution of distressed financial services providers requires special arrangements in order to take into account all the interests at stake, including those of consumers', and that '[c]onsumer protection and the need to keep consumers' trust in the financial system require that special arrangements are in place so that consumers bear limited losses when a financial services provider is wound up'.[73]

education and awareness policies; they do not address the sectoral issues addressed by the BCBS, the IAIS and the IOSCO.

67 Available at www.oecd.org/daf/fin/financial-markets/48892010.pdf.

68 Available at http://acts.oecd.org/Instruments/ShowInstrumentView.aspx?InstrumentID=282.

69 Ibid., p. 4. The seventh High Level Principle in particular refers to the protection of consumer assets against fraud and misuse, stating that relevant information, control and protection mechanisms should protect consumers' deposits, savings and similar assets against such risks.

70 See the relevant 2012 Action Plan of the G20/OECD Task Force, available at www.oecd.org/daf/fin/financial-education/FCPTaskForceActionPlan.pdf.

71 The first effective approaches concerned the fourth, sixth and ninth High Principles.

72 Available at www.oecd.org/daf/fin/financial-education/G20-OECD-Financial-Consumer-Protection-Principles-Implementation-2014.pdf. In this document, the notion of consumer in the context of said High Principles is understood as referring to that of 'retail consumer rather than high-net worth individuals or institutions'; ibid., p. 6.

73 Ibid., p. 34, paras 183 and 184, respectively. The notion of financial services providers refers, in the context of the High Principles, to 'all independent entities that provide, or offer, financial products and services in the market place'; ibid., p. 6. Concerning investment services, a common effective approach in relation to external frauds (i.e. frauds perpetrated against financial consumers by entities different from financial services providers) noted by the G-20/OECD Task Force is that 'financial services providers perform due diligence in choosing any third party where the consumers and/or client's assets are deposited'; ibid., p. 34, para. 189. The notion of 'client' is not defined in said document. In relation to internal frauds (i.e. frauds from within financial services providers), a common effective approach noted by the G-20/OECD Task Force is that financial services providers must refund or compensate consumers for financial loss unless it can be proved that the loss occurred was due to the negligence or fraudulent behaviour of the consumers. Also, concerning misappropriation or misuses, the common effective approaches noted by the Task Force include segregation of consumers' assets from those of the financial services providers, keeping records clear

In particular, in relation to winding-up procedures, the G-20/OECD Task Force inter alia noted that in cases where an FI failure is certain, the actions that can be taken are that law protects clients' ownership rights to property on their assets, and consumers' assets are regarded as trust property (separate from the FSP's general assets). In cases where consumers' assets are not separated, protection may be effected through a preferred claim in the winding-up procedure and/or the organisation of an efficient guarantee scheme.[74]

The requirement for FIs to be members of a compulsory guarantee scheme or a deposit insurance policy is connected, according to the Task Force, to the protection of 'consumers', depositors', policyholders' or investors' assets, and to maintain the stability of the financial system'.[75]

While the adoption by the G-20 and the OECD of the *High Level Principles on Financial Consumer Protection* constitutes an important step in the direction of discussing this issue at the global level, with a view to addressing it in an effective way, the approach adopted is, in our view, inevitably generic.

This is reasonable, as it has to take into account views, traditions, developments, binding or non-binding instruments, aims as well as reservations across a wide array of jurisdictions, and political and economic ethos.

However, it does not allow, in our view, scrutiny of the differences between the status of depositors vis-à-vis retail investors, and consideration as to whether the protection of consumers, as defined in the *High Level Principles*, constitutes a valid and autonomous aim of financial law.

The 2012 World Bank Good Practices for Financial Consumer Protection

Furthermore, in 2012, the World Bank published its *Good Practices for Financial Consumer Protection* (*Good Practices*),[76] as a diagnostic tool for international organisations and states aiming to provide comprehensive guidance for financial consumer protection on a cross-sectoral dimension.[77]

The *Good Practices* complement the 2011 OECD *High Level Principles* at a practical level, and take into account international best practices and a wide array of financial consumer protection issues across the financial sector. They recognise the existence of gaps in the protection awarded and aim to help policy-makers in identifying issues and designing 'coherent, comprehensive and coordinated regimes for the protection of financial consumers'.[78]

and readily in order, to allow for verification of positions in securities, cash and pending transactions, particularly in the event of insolvency of the FI; ibid., p. 37, paras 210–13.

74 Ibid., p. 39, paras 230–31.

75 Ibid., p. 40, para. 233.

76 Available at http://siteresources.worldbank.org/EXTFINANCIALSECTOR/Resources/Good_Practices_for_Financial_CP.pdf.

77 Financial consumers are not defined in the *Good Practices*, but include depositors, (retail) investors as well as policy-holders.

78 The 2012 World Bank *Good Practices for Financial Consumer Protection*, p. 3.

Financial consumer protection is achieved, according to the *Good Practices*, in two ways: through financial regulation, and through financial education.[79]

In relation to financial regulation, the *Good Practices* include in the field of envisaged protection compensation (guarantee) and insolvency issues, through a cross-sectoral common approach as well as on a sectoral approach.

With regard to protection of financial consumers in the event of FI insolvency, they propose as common good practices inter alia that '[a]ny law on financial insurance or a guarantee fund is clear on the insurer, the classes of depositors who are insured, the extent of insurance coverage, the contributor(s) to the fund, each event that will trigger a pay-out, and the mechanisms to ensure timely pay-out to all insured persons'; and that '[d]epositors, life insurance policyholders, securities and derivatives account holders, and pension fund members enjoy higher priority that other uninsured creditors in the liquidation process of a relevant financial institution'.[80]

Beyond the common good practices, they propose good practices per sector. In relation to the banking sector, the *Good Practices* note, in particular, that trust and confidence between banks and consumers are crucial for the development of any banking system,[81] also noting that '[t]he laws of central banks or banking supervisory agencies typically contain no reference to "consumer protection" as a function of the banking supervisor'.[82]

Concerning in particular depositor protection, they provide a number of practically useful approaches, commenting in addition that: '[a] deposit insurance system should be able to deal with a limited number of simultaneous bank failures, but the resolution of a systemic banking crisis requires that all financial system safety-net participants work together effectively'.[83]

In the field of investment services, the *Good Practices* connect consumer protection to the development and depth of the securities markets, as defined therein,[84] and provide guidance in relation to investor protection. In terms of guarantee schemes and insolvency, they note the importance of segregation of funds and they inter alia propose that: '[t]he law on the investors' guarantee fund, if there is one, should be clear on the funds and financial instruments that are covered under the law'.[85]

Although the *Good Practices* provide useful guidance for financial consumer protection at a cross-sector level, in our view, they do not enter into a discussion as to the aim of financial law in relation to financial consumer protection, nor to a discussion as to the distinction between depositor and retail investor protection, as usually provided by financial law.

However, although the *Good Practices* do not discuss these issues – which is

79 Ibid., p. 89.
80 Ibid., p. 9, paras 30 and 31, respectively.
81 Ibid., p. 11.
82 Ibid., p. 13.
83 Ibid., p. 28.
84 Ibid., p. 33.
85 Ibid., p. 41.

reasonable since their aim is to provide practical guidance at a very general level – they do not fail to note them, even if subtly.

In relation to the first issue, noting that the rationale for financial regulation ultimately rests on the objectives of mitigating systemic risk and protecting consumers, and that the two objectives are complementary over the long-term, the *Good Practices* also point out that there are instances where the objectives may be in conflict.[86]

In relation to the second issue, the *Good Practices* do define the sectors of the financial market and the participants therein, but refer to the instruments of various legal orders and the work of organisations per sector of the financial market.[87] Noting, on the one hand, that each sector of the financial market has its own peculiarities,[88] and, on the other hand, the danger of regulatory arbitrage when disparities appear between the legal characterisation and the functional operation of a financial services contract,[89] they conclude that a cross-sectoral and comprehensive approach to consumer protection is necessitated by the integration of many FIs into conglomerates, and by the increasing sophistication of financial 'products'.[90]

Indeed, in particular after the GFC, many jurisdictions have considered the issue of providing protection to financial consumers through a single entity, albeit in many cases according to different conditions reflecting a sector-based approach. In such cases, 'integrated protection schemes' have been developed, on the basis of different institutional structures across jurisdictions.[91] This development reflects the recognition, that:

> [w]ith the blurring of demarcation lines between financial sectors and the emergence of innovative financial products, financial services have become increasingly complex, and many [FIs] have restructured to become financial conglomerated or financial holding companies.[92]

86 Ibid., p. 91, wherein there are further references.

87 Ibid., *passim*; in particular table 2, pp. 32–33, and table 3, p. 43.

88 Ibid., p. 93.

89 Ibid.

90 Ibid., pp. 4, 94.

91 See in this regard the 2015 IADI Research Paper 'Integrated Protection Schemes', available at www.iadi.org/docs/IPS_Research_Paper_March_2015_FINAL_Version.pdf. Out of 61 jurisdictions (OECD and non-OECD) analysed in this Research Paper, 17 had integrated protection schemes, out of which 12 protect both depositors and investors; ibid., p. 8. These were, at the time of the research, Austria, Belgium, Quebec (Canada), Denmark, France, Germany, Greece, Iceland, Luxembourg, Sweden. Also, the UK and Korea covered all three categories of financial consumers (depositors, investors and policyholders), while Australia, Malaysia and Singapore covered both depositors and policyholders. See ibid., pp. 8–9, 15–16, 19. It is interesting to note that Korea, whose financial market and FSN was affected by the 1997 Asian financial crisis, adopted integrated systems for both financial supervision and consumer protection and resolution, and applies a uniform limited coverage level for all financial sectors; ibid., pp. 34, 39.

92 Ibid., p. 11. The IADI notes in this Research Paper that 'a search of current literature for a theoretical basis for IPS yielded no results', as did previous relevant analyses; ibid., p. 32. IADI also refers to pros and cons of adopting an integrated protection scheme, and to design features for consideration in adopting such a scheme, IADI notes in conclusion that '[d]ue to limited data and

Interim concluding remarks

As a result of the GFC, a consensus was built at the international level on the need to disconnect the protection of failing FIs from sovereigns and public funds to bail them out, by the introduction of a new resolution regime.

In this context, the reassessment of the *ratio* and aims of financial law took place on the basis of both a sector-based and a cross-sector analysis by international *fora*, revealing the disparities in protection of retail depositors vis-à-vis retail investors, without objective justification as to their reasoning and purpose, especially in the case of FI failure.

While the enhancement of financial consumer protection, as an aim of financial law, has been the object of research and proposals of international *fora*, the new analysis on the resolution of FIs and the new bail-in regime appears to be creating a hierarchy among the aims of financial law; according to this hierarchy, financial consumer protection in case of FI failure is placed below systemic risk considerations.

At the same time, differentiation in the protection awarded to financial consumers, whether as retail depositors or retail investors, appears all the more difficult to explain and justify, in particular in case of FI failure.

insufficient literature, this study can only provide an overview and describe some design features of [integrated protection schemes]. More detailed theoretical and empirical analysis of [integrated protection schemes] remains for future research'; ibid., p. 41.

4 Development and objectives of EU financial law on financial consumer protection prior to the GFC

Focusing on the creation of a single market

Introductory note

EU financial (banking and investment services) law is part of the greater system of rules that compose EU internal market law, and also has to be examined and taken into account from this perspective.[1]

In this respect, EU financial law followed the difficulties faced in creating a single European market, as planned by the EEC Treaty in 1952, from its initial stages to the period introduced by the 1985 Commission White Paper,[2] the *Cassis* and *Keck and Mithouard* case law and the mutual recognition mechanism.[3]

1 For an overview and an account of the evolution of EU financial law, see, generally, HAENTJENS, M., and De GIOIA-CARABELLESE, P. (2015) *European Banking and Financial Law*, London and New York: Routledge; MOLONEY, N. (2014) *EU Securities and Financial Markets Regulation*, 3rd edition, Oxford: OUP, Oxford European Union Law Library; LASTRA, R. and LOUIS, J.-V. (2013) 'European Economic and Monetary Union: History, Trends, and Prospects', *YEL*, vol. 32, issue 1, pp. 57–206; MOLLE, W. (1997) *The Economics of European Integration – Theory, Practice and Policy*, 3rd edition, London: Ashgate; TRIDIMAS, T. (2011) 'EU Financial Regulation: Federalization, Crisis Management, and Law Reform' in CRAIG, P. and De BURCA, G. *The Evolution of EU Law*, 2nd edition, Oxford: OUP, pp. 783–804; *idem* (2010) 'EU Financial Regulation: From Harmonisation to the Birth of EU Federal Financial Law' in BIRKENSHAW, P. and VARNEY, M. (eds) *The European Union Legal Order after Lisbon*, The Hague: Kluwer Law International; WALKER, G. A. (2007) *European Banking Law – Policy and Programme Construction*, The Hague: Kluwer Law International Ch. 1 (n. 1).

2 Commission (1985) *Completing the Internal Market – White Paper from the Commission to the European Council*, COM(85) 310 final, 14 June 1985. This White Paper did not refer to the investment services market, but only to banking and insurance markets, in which inter-state provision of services was more developed at the time. It further referred to mutual recognition as a general principle which should be approved under certain conditions (ibid., para 58 *et seq.*). For an analysis of single market law, see BARNARD, C. (2007), *The Substantive Law of the EU: The Four Freedoms*, 2nd edition, Oxford: OUP.

3 The principle of mutual recognition introduced by the 1985 White Paper had already been used (although not expressly referred to) in the ECJ decision of 20.02.1979 in Case 120/78, *Rewe-Zentrale AG v Bundesmonopolverwaltung fur Branntwein ('Cassis de Dijon')* [1979] ECR 649. For an analysis of the case, including consumer groups' response to it, see WALKER G. A. (2007) *European Banking Law – Policy and Programme Construction*, (n. 1), pp. 120 *et seq.*, wherein there are further references. See also ORTINO, M. (2007) 'The role and functioning of mutual recognition

In relation to the freedom of establishment and the freedom to provide services, the ECJ has recognised the direct effect of the relevant Treaty provisions.[4] Establishment is to be distinguished from provision of services on the basis of 'periodicity, continuity and regularity' of the activity conducted.[5]

In the area of financial services, the principle of equivalence as expressed by the rule of mutual recognition entails that financial market participants are to be allowed to provide financial services in any Member State, provided they had received authorisation in the Member State of origin (the home Member State) by the competent national authorities and according to national law which (correctly) incorporates requirements of EU law ('passporting').[6]

Such authorisation entails that other Member States are unable to impose additional licensing requirements, as these would amount to measures having the equivalent effect of restrictions and thus to protectionist measures, except where such (non-discriminatory in relation to nationality) restrictions relate to imperative national reasons in areas where national laws have not been harmonised, or fall within the derogations permitted by primary EU law in areas where harmonisation has been achieved.

According to the philosophy of the Commission's 1985 White Paper approach, financial markets integration would be achieved on the basis of mutual recognition, minimum harmonisation as well as home Member State control, while host Member State control would be exercised up to parallel in relation to Conduct of Business (CoB) rules for the sake of public interest and general good considerations.

Considering the effect of non-discriminatory national measures on the exercise of such freedoms, the ECJ developed relevant criteria which take into account the effects of the national restrictive measure and its possible justification under the

in the European market of financial services', *ICLQ*, vol. 56, issue 2, pp. 309–38. The *Cassis de Dijon* ruling was relevant to the ECJ decision of 11.07.1974 in Case 8/74, *Procureur du Roi v Benoît and Gustave Dassonville* [1974] ECR 837, relating to the notion of national measures having an equivalent effect to trade restrictions. For discussion of *Dassonville* and relevant case law, see WEATHERILL, S. and BEAUMONT, P. (1999) *EU Law*, London: Penguin, pp. 532 *et seq.* The *Cassis de Dijon* case law was partly re-examined by the ECJ decision of 24.11.1993 in Cases C-267/91 and 268/91, *Criminal Proceedings against Bernard Keck and Daniel Mithouard* [1993] ECR I-06097. For an analysis and discussion of this 'post-*Keck*' line of case law, see CHALMERS, D. (1994) 'Repackaging the internal market – the ramifications of the Keck judgment', *ELRev*, vol. 19, pp. 385–403; GORMLEY, L. (1994) 'Reasoning renounced? The remarkable judgment in Keck & Mithouard', *EBLR*, vol. 5, issue 3, pp. 63–67; POIARES MADURO, M. (2002) 'Harmony and Dissonance in Free Movement' in ANDENAS, M. and ROTH, W.-H. (eds) *Services and Free Movement in EU Law*, Oxford: OUP.

4 See e.g. ECJ decision of 21.06.1974 in Case 2/74, *Reyners v Belgian State* [1974] ECR 631; ECJ decision of 03.12.1974 in Case 33/74, *Johannes Henricus Maria van Bisbergen v Bestuur van de Bedrijfsvereniging voor de Metaalnijverheid* [1974] ECR 1299.

5 See e.g. ECJ decision of 30.11.1995 in Case C-55/94, *Reinhard Gebhard v Consiglio dell'Ordine degli Avvocati e Procuratori di Milano* [1995] ECR I-4165.

6 See, generally, LOMNICKA, E. (2000) 'The home country control principle in the financial services Directives and case law', *EBLR*, pp. 324–36; CREMONA, M. (1994) 'A European passport for investment services', *JBL*, p. 195.

'imperative reasons' doctrine announced in *Cassis* and the following formulation of *Keck* and 'post-*Keck*' case law.[7]

It might be argued in this sense, that integration has evolved by adapting to national concerns revealed through 'public interest' or 'general good' considerations.[8]

Discrepancies in the integration of the European financial market through this process led to the 1997 European Financial Services Action Plan (FSAP)[9] and the 2000 '*Lamfalussy* process'.[10]

7 See e.g. ECJ decision of 03.12.1974 in Case 33/74, *van Binsbergen* (n. 4, above) ECJ decision of 18.01.1979 in Joined Cases 110/78 to 111/78, *Ministère public and 'Chambre syndicale des agents artistiques et impresarii de Belgique' ASBL v Willy van Wesemael and Others* [1979] ECR 35; ECJ decision of 18.03.1980 in Case 62/79, *SA Compagnie générale pour la diffusion de la télévision, Coditel, and Others v Ciné Vog Films and Others* [1980] ECR 881; ECJ decision of 17.12.1981 in Case 279/80, *Criminal Proceedings against Alfred John Webb* [1981] ECR 3305; ECJ decision of 25.07.1991 in Case C-76/90, *Manfred Säger v Dennemeyer & Co Ltd* [1990] ECR I-422; ECJ decision of 25.07.1991 in Case C-288/89, *Stichting collectieve Antennevoorziening Gouda and others v Commissariaat voor de Media* [1991] ECR I-4007; ECJ decision of 31.03.1993 in Case C-19/92, *Dieter Kraus v Land Baden-Württemberg* [1993] ECR I-1663. For analysis, see BARNARD, C. (2007), *The Substantive Law of the EU* (n. 2). See also DASHWOOD, A., DOUGAN M., RODGER B., SPAVENTA E. and WYATT, D. (2011) *Wyatt and Dashwood's European Union Law*, sixth edition, Oxford: Hart Publishing, pp. 407–61.

8 See evaluation of the home Member State principle in financial integration law by the ECJ in its decision of 13.05.1997 Case C-233/94, *Germany v European Parliament and Council* [1997] ECR I-2441, para. 64, and the relevant Opinion of AG Léger, points 126–29. The ECJ, concurring with the AG, ruled that while this principle has been the guiding principle in the harmonisation of the financial services sector, the Community authorities are entitled to depart from it if so deemed appropriate (as in the case of the DGSD in relation to certain issues).

9 Despite the new mutual-recognition approach, the completion of the single European financial market had not been achieved at the end of the 20th century, and the financial market remained fragmented. In an effort to address this issue, the Commission issued in 1997 a Communication to the European Council on an *Action Plan for the Single Market*, CSE(1997) 1 final, 4 June 1997, and in 1998 a Communication on *Financial Services: Building a Framework for Action*, COM(1998) 625 final, 28 October 1998. These Communications were followed in 1999 by the Commission Communication of 11 May 1999 *Financial Service: Implementing the Framework for Financial Markets: Action Plan* (FSAP), which provided a framework for action and a timetable to achieve the establishment of a single market in wholesale financial services, increasing investor protection and transparency in retail markets, and strengthening prudential supervision.

10 In 2000, the Council appointed an expert Committee chaired by Baron Alexander Lamfalussy to assess the progress of financial markets integration in the EU. The Committee issued an Initial Report in 2000 and in 2001 the Final Report of the Committee of Wise Men on the Regulation of the European Securities Markets *(Lamfalussy Report)*. The *Lamfalussy Report* exercised criticism on the normative formation and implementation of measures to achieve the internal financial market, and proposed a series of measures to achieve the FSAP. The *Lamfalussy Report*, endorsed by the Stockholm Council and by the European Parliament in 2001, proposed the adoption of a new normative structure for achieving the internal financial market. Initially, the *Lamfalussy Report* recommendations referred to the securities sector, but were also subsequently extended to the banking and insurance sector. The Report proposed as new normative structure: (a) a principle-based legislation adopted on the basis of the co-decision procedure ('Level 1'), (b) implementing measures, adopted by the Commission under powers conferred by Level 1 measures, which is to be assisted by the Committee of European Securities Regulation (CESR) and the European Securities Committee (ESC) ('Level 2'), (c) enhanced cooperation between members of the CESR in order to achieve implementation of Level 1 and Level 2 measures ('Level 3'), and (d) effective

The *Lamfalussy* process illustrates the lengthy effort of the EU institutions and of the Member States to establish a single market in the area of financial services, which has followed the historical evolution and the different stages of political development of the EU.[11]

During this process, the political and legal machinery of integration moved from maximum harmonisation to minimum harmonisation and mutual recognition, and then to a new effort towards focused maximum harmonisation and centralisation of institutional control.[12]

In order to examine the *ratio* of EU financial law, with regard to financial consumer protection and in particular in relation to how retail investor protection interrelates to retail depositor protection, it will be necessary to take into account certain main features of EU financial law as it developed until the global financial crisis (GFC), before proceeding to examine how it has been affected by the financial crisis.

This development of EU financial law up to the GFC will be briefly examined, taking into account the main features of the evolution of EU banking and investment services law, the banking Directives and focusing mainly on the ISD and the Markets in Financial Instruments Directive (MiFID), as they are related to investigating the nature and status of retail depositors vis-à-vis retail investors under EU law.

4.1 Development of EU banking law prior to the GFC

The EEC Treaty did not make explicit reference to the banking sector, except for providing that necessary measures had to be adopted on the basis of unanimity, and, in line with the liberalisation of capital movements,[13] efforts were made to achieve approximation of national rules in the area of banking on the basis of general Treaty provisions on freedom of establishment and freedom to provide services.[14]

enforcement of compliance by the Commission ('Level 4'). See in general MOLONEY, N. (2003) 'II. The Lamfalussy legislative model: A new era for the EC securities and investment services regime', *ICLQ*, vol. 52, no. 2, pp. 509–20. The influence of the *Lamfalussy Report* has been important, in terms of legislative production. However, the division of responsibilities between home Member State and host Member State, according to the *Lamfalussy* process, raised concerns: see e.g. CESR (2007) *'The Passport under MiFID' CESR/07-337b.*

11 In relation to market integration achieved in the EU before the financial crisis, see inter alia Commission Staff Working Document, 'Financial Integration Monitor 2006', SEC(2006) 1057, 26.07.2006; Commission, White Paper, *Financial Services Policy 2005–2010*, COM(2005) 629 final.

12 For an assessment of the *Lamfalussy* process, see European Parliament Communication of 9 October 2008 with recommendations to the Commission (OJ C 9E, 15.1.2010, p. 48). For an overview, see FERRAN, E. and GREEN, D. (2007) 'Are the Lamfalussy Regulatory Networks Working Successfully?' European Policy Forum; LASTRA, R. M. (2003) 'Regulating European Securities Markets: Beyond the Lamfalussy Report' in ANDENAS, M. and AVGERINOS, Y. (eds) *Financial Markets in Europe: Towards a Single Regulator?*, The Hague: Kluwer International, pp. 211–22.

13 EEC Treaty, Article 61.

14 For an overview, see BARNARD, C. (2007), *The Substantive Law of the EU: The Four Freedoms* (above,

Such important initiatives were reflected in the Banking Directives, providing the context for the operation of credit institutions in the EEC, as the gradual liberalisation of capital movement permitted the first efforts to harmonise banking activities throughout the EEC.

The First Banking Directive,[15] adopted in 1977, provided the basic rules for authorisation of credit institutions, taking into account BCBS recommendations. The Second Banking Directive,[16] adopted in 1989, introduced principles of home Member State licensing and prudential supervision for credit institutions, thus implementing the EEC 'passporting' regime.[17]

The definition of a credit institution in both the First and the Second Banking Directives is that of an institution 'whose business is to receive deposits or other repayable funds from the public and to grant credits for its own account'.[18]

The First Banking Directive did not expressly refer to depositor (consumer) protection as the *ratio* for its adoption.[19]

The gradual regulation of the banking sector by harmonisation through the EEC was effected at this stage inter alia by the adoption of the Own Funds Directive,[20] the Solvency Ratio Directive,[21] both adopted in 1989, later the Large

n. 2); WALKER, G. A. (2006) *European Banking Law*, London: British Institute of International and Comparative Law; DASSESSE, M., STUART, I. and PENN, G. (1994) *EC Banking Law*, London: LLP.

15 Directive 77/780/EEC, OJ L 322/30., 17.12.1977. Repealed by Directive 2000/12/EC (CBD).

16 Directive 89/646/EEC, OJ L 386/1, 30.12.1989. Consolidated in Directive 2006/48/EC (recast), OJ L 177/1, 30.06.2006. Repealed by CRD IV.

17 Cf. Commission Interpretative Communication (1997) *Freedom to provide services and the interests of the general good in the Second Banking Directive* (OJ 97/C 219/04). See also DASSESSE, M. (1997) 'The European Commission's interpretative communication on freedom of services and the general good in the Second Banking Directive', *YIFEL*, pp. 45–63.

18 First Banking Directive, Article 1; Second Banking Directive, Article 1(1). Regarding deposit taking from the public see also ECJ decision of 11.02.1999 in Case C-366/97, *Criminal Proceedings against Massimo Romanelli and Paolo Romanelli* [1999] ECR I-00855.

19 See ECJ decision of 09.07.1997 in Case C-222/95, *Société Civile Immobilière Parodi v Banque Albert de Bary* [1997] ECR 3899, where the ECJ examined the issue of additional authorisation to provide banking services in the host Member State taking into account consumer protection considerations. The ECJ took into account that it is necessary to protect consumers against the harm that they would suffer through banking transactions effected by institutions not complying with the requirements relating to solvency and whose managers do not have the necessary professional qualifications or integrity. The ECJ accepted the existence of certain imperative reasons in the banking sector which related to the public interest that could justify measures adopted by the host Member State imposing additional authorisation requirements to credit institutions operating in its territory (ibid., paras 25–26). Furthermore, it referred expressly to consumer protection issues which are connected to individual protection (such as contractual terms and conflicts of interest) rather than control of the systemic risk. For a critical review of *Parodi*, see WALKER, G. A. (2006) *European Banking Law*, (n. 14), p. 176.

20 Directive 89/299/EEC, OJ L 124/16, 05.05.1989. Consolidated in Directive 2006/49/EC (recast), OJ L 177/201, 30.06.2006. Repealed by CRD IV.

21 Directive 89/647/EEC, OJ L 386/14, 30.12.1989. Consolidated in Directive 2006/49/EC, and repealed by CRD IV.

Exposures Directive,[22] adopted in 1992, and the Capital Adequacy Directive,[23] adopted in 1993, and then the Capital Adequacy II Directive,[24] adopted in 1998, which sought to harmonise prudential standards for credit institutions, in order to control systemic risk. The influence of the relevant BCBS proposals is noted.[25] Furthermore, consolidated supervision of banking groups was introduced by the First Consolidated Supervision Directive,[26] adopted in 1983, which was later replaced by the Second Consolidated Supervision Directive,[27] adopted in 1992. Further, another step on the difficult issue of supervising groups of financial companies was taken by the adoption in 2002 of the Financial Conglomerates Directive.[28]

While general EU law in the area of insolvency has been limited to an essential coordination of insolvency proceedings, in the context of judicial cooperation in civil matters,[29] minimum harmonisation measures were introduced before the

22 Directive 92/121/EEC, OJ L29/1, 05.02.1993. Consolidated in Directive 2006/49/EC, and repealed by CRD IV.

23 Directive 93/6/EEC, OJ L 141/1, 11.06.1993. Consolidated in Directive 2006/49/EC, and repealed by CRD IV.

24 Directive 98/31/EC, OJ L 204/13, 21.07.1998. Consolidated in Directive 2006/49/EC, and repealed by CRD IV.

25 See Ch. 2.1.

26 Directive 83/350/EEC, OJ L 193/18, 18.07.1983.

27 Council Directive 92/30/EEC, OJ L 110/52, 28.04.1992.

28 Directive 2002/87/EC, OJ L 035/1, 11.02.2003. Amended by CRD IV. See also Judgment of the EFTA Court of 18 October 2010 in Case E-3/10, *EFTA Surveillance Authority v Republic of Iceland* [2010] EFTA Court Reports 189.

29 The main EU law instrument was the *Insolvency Regulation* (Council Regulation 1346/2000, OJ L 160/1, 30.06.2000) which was updated a number of times through implementing Regulations in relation to the proceedings and persons falling within its field of application, the last before its repeal being Council Regulation 583/2011, OJ L 160/52, 18.06.2011. It has been repealed by the new Regulation (EU) 2015/848 of the European Parliament and of the Council of 20 May 2015 on insolvency proceedings, OJ L 141/19, 05.06.2015 (new Insolvency Regulation). Insolvency Regulation 1346/2000/EC aimed to achieve efficient and effective operation of cross-border insolvency proceedings, and to control forum shopping, which is a requirement to the proper functioning of the internal market (Regulation 1346/2000, Preamble, recitals 2 and 4). As substantive bankruptcy laws widely differ among Member States, the 2000 Insolvency Regulation did not introduce insolvency proceedings with universal scope in the EU (ibid., recital 11); it enabled the main insolvency proceedings to be opened in the Member State where the debtor has the centre of his main interests (ibid., recital 12 and Article 3) and provided for the immediate recognition of judgments concerning the opening, conduct and closure of insolvency proceedings which fall within its scope and of judgments handed down in direct connection with such insolvency proceedings (ibid., recital 22 and Articles 16–26). Following the opening of main proceedings, secondary insolvency proceedings could be opened in another Member State without the debtor's insolvency being examined in that other State (ibid., Article 27). However, insolvency proceedings concerning insurance undertakings, credit institutions, investment undertakings which provide services involving the holding of funds or securities for third parties, or to collective investment undertakings, did not fall within the scope of application of this Regulation (ibid., Article 1(2)). The law applicable to insolvency proceedings and their effects was stated to be the law of the Member State within the territory of which such proceedings were opened (ibid., Article 4; see also Article 5 regarding third parties' rights *in rem*). In relation to claim verification rules, Regulation 1346/2000 referred to applicable national law without providing more specific rules. For analysis, see MOSS, G., FLETCHER, I. and ISAACS, S. (eds) (2009) *The EC Regulation on Insolvency Proceedings – A*

GFC – in relation to the reorganisation and winding-up of credit institutions, which should briefly be examined.

Winding-up Directive

The insolvency of credit institutions, as a sectoral and important issue, was treated in the EU before the GFC – by the introduction of Directive 2001/24/EC (the Winding-up Directive),[30] an instrument of minimum harmonisation in specific issues, aiming at mutual recognition of reorganisation and winding-up procedures between Member States, while the application of (unharmonised) national law remained the norm.[31]

While the single-passport regime meant that supervision of a credit institution (and its branches) was provided by the competent authorities of the Member State where authorisation was granted, according to Consolidation Banking Directive, the same did not apply to reorganisation measures or open winding-up procedures.[32] In this context, mutual recognition of measures adopted by one Member State in relation to the reorganisation of a credit institution should be acceptable and effective in all Member States.[33]

Furthermore, the principle of equal treatment between creditors entails that creditors in the host Member State should be able to exercise their rights to take action within the applicable time limit;[34] also, that the credit institution is wound up according to the principles of unity (i.e. that the competent administrative and judicial authorities of the home Member State have sole jurisdiction) and universality (i.e. that the decisions of said competent authorities of the home Member State are recognised and have legal effect in all other Member States without any formality).[35]

Winding-up proceedings are defined by the Winding-up Directive as 'collective proceedings opened and monitored by the administrative or judicial authorities of a [Member State] with the aim of realising assets under the supervision of those authorities, including where the proceedings are terminated by a composition or

Commentary and Annotated Guide, 2nd edition, Oxford: OUP. See also VIRGOS, M., SCHMIT, E. (1996) *Report on the Convention on Insolvency Proceedings*, EU Council Document 6500/96.

30 Directive 2001/24/EC, OJ L 125/15, 05.05.2001. The Winding-up Directive was proposed to be amended by COM(2012) 0280 final; it has now been amended by the BRRD. The original proposal of the Commission for the adoption of this Directive was issued in 1985 (OJ C356/55, 31.12.1985 and OJ C 36/1, 08.02.1988), the opinion of the EESC on the proposal was issued in 1986 (OJ C 263/13, 20.10.1986), while the opinion of the European Monetary Institute was issued in 1998 (OJ C 332/13, 30.10.1998). The Directive entered into force many years after it was proposed, on 04.04.2001, and the time limit for its transposition was 05.05.2004 (Directive 2001/24/EC, Articles 34 and 35). See also MOSS, G., WESSELS, B. (2006) *EU Banking and Insurance Insolvency*, Oxford: OUP, p. 47 *et seq.*

31 For a general discussion of bank insolvency in advanced Western economies at the time, see HÜPKES, E. (2000) *The Legal Aspects of Bank Insolvency. A Comparative Analysis of Western Europe, the United States and Canada*, The Hague: Kluwer Law International.

32 Directive 2001/24/EC, Preamble, recitals 3 and 4.

33 Ibid., recitals 5 to 7.

34 Ibid., recital 12.

35 Ibid., recital 16.

other, similar measure',[36] governed by the substantive and procedural law of the home Member State (unless otherwise provided in the Directive).[37]

While the above issues are left to national law, the Directive provides that any creditor who has his domicile, normal place of residence or head office in a Member State other than the home Member State, including Member States' public authorities, shall have the right to lodge claims or to submit written observations relating to claims, further providing that the claims of creditors in other Member States than the home Member State shall be treated in the same way and accorded the same ranking as claims of an equivalent nature in the home Member State.[38]

Also, while the lodging, verification and admission of claims is governed by national law,[39] the Directive provides that a creditor 'shall send copies of supporting documents, if any, and shall indicate the nature of the claim, the date on which it arose and its amount, as well as whether he alleges preference, security in re or reservation of title in respect of the claim and what assets are covered by his security'.[40]

The amendments brought to the Winding-up Directive by the BRRD have not materially affected its rules, on the reorganisation and winding-up of credit institutions; most important, the BRRD amendments have extended its field of application to include also investment firms, and their branches located in Member States other than those where their head offices.[41]

Thus, it may be considered that the *corpus* of European banking legislation has historically sought to control systemic risk in the banking sector, while creating a level playing field for banks to compete, aiming to achieve a single European market for the banking sector.

4.2 Development of EU investment services law prior to the GFC

EU investment services law[42] has long stated that its aim is dual: the protection of investors and the protection of financial markets.[43]

36 Ibid., Article 2 (now amended by BRRD, Article 117).

37 In particular, the law of the home Member State determines: '(a) ...;(f) the claims which are to be lodged against the credit institution and the treatment of claims arising after the opening of winding-up proceedings;(g) the rules governing the lodging, verification and admission of claims'; Directive 2001/24/EC, Article 10(2).

38 Ibid., Article 16(1) and (2).

39 Ibid., Article 10(2)(g).

40 Ibid., Article 16(3).

41 As defined in CRR, Article 4(1), point (2); BRRD, Article 117(1).

42 For an overview, see MOLONEY, N. (2014) *EU Securities and Financial Markets Regulation*, 3rd edition, Oxford: OUP, Oxford European Union Law Library; BLAIR, M., WALKER, G. A. and PURVES, R. (eds) (2009) *Financial Services Law*, 2nd edition, Oxford: OUP; PANASAR, R. and BOEKMAN, P. (2010) *European Securities Law*, Oxford: OUP; FERRAN, E. (2004) *Building an EU Securities Market*, Cambridge: Cambridge University Press.

43 See Communication from the Commission, 'The application of conduct of business rules under

It has also acknowledged that in the event of an investment firm failure, the damage sustained by the affected investors may also affect the financial market at large – if not as a signal causing systemic disturbances, at least as a factor causing distress to investors' confidence in the market.[44]

Harmonisation of EU investment services law followed the model which had been used in the European banking sector, applying the 'passporting' regime to investment firms, to be prudentially regulated and supervised by their home Member State competent authorities.

While the development of relevant secondary European financial legislation on free movement is in general connected to investor protection considerations (since every measure is protecting market transparency, efficiency and stability protects participants' legitimate interests), it is not directly connected to the issue of retail investor protection in the event of an investment firm failure. As an in-depth examination of all relevant European law instruments falls outside the scope of this study,[45] it will be important briefly to examine certain features of the ISD and the MIFID, especially in relation to the delineation of the notion of retail investor, and to the notion of investor protection and to corresponding supervisory and competent authorities' responsibilities, as may be relevant to a FI's failure.[46]

The Investment Services Directive (ISD)

The ISD, adopted in 1992, built on the experience of harmonisation in the banking sector. Numerous references to investor protection were made in the preamble to the ISD, which has to be taken into account in determining its *ratio*.[47]

Article 11 of the investment services directive (93/22/EEC)', COM(2000) 0722 final; MiFID, Preamble, recitals 26, 31, 44, 61 and 71.

44 See e.g. DGSD, Preamble, recital 25.

45 Such development included the introduction, as part of the FSAP, inter alia of the Markets Abuse Directive: Council Directive 2003/6, OJ L 96/16, 12.04.2003; the Prospectus Directive: Council Directive 2003/71, OJ L 345/31, 31.12.2003; the Transparency Directive: Council Directive 2004/109, OJ L 390/38, 31.12.2004; and MiFID.

46 With regard to the notion and the reason to protect retail investors and the design of a retail investor regime with regard to the provision of services, as the relevant problematic unfolded in the early stages of the financial crisis, see MOLONEY, N. (2010) How to Protect Investors: Lessons from the EC and the UK, Cambridge: Cambridge University Press, pp. 45–133.

47 The Preamble to the ISD stated inter alia that: 'firms that provide the investment services covered by [ISD] must be subject to authorisation by their home Member States in order to protect investors and the stability of the financial system' (Preamble, recital 2); that 'it is necessary, for the protection of investors, to guarantee the internal supervision of every firm, either by means of two-man management or, where that is not required by [ISD], by other mechanisms that ensure an equivalent result' (Preamble, recital 5); that 'in order to protect investors an investor's ownership and other similar rights in respect of securities and his rights in respect of funds entrusted to a firm should in particular be protected by being kept distinct from those of the firm' (Preamble, recital 29); that 'one of the objectives of [ISD] is to protect investors; … it is therefore appropriate to take account of the different requirements for protection of various categories of investors and of their levels of professional expertise' (Preamble, recital 32); and that 'with the two-fold aim of

The ISD defined an investment firm as 'any legal person the regular occupation or business of which is the provision of investment services for third parties on a professional basis'.[48]

Thus, the ISD definition of an investment firm for the purpose of its application was based on a functional criterion, according to which a firm fell within its field of application if it wished to provide at least one of the investment services listed in Section A of the Annex to ISD, in which case it had to achieve specific licensing for the specific investment service to be provided.

The ISD provided for certain obligations of national competent authorities regarding the conditions for providing authorisation to investment firms, which had to specify the investment services they were licensed to provide:[49] national competent authorities had to verify inter alia that an investment firm had sufficient initial capital in accordance with CAD rules having regard to the nature of the investment service in question, and that the direction of the investment firm's business was decided by at least two persons – the 'four eye rule' – of sufficiently good repute and sufficiently experienced.[50] The latter requirement being very broad, it was left to national competent authorities to regulate on the conditions for this crucial criterion, of 'fit and proper' management of an investment firm, to be satisfied.

The ISD provided certain further obligations that investment firms had to comply with, on an ongoing basis, and under the supervision of competent national authorities.[51]

Furthermore, the ISD introduced a specific supervisory regime in relation to CoB rules, which departed from the principle of home Member State regulation and supervision of investment firms, and provided that both the home Member State and the host Member State were competent for issuing and enforcement of CoB rules.[52]

The introduction of this rule may be regarded as relevant to the *Cassis* rule of

protecting investors and ensuring the smooth operation of the markets in transferable securities, it is necessary to ensure that transparency of transactions is achieved and that the rules laid down for that purpose in [the ISD] for regulated markets apply both to investment firms and to credit institutions when they operate on the market' (Preamble, recital 42). See also, however, ECJ decision of 21.11.2002 in Case C-356/00, *Antonio Testa and Lido Lazzeri v Commissione Nazionale per la Società e la Borsa (Consob)* [2002] ECR I-10797, paras 3 and 33.

48 ISD, Article 1(2). Investment services were defined as 'any of the services listed in Section A of the Annex relating to any of the instruments listed in Section B of the Annex that are provided for a third party': ibid., Article 1(1).

49 Ibid., Article 3(1).

50 ISD, Article 3(3).

51 Such prudential requirements were relevant to administrative and accounting procedures, control and safeguard arrangements for electronic data processing, internal control mechanisms, safeguarding ownership rights of investors especially in the event of the investment firm's insolvency, the prevention of the use of investors' instruments by the investment firm for its own account, the record keeping of transactions executed, and conflict of interest avoidance; ibid., Article 10.

52 See ANDENAS, M. (1994) 'Rules of conduct and the principle of subsidiarity', *Company Lawyer*, p. 60; WOUTERS, J. (1993) 'Rules of conduct, foreign investment firms and the ECJ's case-law on services', *Company Lawyer*, p. 194.

host State competence where national rules adopted in the general good are applicable. The reasoning of such supervisory competence allocation was connected to general good (protection of investors) considerations of the Member State where services were provided.[53]

The ISD provided that CoB rules should be applied taking into account the professional nature of the person for whom the service is provided.[54] However, the ISD did not provide any definition of such professional nature, nor did it provide any criteria under which a person might be characterised as professional for the purpose of CoB rules application.

The issue of CoB rules specifically in the area of financial services, and in the context of consumer protection as a public interest restriction on the free provision of services in the securities sector,[55] was examined by the ECJ in the *Alpine Investments* case.[56] The ECJ accepted that the need to protect the reputation of the financial markets and investors could constitute imperative reasons of public interest justifying certain restrictions (as in that case, of 'cold calling').[57]

It is interesting to note in this regard that the protection of investors was taken into consideration by the ECJ mainly in the context of the protection of the trust of investors to the financial market; in that sense, the protection of the integrity of financial markets was at the centre of the notion of 'market reputation' protection.[58]

While the ISD was provided with certain rules relevant to retail investor protection, it did not achieve full market integration.[59]

The ISD was replaced by the MiFID, adopted in the context of the *Lamfalussy* process.

53 See 1997 Commission Interpretative Communication (n. 17).

54 ISD, Article 11(1).

55 In relation to public interest concerns in the area of insurance, see ECJ decision of 04.12.1986 in Case 220/83, *Commission v French Republic* [1986] ECR 3663; ECJ decision of 04.12.1986 in Case 252/83, *Commission v Kingdom of Denmark* [1976] ECR 3713; ECJ decision of 04.12.1986 in Case 205/84, *Commission v Federal Republic of Germany* [1986] ECR 3755; ECJ decision of 04.12.1986 in Case 206/84, *Commission v Ireland* [1986] ECR 3817 (the '*Co-insurance Cases*'). It is interesting to note that the ECJ took into account, as a factor of the sensitivity of the insurance market in relation to consumer protection and public interest national rules, the nature of the service provided (uncertainty of the occurrence of events at the time of conclusion of the insurance contract) and the difficulty for consumers to foresee whether they would receive payment in relation to insurer's future financial position, as well as the great number of consumers such contracts concerned; cf. Case 220/83 above, para. 30.

56 See ECJ decision of 10.05.1995 in Case C-384/93, *Alpine Investments BV v Minister van Financiën* [1995] ECR I-1141, [1995] 2 *CMLRev* 209. See ANDENAS, M. (1995) 'Investment Services: Cross-border Cold Calling and the Right to Provide Services', *Company Lawyer*, p. 249. See also HATZOPOULOS, V. (1995) 'Case C-384/93 Alpine Investments BV v Minister van Financiën, Judgment of 10 May 1999, NYR (1995)' 32 *CMLRev* 1427.

57 *Alpine Investments*, para. 47.

58 Ibid., paras 42–43.

59 See also Commission Communication (2000) 'Upgrading the Investment Services Directive', COM(2000) 729, 16.11.2000.

It is then necessary to carefully examine certain aspects of the MiFID, which are important to this study.

The Markets in Financial Instruments Directive (MiFID)

The introduction of the MiFID,[60] as the ISD before it, aimed at protecting both the stability of the financial market and investors.[61]

The MiFID entered into force on 30 April 2004, providing for a transposition period which ended on 31 January 2007, i.e. a short time before the occurrence of the GFC.[62] Since its publication it has been amended several times.[63]

The MiFID took EU financial law into a new dimension, in an effort 'to encompass the full range of investor oriented activities';[64] many ISD provisions were amended by the MiFID, new rules were introduced, and the ISD was repealed.[65]

The field of application of the MiFID is wider than that of the ISD.[66] Authorised credit institutions, when providing investment services to their clients, fall within the scope of application of the MiFID, without the need for further licensing under it;[67] furthermore, investment firms providing investment

60 Directive 2004/39/EC, OJ L 145/1, 30.04.2004. See in general AUBRY, N. and McKEE, M. (2007) 'MiFID: Where did it come from, where is it taking us', *JIBLR*, vol. 22, no. 4, pp. 177–86; CESR (2007) 'The Passport under MiFID', CESR/07-335b, Paris: CESR.

61 MiFID, Preamble, recitals 2, 17, 31, 44 and 71. In its decision of 22.03.2012 in Case C-248/11, *Criminal Proceedings against Rareş Doralin Nilaş and Others*, ECLI:EU:C:2012:166, the ECJ ruling on a preliminary reference on the interpretation of Articles 4(1)(14) and 47 of the MiFID, inter alia considered that 'as is clear in particular from recitals 2, 5 and 44 in the preamble to Directive 2004/39, that its objectives consist, inter alia, in protecting investors, preserving the efficient and orderly functioning of financial markets and the transparency of transactions' (ibid., para. 48). However, the ECJ, considering such a conclusion to be clear, did not discuss it in view of its general case law relevant to the matter, to which it did not refer. See also ECJ decision of 30.05.2013 in Case C604/11, *Genil 48 SL, Comercial Hostelera de Grandes Vinos SL v Bankinter SA, Banco Bilbao Vizcaya Argentaria SA*, ECLI:EU:C:2013:344 (*Bankinter* case), para. 39.

62 Ibid., Article 70.

63 The MiFID is repealed by the MiFID II with effect from 03.01.2017, so until then it remains in force. MiFID II has to be transposed into national legal orders according to the relevant time limits: see MiFID II, Articles 93 and 94.

64 MiFID, Preamble, recital 2.

65 See ESME (2008) 'Differences between the Definitions of "Qualified Investor" in the Prospectus Directive and "Professional Client" and "Eligible Counterparty" in MiFID – Is Alignment Needed?'; FERRANINI, G. and WYMEERSCH, E. (eds) (2006) *Investor Protection in Europe: Corporate Law Making, The MiFID and Beyond*, Oxford: OUP.

66 *Ratione materiae*, it includes also investment advice as an investment service, taking into account 'the increasing dependence of investors on personal recommendations'; MiFID, Preamble, recital 3. Furthermore, commodities and other derivatives have been introduced in the list of financial instruments, taking into account the need to regulate their trading in the financial market. *Ratione personae* it encompasses also regulated markets: MiFID, Articles 36–47. In relation to the criteria of the MiFID regarding a regulated market, see ECJ judgment of 22.03.2012 in Case C-248/11 (above, n. 61). It also encompasses alternative trading systems (Multilateral Trading Facilities, MTFs): MiFID, in particular Articles 14, 29, 30 and 35.

67 Ibid., Preamble, recital 18; Article 1.

services for which they are not licensed under the MiFID do not need additional authorisation for the provision of such services, if they provide them on a non-regular basis.[68]

In relation to the definition of investment firm and investment service, the MiFID follows the same normative structure as the ISD,[69] and is completed by the implementing Directive 2006/73/EC and Implementing Regulation EC (No.) 1287/2006.[70]

The normative system introduced by the MiFID provides for more detailed conditions and procedures for authorisation of investment firms than the ISD.[71] In relation to the 'fit and proper' requirement regarding the persons who effectively direct the business of the investment firm, the MiFID provides broad criteria, not different in essence from those provided by the ISD: The 'four eye rule' being *a priori* applicable,[72] Member States had to require that such persons were 'of sufficiently good repute and sufficiently experience as to ensure the sound and prudent management of the investment firm'.[73] Further, the competent national authority has to refuse authorisation not only if not satisfied that the persons effectively directing the business of the investment firm are of sufficiently good repute or sufficiently experienced, but also 'if there are objective and demonstrable grounds for believing that proposed changes to the management of the firm pose a threat to its sound and prudent management'.[74]

Other organisational requirements are provided by the MiFID for investment firms, the home Member State being responsible for achieving compliance: inter alia that an investment firm shall establish adequate policies and procedures sufficient to ensure compliance,[75] shall take measures to prevent conflicts of interests,[76] shall take steps to ensure continuity and regularity in the performance of investment services and activities,[77] shall have sound administrative and accounting procedures, internal control mechanisms, effective procedures for risk assessment, and effective control and safeguard arrangements for information processing systems,[78] shall arrange for records to be kept of all services and transactions undertaken by it which shall be sufficient to enable the competent authority to monitor compliance,[79] and shall make adequate arrangements so as

68 Ibid., Preamble, recital 19; Article 2.

69 Ibid., Article 4.

70 Commission Directive 2006/73/EC, OJ L 241/26, 02.09.2006, and Regulation (EC) No. 1287/2016, OJ L241/1, 02.09.2006, respectively. The time limit for the application in the national legal orders of the provisions transposing this Directive was 01.11.2007; ibid., Article 53(2).

71 MiFID, Chapter I.

72 Ibid., Article 9(4).

73 Ibid., Article 9(1).

74 Ibid., Article 9(3).

75 Ibid., Article 13(2).

76 Ibid., Article 13(3); Article 18. Cf. Directive 2006/73/EC, Article 21.

77 MiFID, Article 13(4).

78 Ibid., Article 13(5).

79 Ibid., Article 13(6). See also Directive 2006/73/EC, Article 51 and Regulation (EC) No. 1287/2006. Regarding record keeping see Directive 2006/73/EC, Article 16.

to safeguard clients' ownership rights, especially in the event of the investment firm's insolvency.[80]

Taking into account the above general context of the MiFID rules on retail investor protection, as specified also by implementing Directive 2006/73/EC, it is useful to examine the rules provided by the latter in relation more specifically to investor protection.

First, a licensed investment firm must comply at all times with the conditions for its initial authorisation[81] and Member States are under an obligation to ensure that national competent authorities monitor the activities of investment firms, in the context of ongoing supervision.[82]

In relation to the level of investor protection,[83] the MiFID differentiates the status of protection by setting out three categories of investors: retail investors (clients), professional investors (clients) and counterparties.[84]

The MiFID defines as 'client' any natural or legal person to whom an investment firm provides investment and/or ancillary services.[85]

A 'retail client' is defined as a client who is not a professional client,[86] and a 'professional client' is one meeting the criteria laid down in Annex II of the Directive.[87]

Professional clients are, according to the MiFID, entities required to be authorised or regulated to operate in the financial markets and other institutional investors whose main activity is to invest in financial instruments.[88] These entities are defined *ex lege* as professional investors (clients). However, they are allowed to request non-professional treatment in order to enjoy a higher level of protection, and following a written agreement with the investment firm to that effect, in which the particular services or transactions to which it applies have to be specified.[89]

Furthermore, the MiFID provides for a particular sub-category of retail investors (clients), who although being categorised according to the terms of the Directive as non-professional, may be treated as professional investors on request.[90]

However, even if treated as professional investors, such persons may not be presumed to possess market knowledge and experience comparable to that of

80 MiFID, Article 13(7) and (8).

81 Ibid., Article 16(1).

82 Ibid., Article 17(1). See, e.g., ECJ decision of 12.11.2014 in Case C-140/13, *Annett Altmann and Others v Bundesanstalt für Finanzdienstleistungsaufsicht*, ECLI:EU:C:2014:2362, para. 28, where the Court considered that '… under Article 17(1) of [MiFID], the Member States must ensure that the competent authorities continuously monitor the activities of investment firms so as to assess compliance with their obligations'.

83 Regarding market transparency and integrity protection, see ibid., Articles 25–30.

84 Ibid., Preamble, recital 31.

85 Ibid., Annex I(1), point 10.

86 Ibid., Annex I(1), point 12.

87 Ibid., Annex I(1), point 11.

88 Ibid., Annex II, Article I(1).

89 Ibid.

90 Ibid., Annex II, Article 2.

professional investors, and waiver of the protection afforded to them by CoB rules is conditional.[91]

In this way, despite providing for enhanced retail investors protection especially by CoB rules, and by reference to the ICSD regime,[92] MiFID allows for exceptions from this regime on a voluntary basis and according to a procedure taking place between the interested investor and the investment firm.

Additional requirements may be posed by Member States 'only in those exceptional cases where such requirements are objectively justified and proportionate so as to address specific risks to investor protection or to market integrity that are not adequately addressed by this Directive',[93] i.e. for imperative reasons.

In relation to CoB rules, the MiFID provides for an obligation of Member States to require that in the provision of investment services, an investment firm acts 'honestly, fairly and professionally in accordance with the best interests of its clients',[94] complying in particular with relevant principles regarding fair, clear and not misleading transmission of information,[95] provision of appropriate information about the investment firm and its services, financial instruments and proposed investment strategies,[96] execution venues and costs and associated charges,[97] presented so as to enable clients to understand the nature and risks of the investment service envisaged and to take investment decisions on an informed basis.[98] The investment firm must keep a record of documents agreed with the client, and must provide the client with adequate reports on the service provided and the costs associated with it.[99]

More generally, regarding CoB rules, the MiFID attempts to resolve the problems that had emerged under the ISD regime, mainly by introducing the sole competence of home Member State on CoB rules; however, with services provided by a branch of an investment firm still falling within the competence of the Member State where provided.

The MiFID rules on requirements regarding initial authorisation and ongoing

91 Ibid., Annex II, Article 2(2).
92 Ibid., Article 11.
93 Directive 2006/73/EC, Article 4(1).
94 MiFID, Article 19(1). Cf. Directive 2006/73/EC, Article 26 regarding inducements.
95 MiFID, Article 19(2). Cf. Directive 2006/73/EC, Article 27.
96 Cf. Directive 2006/73/EC, Article 31.
97 MiFID, Article 19(3). See also Directive 2006/73/EC, Articles 28, 29, 30 and 31.
98 MiFID, Article 19. See also in relation to execution of orders 'in the best interest' of the client, ibid., Article 21. With regard to CoB rules on suitability or appropriateness assessment under MiFID, in particular Article 19 of the MiFID and Articles 35 to 37 of Directive 2006/73 (MiFID implementing Directive), see ECJ decision in Case C-604/11, *Bankinter* (n. 61); see also GRUNDMAN, S. (2013) 'The Bankinter Case on MiFID Regulation and Contract Law', *European Review of Contract Law*, vol. 9, pp. 267–80, TENENBAUM, A. (2014) Les contrats financiers complexes et les obligations d'information: partition d'un dialogue subtil entre la CJUE et les juges nationaux, *Revue des contrats*, pp. 123–26. See also the ECJ decision of 03.12.2015 in Case C312/14, *Banif Plus Bank Zrt. v Márton Lantos, Mártonné Lantos*, ECLI:EU:C:2015:794, in which the Court considered the concept of 'investment services and activities' under MiFID, Article 4(1), in relation to CoB suitability or appropriateness requirements pursuant to Article 19 of the same Directive.
99 Ibid., Article 19(8).

supervision of investment firms, as well as the CoB rules, provide a framework relevant to investor protection, although mostly in terms of *ex ante* protection (before the failure of an investment firm).

However, this issue is also relevant to the question of supervisory liability in tort in case of financial institution (FI) failure, since the initial authorisation and the ongoing supervision of an investment firm by the competent authorities is closely related to retail investor protection considerations. In this context, it is useful to briefly examine the obligations of national competent authorities as provided by the MiFID.[100]

The MiFID provides that '[e]ach [Member State] shall designate the competent authorities which are to carry out each of the duties provided for in this Directive'.[101] There is no specific requirement as to the legal nature of competent authorities, beyond that they have to be public authorities, with the option of delegating tasks to other entities where permitted and on the conditions provided by the MiFID.[102] The criterion set by the MiFID, for Member States to allow such delegation, is connected to effectiveness: Member States have to require that competent authorities take all reasonable steps to ensure that the delegate has the capacity and resources to execute the delegated tasks effectively.[103]

The MiFID further provides that competent authorities have to be given all-encompassing supervisory and investigatory powers, according to national law.[104] In relation to the powers that competent authorities must have, as a minimum, the MiFID provides a list of competences, which relate to: (a) collecting information (accessing documents,[105] demanding information from any person[106] including auditors,[107] carrying out of on-site inspections,[108] requiring existing telephone and data traffic records,[109] requiring auditors to provide information, allowing auditors or experts to carry out verifications or investigations),[110] (b) taking provisional and permanent measures to control any illegal practice (requiring the cessation of any such practice,[111] requesting the temporary prohibition of professional activity[112] or the suspension of trading in a financial instruments,[113] or the removal of such instrument

100 An issue of interpretation and application of the relevant provisions emerges in particular if such competence is not exercised by national competent authorities but by EU institutions or agencies, in the context of the new EU financial supervision framework.
101 MiFID, Article 48(1).
102 Ibid., Article 48(2).
103 Ibid.
104 Ibid., Article 50(1).
105 Ibid., Article 50(2), point (a).
106 Ibid., point (b).
107 Ibid., point (h).
108 Ibid., point (c).
109 Ibid., point (d).
110 Ibid., point (m).
111 Ibid., point (e).
112 Ibid., point (g).
113 Ibid., point (j).

from trading),[114] (c) taking measures to protect pecuniary claims (requesting freezing and/or sequestration of assets),[115] (d) referring matters for criminal prosecution,[116] and (e) in general, adopting 'any type of measure to ensure that investment firms and regulated matters continue to comply with legal requirements'.[117]

This minimum harmonisation approach of the MiFID leaves unspecified how each competence is to be exercised by national competent authorities, which has to be determined by national law with a view to achieving the aim of the Directive.

Further rules are provided in relation to the powers of the host Member State to take precautionary measures in order to control the illegal activity of an investment firm (or a regulated market or a multilateral trading facility (MTF))[118] operating in its territory if, despite having notified the competent authorities of the home Member State, the investment firm fails to comply with its obligations, or where the measures taken by the competent authorities of the home Member State prove 'inadequate'.[119]

Such action by the host Member State competent authorities is justified under the MiFID when the investment firm acts 'in a manner that is clearly prejudicial to the interests of host [Member State] investors or the orderly functioning of the markets'[120] and the host Member State could take 'all the appropriate measures needed in order to protect investors and the proper functioning of the markets'.[121]

The provisions of the MiFID regarding the adoption of administrative measures and the imposition of administrative sanctions by Member States are also very broad;[122] Member States are called to ensure that such measures are effective, proportionate and dissuasive.[123]

On the other hand, it is interesting to note that the MiFID provides for *locus standi* of bodies (public bodies, consumer organisations and professional organisations), which could take action 'in the interest of consumers'[124] before the national

114 Ibid., point (k).
115 Ibid., point (f).
116 Ibid., point (l).
117 Ibid., point (i).
118 Ibid., Article 62(1) and (3).
119 Ibid., Article 62(1), as amended by Directive 2010/78/EU [2010] OJ L 331/120.
120 Ibid.
121 Ibid.
122 Ibid., Article 51(1)–(3).
123 Ibid., Article 51(1). See also ECJ decision of 30.05.2013 in Case C-604/11, *Bankinter* (n. 61). The ECJ considered inter alia that, although MiFID Article 51 provides for the imposition of administrative measures or sanctions against the parties responsible for non-compliance with the provisions adopted pursuant to it, it does not state either that Member States must provide for contractual consequences in the event of contracts being concluded which do not comply with the obligations under national legal provisions transposing MiFID, Article 19(4) and (5), or what those consequences might be; and that in the absence of EU legislation on the point, it is for the internal legal order of each Member State to determine the contractual consequences of non-compliance with those obligations, subject to observance of the principles of equivalence and effectiveness (para. 57 and the case law cited therein).
124 The term 'consumer' is not defined in the MiFID. On the relevant problematic of the legal status of investors, see also MOLONEY, N. (2012) 'The investor model underlying the EU's investor

courts or competent administrative bodies 'to ensure that the national provisions for the implementation of [the MiFID] are applied'.[125]

In the context of the changes brought to EU financial legislation by the onset of the GFC, the MiFID was recast and partly replaced by the MiFID II and the MiFIR, establishing a new system of EU law regulating investment firms and markets.

Interim concluding remarks

EU financial law was shaped, prior to the GFC, on the basis of the initial EEC Treaty freedoms, gradually and through a long process in the context of which the impetus to integrate the wider EU market, reflecting the operation of the real economy, led to efforts to integrate the financial market as well.

The model for investment services law was generally built according to that of the banking sector, while the two sectors were considered and treated differently, with prudential supervision and regulation focusing on banks perceived as systemically sensitive.

While concerns with regard to the treatment of financial consumers led to acceptance under conditions of national imperative reasons, to the *communitarisation* of CoB rules and to the introduction of an exceptional supervisory regime for their application, in general supervision and regulation of investment firms remained a national issue, with competent authorities of the home Member State applying national law (in many areas of EU secondary law origin).

In this context, the participation of financial consumers in the EU financial market related to the activity of FIs regulated and supervised by national competent authorities which were obliged to interpret and apply national law (of EU origin) under the light of harmonising EU law. Beyond the competence of the ECJ to provide a single and obligatory interpretation of EU law for Member States and EU institutions, the interpretation and application of financial law remained at the national level without any unifying mechanism at the EU level.

Thus, while FIs, whether large conglomerates or smaller firms, had become closely connected in a nexus of legal and financial relations across the EU and global markets, EU financial law remained fragmentary, in many cases internally inconsistent, and its application segmented across national legal orders.

protection regime: consumers or investors?', *European Business Organization Law Review*, vol. 13, no. 2, p. 169.

125 MiFID, Article 52(2). While there is no reference in this provision as to the nature of the remedy or the claim such action may have, it connects the interests of consumers with application of national law implementing the Directive. And as it refers to national law to regulate this matter (not only at the procedural level, but also at the substantive level), it may entail, under the conditions provided by national law and case-law, that action may be brought by such bodies against competent authorities, for failure to exercise their duties according to national law implementing the MiFID. This issue is connected to the wider problematic of supervisory authorities' liability under EU law, and relates to the question of whether national law may provide for such liability even if EU law does not.

As a result, when the GFC hit the European financial markets, they were soon found isolated, searching for national solutions to protect national financial markets from systemic risk, and to protect financial consumers according to national policy considerations.

5 Effect of the GFC on EU financial supervisory architecture

Centralisation and concentration of powers at the EU level

Introductory note

Together with initiatives at the international level, by *fora* and organisations such as the World Bank, the IMF, the BCBS, the IOSCO and others, and by important new programmes by states with developed financial markets, as in particular the USA, the EU has been undergoing fundamental changes to its financial architecture and law, as a consequence of the global financial crisis (GFC).

In the wake of the GFC, the EU adopted a new single rulebook for financial institutions (FIs), aiming at coherence that will promote the creation of an integrated EU financial market, while also facilitating effective regulation and supervision of FIs and markets.[1]

Most important, a new EU architecture of financial supervision and regulation has been established, by the adoption of a new *corpus* of EU instruments creating new EU agencies with enhanced powers.[2]

1 For a general overview of current EU banking and financial law, see HAENTJENS, M. and De GIOIA-CARABELLESE, P. (2015) *European Banking and Financial Law*, London and New York: Routledge.

2 With regard to the institutional reaction of the EU to the GFC, see FERRAN, E., MOLONEY, N. and PAYNE, J. (eds) (2015) *The Oxford Handbook of Financial Regulation*, Oxford: OUP; MOLONEY, N. (2014) *EU Securities and Financial Markets Regulation*, 3rd edition, Oxford: OUP, Oxford European Union Law Library; WYMEERSCH, E., HOPT, K. J. and FERRANINI, G. (eds) (2012) *Financial Regulation and Supervision: a Post-crisis Analysis*, Oxford: Oxford University Press; FERRAN, E. (2012) 'Crisis-driven EU Financial Regulatory Reform', *Legal Studies Research Paper Series*, vol. 6, March, http://ssrn.com/abstract=2028003; MOLONEY, N. (2012) 'The legacy effects of the financial crisis on regulatory design in the EU' in FERRAN, E., HILL, J., MOLONEY, N. and COFFEE, J. (eds) *The Regulatory Aftermath of the Global Financial Crisis*, Cambridge: Cambridge University Press, pp. 111–202; *idem* (2012) 'Supervision in the wake of the financial crisis: achieving effective "law in action" – a challenge for the EU' in WYMEERSCH, E., HOPT, K. J. and FERRANINI, G. (eds) *Financial Regulation and Supervision: a Post-crisis Analysis*, Oxford: OUP; TRIDIMAS, T. (2011) 'EU Financial Regulation: Federalization, Crisis Management, and Law Reform' in CRAIG, P. and De BURCA, G. (2011) *The Evolution of EU Law*, 2nd edition, Oxford: OUP, pp. 783–804; MOLONEY, N. (2010) 'EU financial market regulation after the global financial crisis: "more Europe" or more risks?', *CMLRev*, vol. 47, no. 5, pp. 1317–83; AVGOULEAS, E. (2009) 'The global financial crisis, behavioural finance and financial regulation: in search of a new orthodoxy', *Journal of Corporate Law Studies*, vol. 9, no. 1, April, pp. 23–59.

It is useful for the purposes of this study to take into consideration the gradual development of EU law in this area, so as to also examine their relation to financial consumer considerations, in the event of FI failure.

5.1 The new EU rules on licensing and prudential supervision of FIs

In June 2013, the EU took an important step forward in order to achieve effective operation of the financial market, in the direction of unifying prudential requirements and supervisory mechanisms for credit institutions and investment firms, since both have been acknowledged as being prone to systemic dangers, by the adoption of the Capital Requirements Regulation[3] and of the Capital Requirements Directive IV.[4]

The European Single Rule Book – Capital Requirements Regulation (CRR) / Capital Requirements Directive IV (CRD IV)

While the CRR Regulation mainly provides the (micro)prudential requirements for FIs that relate strictly to the functioning of banking and financial services markets, the CRD IV contains rules on the access to the activity of FIs, capital adequacy rules, the modalities for their governance, and their supervisory framework.[5]

Together, the CRR and the CRD IV aim to form the legal framework for the access to the activity, the supervisory framework and the prudential rules for all FIs, and thus to establish a coherent and transparent 'single rulebook' for FIs. The creation of such a single rulebook was considered necessary for reasons of legal certainty and in order to create a level playing field for all participants in the financial market within the EU.[6]

In this direction, maximum harmonisation was preferred in relation to minimum prudential requirements,[7] so that those requirements will be directly applicable in the national legal orders.[8] The effort to achieve balance between the requirements for legal certainty and flexibility aims at addressing regulatory arbitrage and at achieving market confidence especially in times of crisis.[9]

It is interesting that the new EU law on FIs endorses a clear and critical position in relation to the role of banking activities, noting that:

> [c]onsidering the devastating effects of the latest financial crisis the overall objectives of this [CRR] are to encourage economically useful banking

3 Regulation (EU) No. 575/2013, OJ L 176/1, 27.06.2013.

4 Directive 2013/36/EU OJ L 176/338.

5 See Commission Report to the European Parliament and the Council 'on the rules governing the levels of application of banking prudential requirements', COM(2015) 388 final, 05.08.2015, referring inter alia to consistency of such EU rules with BCSB standards.

6 CRR, Preamble, recital 9.

7 Ibid., recitals 9 and 11.

8 Ibid., recital 12.

9 Ibid., recitals 6 and 15.

activities that serve the general interest and discourage unsustainable financial speculation without real added value. This implies a comprehensive reform of the way savings are channeled into productive investments.[10]

The Capital Requirements Regulation (CRR)

The CRR, on the prudential requirements for FIs, explicitly refers in its preamble to the G-20 Declaration of 02.04.2009 and the following international initiatives,[11] as well as to the *de Larosière* Report which stressed the need to establish a 'European Single Rule Book' applicable to all FIs in the internal market.[12]

Taking over from Directives 2006/48/EC and 2006/49/EC,[13] the CRR incorporates the EU law provisions applying the Basel II and Basel III frameworks in relation to capital measurement and capital requirements for FIs, taking into account the relevant risk profile of FIs.[14]

Disclosure requirements for FIs are connected by the CRR to the purposes of strengthening market discipline and enhancing financial stability which are further connected in order 'to ensure that investors and depositors are sufficiently well informed about the solvency of institutions'.[15]

While the CRR illustrates a reform of EU banking law in the direction of ensuring that credit institutions provide vital services to the real economy,[16] it does not proceed to a structural separation of retail and investment banking activities within a banking group, which it allows Member State to regulate, while requiring the Commission to analyse the issue.[17]

In the same direction, and with a view to protecting depositors and preserving financial stability, the CRR allows for home Member States to require credit institutions to reduce exposures to different legal entities depending on their activities, but only following a future legal act harmonising such measures.[18]

The Capital Requirements Directive IV (CRD IV)

The CRR provides (micro)prudential rules of a highly technical nature for FIs,[19] it is necessary to examine in turn the main features of the CRD IV, which provides the new EU framework for the authorisation, operation and supervision of FIs.

10 Ibid., recital 32.

11 Ibid., recital 1.

12 Ibid., recital 2. A credit institution is defined by the CRR as 'an undertaking the business of which is to take deposits or other repayable funds from the public and to grant credits for its own account'. Ibid., Article 4(1), point 1. For the definition of an investment firm for the purposes of the CRR, see ibid., Article 4(1), point 2.

13 Repealed by the CRD IV.

14 CRR, Preamble, recital 41 *et seq.*

15 Ibid., recital 76; cf. ibid., recital 120. See also ibid., Articles 431–34.

16 Ibid., recital 122; cf. ibid., recital 32.

17 Ibid., recital 122.

18 Ibid., recital 123.

19 Ibid., Article 521.

The CRD IV is an instrument adopted with a view to ensure a coherent application of EU law on the taking up and pursuit of the business of credit institutions and on the capital adequacy of FIs;[20] it provides rules for the authorisation of the business, the acquisition of qualifying holdings, the exercise of the freedom of establishment and of the freedom to provide services, the powers of supervisory authorities of home and host Member States in this regard and the provisions governing the initial capital and the supervisory review of FIs.[21]

It takes into account that the scope of relevant measures should be as broad as possible 'covering all institutions whose business is to receive repayable funds from the public, whether in the form of deposits or in other forms such as the continuing issue of bonds and other comparable securities and to grant credits for their own account'.[22]

While the principles of mutual recognition of authorisation and of prudential supervision systems are to be respected, they are understood by the CRD IV in conjunction with a requirement of effectiveness, in the sense that authorisation should not be granted or should be withdrawn in cases of regulatory arbitrage[23] or where supervisory authorities are liable to be prevented from effectively exercising their supervisory functions.[24]

The requirement for supervision to be effective further necessitates that supervision on a consolidated basis should be applied to all banking groups, its aim being 'to protect the interests of depositors and investors of institutions and to ensure the stability of the financial system',[25] while it is acknowledged by the CRD IV that illegal behaviour (such as fraud) is liable to affect the stability and integrity of the financial system.[26]

Moreover, the CRD IV takes into account that:

> weaknesses in corporate governance … have contributed to excessive and imprudent risk taking in the banking sector which has led to the failure of individual institutions and systemic problems in [Member States] and globally. … The unclear role of the competent authorities in overseeing corporate governance systems in institutions did not allow for sufficient supervision of the effectiveness of the internal governance processes.[27]

The CRD IV does not apply to the access to the activity of investment firms insofar as regulated by MiFID/MiFID II.[28] However, it provides a new, enhanced

20 CRD IV, Preamble, recital 1.
21 Ibid., recital 2. See also ibid., Article 1.
22 Ibid., recital 14.
23 Ibid., recital 16.
24 Ibid., recital 17.
25 Ibid., recital 47.
26 Ibid., recital 30.
27 Ibid., recital 53.
28 Ibid., Article 2(5)(1). The terms 'credit institution' and 'investment firm' are defined as in CRR, Article 4; see CRD IV, Article 3.

framework for the powers of competent authorities in connection to its scope: Member States are under the obligation to ensure that competent authorities monitor the activities of FIs, so as to assess compliance with the CRR, and to ensure that appropriate measures are in place to enable competent authorities to obtain information to investigate breaches of applicable requirements, and to carry out their functions.[29]

In relation especially to prudential supervision, the CRD IV provides for enhanced supervisory measures and powers, already at an early stage, to address problems regarding fulfilment of CRD IV/CRR requirements.[30]

Furthermore, for the purpose of satisfying the prudential requirements of the CRR, competent authorities are provided by the CRD IV with an array of important powers (which may be further enhanced by Member States) and which include inter alia requiring FIs to hold extra own funds, to reinforce internal arrangements, processes, mechanisms, etc., to restrict or limit their business, operations or network or to diversify their activities, to reduce risk in their activities, etc.[31]

According to the CRD IV, competent authorities are inter alia under the obligation to publish not only the legal instruments, administrative rules and general guidance adopted in their legal order in the field of prudential regulation, but also to proceed to disclosure in relation to a number of features relevant to the exercise of their duties under national law.[32]

The new MiFID II and MiFIR

As part of the reforms in EU financial law necessitated by the GFC, the Commission proposed the replacement of the MiFID by a new Directive on markets in financial instruments, with a view to enhance existing rules,[33] and a new Regulation to complement it.[34]

The proposals for new rules included inter alia provisions to strengthen the

29 CRD IV, Article 4.

30 Ibid., Article 102.

31 Ibid., Article 104.

32 Ibid., Articles 143–44.

33 See COM(2011) 656 final, 20.10.2011. This proposal related to requirements on the provision of investment services, the scope of exemptions from the MiFID, organisational and CoB requirements for investment firms, organisational requirements for trading venues, powers available to competent authorities, sanctions, and rules applicable to third-country firms operating via a branch. See also MOLONEY, N. and FERRANINI, G. (2012) 'Reshaping order execution in the EU and the role of interest groups under MiFID II', *European Business Organization Law Review*, vol. 13, no. 4, pp. 557–97.

34 See COM(2011) 652 final. The Commission proposal for MiFIR intended to establish uniform and directly applicable requirements in relation to disclosure of trade transparency data to the public and transaction data to competent authorities, removing barriers to non-discriminatory access to clearing facilities, mandatory trading of derivatives on organised venues, specific supervisory actions regarding financial instruments and positions in derivatives and the provision of services by third-country firms without a branch.

framework for the provision of investment advice and portfolio management, and to clarify the conditions for minimum protection awarded by investment firms to investors in relation to transactions in non-complex financial instruments. Furthermore, the requirements for the handling of funds or instruments belonging to clients by investment firms were proposed to be strengthened. According to the Commission proposal, the safe-keeping of financial instruments on behalf of clients should be classified as an investment service.[35]

The ECB in its Opinion on the proposal to adopt the MiFID II and the MiFIR[36] inter alia expressed its strong support to the development of a single EU rulebook for all FIs and recommended ensuring that only framework principles 'reflecting basic political choices and substantive matters' remain subject to the ordinary legislative procedure, whereas technical rules are adopted through delegated or implementing acts; also, that the new EU legislation should ensure cross-sectoral consistency.[37] It further welcomed the strengthening and aligning of supervisory authorities, and the strong role of the ESMA in this framework.[38] In particular, in relation to investor protection according to the Commission proposals, the ECB welcomed the proposed empowerment of the ESMA temporarily to prohibit or restrict certain financial instruments or activities,[39] and the extension of CoB and other requirements to credit institutions selling or advising structured deposits; at the same time, the ECB underlined 'the necessity of (i) clarifying the definition of "structured deposits"; (ii) specifying the consumer protection regime applicable to the financial products; and (iii) ensuring a consistent approach across the different Union legislative initiatives'.[40]

The EESC in its Opinion on the proposal to adopt the MiFID II and the MiFIR[41] expressed its general support, but also made some remarks, including that the legal basis opted for by the Commission may be inadequate,[42] since 'consumer protection and consolidation and development of the internal market ... are underpinned by better-defined, more comprehensive legal bases and ensure a more effective role and involvement for representative bodies';[43] it also expressed its opposition to 'excessive, disproportionate use of delegated acts'.[44]

35 Ibid.

36 OJ C161, 07.06.2012, p. 3. The ECB Opinion also included the position of the ECB on the Commission proposals (at the time) to modify the EU regime on protection from market abuse by the introduction of a new Market Abuse Directive II and a Market Abuse Regulation; COM(2011) 651 final and COM(2011) 654 final, respectively. See Directive 2014/57/EU, OJ L173/179, 12.06.2014, and Regulation (EU) No. 596/2014, OJL 173/1. 12.06.2014.

37 ECB Opinion, (n. 36), paras. 2.2 and 2.3.

38 Ibid., para. 3.1.

39 Ibid., para. 12.1.

40 Ibid., para. 12.1.

41 OJ C191/80, 29.06.2012.

42 I.e. TFEU, Article 53(1).

43 EESC Opinion, (n. 41), para. 1.3.

44 Ibid., para. 1.6.

The Commission proposals were endorsed by the European Parliament and the Council, which adopted in 2014 the MiFID II[45] and the MiFIR.[46]

The MiFIR

The MiFIR,[47] functioning as a complement to the MiFID II, provides directly applicable rules on investment services relating in particular to disclosure of trade data to the public, reporting of transactions to competent authorities, trading of derivatives on organised venues, non-discriminatory access to clearing and to trading in benchmarks, product intervention powers of competent authorities and ESAs, powers of the ESMA on position management, controls and limits.[48] It also confers extensive powers to the Commission to adopt delegated acts for its implementation.[49]

The MiFID II

The MiFID II builds on the structure and refines the normative content of the MiFID, relating primarily to the conditions for the authorisation and operation of investment services by FIs and markets and not directly to the protection of financial consumers in case of FI failure; its discussion will be limited to the scope of this study and, in particular, to the definition of the status of retail investors and the nature of financial instruments considered as relevant to investment services.

The need for the adoption of the MiFID II relates to the recognition that 'the financial crisis has exposed weaknesses in the functioning and in the transparency of financial markets', in particular where trading takes places OTC.[50]

Therefore, it was considered necessary, among other new rules, to include certain complex instruments such as commodity derivatives,[51] derivatives of emission allowances (EUAs), and structured deposits,[52] in regulated financial instruments; to further regulate algorithmic trading and the operation of MTFs and OTFs,[53] to introduce rules on APAs to enhance trade transparency in the OTC domain, requiring CTPs to consolidate data from APAs;[54] to facilitate the financing of

45 Directive 2014/65/EU of the European Parliament and of the Council of 15 May 2014 on markets in financial instruments and amending Directive 2002/92/EC and Directive 2011/61/EU (recast), OJ L 173/349, 12.06.2014.

46 Regulation (EU) No. 600/2014 of the European Parliament and of the Council of 15 May 2014 on markets in financial instruments and amending Regulation (EU) No. 648/2012, OJ L 173/84, 12.06.2014.

47 The MiFIR will apply from 03.01.2017, except for certain provisions that apply from its entry into force and certain others that apply from 03.01.2019; ibid., Article 55.

48 Ibid., Article 1(1).

49 Ibid., Article 50.

50 MiFID II, Preamble, recital 4.

51 Ibid., Articles 57–58.

52 Ibid., recitals 8 and 39; Article 2; Annex I, Section C.

53 Ibid., recitals 59–68; Articles 17–20, 31–32, 34 and 38.

54 Ibid., recitals 112–119; Articles 59–66.

SMEs through financial markets;[55] to provide for the suspension and removal of financial instruments from trading;[56] and to provide for supervisory and enforcement powers, measures and sanctions applicable to all investment firms, market operators, APAs, CTPs, ARMs and other responsible persons controlling FIs.[57]

The MiFID II applies to investment firms, market operators, data reporting service providers (APAs, CTPs and ARMs), and third-country FIs providing services in the EU.[58] It applies partially to credit institutions authorised under the CRD IV (including their obligations under the ICSD/DGSD Recast),[59] when providing investment services or performing investment activities, as well as when selling or advising clients in relation to structured deposits.[60] It also includes a list of exempted persons (such as insurance undertakings),[61] and a list of optional exemptions by Member States.[62]

An investment firm is defined under the MiFID II as 'a legal person whose regular occupation or business is the provision of one or more investment services and/or the performance of one or more investment activities on a professional basis',[63] with such investment services and activities being referred to in Section A of Annex I relating to any of the instruments listed in Section C of Annex I of the MiFID II.[64]

In particular, in relation to structured deposits, these are defined in the MiFID II to be deposits as defined in the relevant exemption rule of the DGSD Recast,[65] i.e. deposits which are fully repayable at maturity:

> on terms under which interest or a premium will be paid or is at risk, according to a formula involving factors such as (a) an index or combination of indices, excluding variable rate deposits whose return is directly linked to an interest rate index …; (b) a financial instrument or a combination of financial instruments; (c) a commodity or combination of commodities or other physical or non-physical non-fungible assets; or (d) a foreign exchange rate or combination of foreign exchange rates.[66]

In relation to such structured deposits, the MiFID II provides that where they are issued by credit institutions which are members of DGSs, under the DGSD (Recast) the obligation to be member of an ICS will be met.[67]

55 Ibid., recitals 132–5; Article 33.
56 Ibid., Article 52.
57 Ibid., recital 140; Articles 67–74.
58 Ibid., Article 1(1).
59 Ibid., Article 14.
60 Ibid., Article 1(3) and (4).
61 Ibid., Article 2.
62 Ibid., Article 3.
63 Ibid., Article 4(1); natural persons may be investment firms under conditions; ibid.
64 Ibid., Article 4(1) and (2).
65 DGSD II, Article 2(1)(c).
66 MiFID II., Article 4(1) and (43).
67 Ibid., Article 14. By regulating structured deposit related investment services, the MiFID II aims

From these arrangements of the MiFID II, in relation to structured deposits it emerges, in our view, that the more financial instruments take complex and hybrid forms, the more difficult it becomes to reconcile the distinction between depositing and investment in terms of risk accepted by financial consumers.

EU initiatives in regulating the financial market appear hesitant to control innovation in the design and offering of new financial instruments to financial consumers, by both credit institutions and investment firms, as long as CoB rules are respected. In this context, the case of structured deposits constitutes a paradigm of the difficulty to make the case for differentiating the legal treatment of retail depositors vis-à-vis retail investors and the protection awarded by DGSs vis-à-vis that offered by ICSs, under EU law.

Furthermore, as in the case of the MiFID, so does the MiFID II regulate the level of protection awarded to investors according to a distinction between professional investors (referred to as 'professional clients') and retail investors (referred to as 'retail clients'), and including an in-between category of 'clients who may be treated as professionals on request'.[68]

'Retail clients' are defined negatively, as clients who are not professional.[69]

Beyond the enumeration of categories of 'professional clients', the MiFID II provides as a general criterion that the '[p]rofessional client is a client who possesses the experience, knowledge and expertise to make his own investment decisions and properly assess the risks that it incurs'.[70] 'Professional clients' include persons such as FIs, large undertakings, governments and public bodies managing public debt, international and EU institutions, institutional investors; however, even such 'professional clients' may request a higher level of protection 'when it deems it is unable to properly assess or manage the risks involved'; in which case, such a client may agree with the investment firm not to be treated as professional for CoB rules-application purposes.[71]

Again in this instance, the criterion of sophistication, as potentially differentiating the status of retail investors vis-à-vis professional investors, becomes more difficult to support in many cases, where the complexity of market, instrument and contractual structures is such that its assessment of risk may be practically impossible even for organised and financially active public bodies or large corporations – so that they may request to be treated as retail investors.

Summing up its objective to be 'creating an integrated financial market in which investors are effectively protected and the efficiency and integrity of the overall market are safeguarded',[72] the MiFID II updates and refines provisions for the authorisation and operating conditions for investment firms, including CoB

to cover a gap in the protection awarded to investors, since structured deposits are not covered by EU law, while other structured investments are covered; ibid., recital 39. See also ECJ decision in Case 671/13, Ch. 6 (n. 75).

68 Ibid., Article 4(1), (10) and (11); Annex II.

69 Ibid.

70 Ibid., Annex II.

71 Ibid.

72 Ibid., recital 164.

rules to ensure investor protection in the provision of investment services;[73] these rules do not present fundamental differences from the respective MiFID rules from a normative point of view.

The MiFID confers extensive powers to the Commission to adopt delegated acts for its implementation, the delegation of powers in many cases being revocable by the European Parliament or the Council at any time.[74]

In addition, the MiFID II, providing for an enhanced enforcement mechanism and more severe sanctions to be imposed by competent authorities, does not explicate on the justiciability of financial consumers' rights, in particular in relation to the non-contractual liability of EU or Member State authorities in relation to its field of application.[75]

5.2 The new European financial supervisory architecture

The GFC entailed a fundamental reformation of the EU financial supervision model.[76]

Following the disruption of European economies and financial markets as a result of the erupting crisis and in order to establish an effective European system of supervision in the area of financial markets, the Commission mandated in October 2008 a group of experts, the *de Larosière* High-level Group of Experts, to submit proposals in this direction.

The de Larosière *report*

The *de Larosière* Group of Experts submitted a report in February 2009,[77] by which it presented its conclusions on the reasons of the GFC and proposed 31 recommendations, in order for financial services supervision to be effective on a pan-EU level and to avoid future systemic crises.

In this direction, it recommended the strengthening of the supervisory framework, the reforming of the structure of supervision of the financial sector in EU by inter alia establishing a European System of Financial Supervisors (ESFS) consisting of three European Supervisory Authorities (ESAs) (one for the banking sector,

73 Ibid., Title II.

74 Ibid., Article 89(2).

75 Ibid., Articles 70–73. It provides for an obligation of Member States to allow for legal action to be taken for the implementation of the MiFID or the MiFIR before national courts or competent authorities by public bodies, consumer or professional organisations, as well as for an extra-judicial mechanism to address consumer complaints; ibid., Articles 74(2) and 75.

76 For an overview and critical analysis of the new EU financial law regime see generally GORTSOS, C. (2015) 'The Crisis-based EU Financial Regulatory Intervention: Are We on the Top of the Prudential Wave?', *ERA Forum Journal of the Academy of European Law*, 16(1) pp. 89–110; FERRAN, E. (2014) 'European Banking Union and the EU Single Financial Market: More Differentiated Integration or Disintegration?', *Cambridge Legal Studies Research Papers* 29/2014, p. 3; THEISSEN, R. (2014) *EU Banking Supervision*, The Hague: Eleven Publishers.

77 Available at http://ec.europa.eu/internal_market/finances/docs/de_larosiere_report_en.pdf.

one for the securities sector and one for the insurance and occupational pensions sector), and by creating a European Systemic Risk Council.[78]

Before examining the formation of the new EU financial architecture, it is useful to take into account the constitutional principal of conferral.

The EU constitutional principal of conferral

Fundamental to the new EU financial regulatory architecture is the issue of conferral of competence to EU institutions and agencies under the Treaties.[79]

With regard to conferral of power from the EU legislature to the Commission to adopt non-legislative acts of general application to supplement or amend non-essential elements of the legislative act, Article 290 of the TFEU is applicable.[80] Furthermore, when uniform conditions for implementing legally binding EU acts are needed, those acts shall confer implementing powers on the Commission, or, in certain cases, on the Council, according to Article 291 of the TFEU.[81]

With regard to the conferral of powers from EU institutions to EU agencies (and other bodies), an important corpus of case law has been developed by the ECJ, with regard in particular to the limits on the exercise of discretionary powers by EU agencies, referred to as the '*Meroni* doctrine' case law. [82] Relevant is also

78 During the same period, a Report on *The Future of EU Regulation and Supervision* was prepared by the European Union Committee of the (UK) House of Lords, published on 17.06.2009 and available at www.publications.parliament.uk/pa/ld200809/ldselect/ldeucom/106/106i.pdf.

79 According to Article 5(1) of the TEU, 'The limits of Union competences are governed by the principle of conferral. The use of Union competences is governed by the principles of subsidiarity and proportionality'. Furthermore, according to Article 5(2) of the TEU, 'Under the principle of conferral, the Union shall act only within the limits of the competences conferred upon it by the Member States in the Treaties to attain the objectives set out therein. Competences not conferred upon the Union in the Treaties remain with the Member States'. According to Article 2(1) of the TFEU, 'When the Treaties confer on the Union exclusive competence in a specific area, only the Union may legislate and adopt legally binding acts, the Member States being able to do so themselves only if so empowered by the Union or for the implementation of Union acts'. The areas of exclusive competence of the EU is *numerus clausus* and is expressly referred to in Article 3 of the TFEU. The areas of internal market, consumer protection and justice are areas of shared competence between the EU and its Member States, according to Article 4(2) of the TFEU. Pursuant to Article 4(1) of the TFEU, which provides that 'The Union shall share competence with the Member States where the Treaties confer on it a competence which does not relate to the areas referred to in Articles 3 and 6'.

80 Article 290 of the TFEU provides strict conditions for such delegation of power, including that the objectives, content scope and duration of the delegation shall be explicitly referred, that essential elements of an area cannot be subject of a delegation of power, and that conditions to which the delegation is subject shall be explicitly referred.

81 For analysis of TFEU Articles 290 and 291 and relevant issues concerning delegation of powers to EU institutions and agencies, see generally SCHÜTZE, R. (2015) *European Union Law*, Cambridge: Cambridge University Press, at pp. 147–84, 221–59 and 302–27.

82 See the ECJ decision of 13.06.1958 in Case 9/56, *Meroni & Co., Industrie Metallurgiche, SpA v High Authority of the European Coal and Steel Community* [1957–1958] ECR 133, ECLI:EU:C:1958:7. The ECJ in *Meroni* controlled the transfer of extensive discretion to EEC (regulatory) agencies as incompatible with the Treaties (specifically, the 1951 European Coal and Steel Community Treaty), considering inter alia that: '[t]he consequences resulting from a delegation of powers are

the ECJ case law in *Romano*,[83] concerning the adoption of measures of general application having the force of law by EU agencies.[84]

The Commission proposals to establish ESAs, the ESRB and the ESFS

Following the *de Larosière* Report, the Commission presented its proposals on a new European financial supervisory architecture, by Communications of March 2009[85] and May 2009.[86]

The Commission proposed to transform the then operating European supervisory committees[87] into three ESAs, the European Banking Authority (EBA), the European Insurance and Occupational Pensions Authority (EIOPA), and the European Securities and Markets Authority (ESMA); and further, to establish an ESFS, which would consist of national supervisors and the new ESAs working together.

This system would allow, according to the Commission proposals, for adequate supervision at a pan-European level, having also input at a micro-prudential level by national regulators, as the European Systemic Risk Board (ESRB) would monitor and assess dangers to financial stability emerging from macro-economic developments,[88] and developments within the whole financial system, and ESAs would contribute to:

very different depending on whether it involves clearly defined executive powers the exercise of which can, therefore, be subject to strict review in the light of objective criteria determined by the delegating authority, or whether it involves a discretionary power, implying a wide margin of discretion which may, according to the use which is made of it, make possible the execution of actual economic policy. A delegation of the first kind cannot appreciably alter the consequences involved in the exercise of the powers concerned, whereas a delegation of the second kind, since it replaces the choices of the delegator by the choices of the delegate, brings about an actual transfer of responsibility'; ibid., p. 152.

83 ECJ decision of 14.05.1981 in Case 98/80, *Giuseppe Romano v Institut national d'assurance maladie-invalidité* [1980] ECR 1241, ECLI:EU:C:1981:104.

84 See WYMEERSCH, E. (2015) 'The European Financial Supervisory Authorities or ESAs' in WYMEERSCH, E., HOPT, K. J. and FERRANINI, G. (eds) (2012) *Financial Regulation and Supervision: A Post-crisis Analysis*, Oxford: OUP; BUSUIOC, M., GROENLEER, M. and TONDAL, J. (eds) (2012) *The Agency Phenomenon in the European Union: Emergence, Institutionalism and Everyday Decision-making*, Manchester: Manchester University Press; BUSUIOC, M. (2013) *European Agencies: Law and Practices of Accountability*, Oxford: OUP; CHAMON, M. (2010) 'EU Agencies: Does the Meroni Doctrine Make Sense', 17, *Maastricht Journal of European and Comparative Law*, p. 281; GRILLER, S. and ORATOR, A. (2010) 'Everything under Control? "The Way Forward" for European Agencies in the Footsteps of the Meroni Doctrine', 35, *ELRev*, p. 3.

85 COM(2009) 114.

86 COM (2009) 252 final, p. 2.

87 I.e. the Committee of European Banking Supervisors (CEBS), the Committee of European Insurance and Occupational Pensions Supervisors (CEIOPS) and the Committee of European Securities Regulators (CESR).

88 In this respect, the Commission noted that '[e]xperience of the financial crisis has exposed important failures in financial supervision, both in particular cases and in relation to the financial system as a whole'; COM(2009) 501 final, 23.09.2009.

> (i) improving the functioning of the internal market, including in particular a high, effective and consistent level of regulation and supervision, (ii) protecting depositors, investors, policyholders and other beneficiaries, (iii) ensuring the integrity, efficiency and orderly functioning of financial markets, (iv) safeguarding the stability of the financial system, and (v) strengthening international supervisory coordination.[89]

Thus, macro- and micro-prudential regulation and regulation, at individual, regional and EU levels, were considered by the Commission to be equally important factors in identifying in a timely manner and addressing sources of systemic risk.

At the same time, the need to protect financial consumers was stated by the Commission as a parameter of the reasoning in establishing the new European financial architecture.

The new system of EU supervisory architecture has been the subject of extensive discussion and debate.[90] It merits to be briefly examined, for the purposes of this study.

The European Systemic Risk Board (ESRB)

The ESRB was established in 2010 by Regulation (EU) No. 1092/2010,[91] in the context of the new system for macro-prudential oversight in the EU, as part of the European System of Financial Supervision (ESFS) also established by the same Regulation.

As stated in its Preamble:

> [t]he ESRB should ... take on all the global responsibilities required in order to ensure that the voice of the Union is heard on issues relating to financial stability, in particular by cooperating closely with the International Monetary Fund (IMF) and the Financial Stability Board (FSB), which are expected to provide early warnings of macro-prudential risks at the global level, and the partners of the Group of Twenty (G-20).[92]

89 Ibid., para. 6.1, p. 4.

90 See, generally, MOLONEY, N., FERRAN, E. and PAYNE, J. (eds) (2015) *The Oxford Handbook of Financial Regulation*, Oxford: OUP; MOLONEY, N. (2014) *EU Securities and Financial Markets Regulation*, 3rd edition, OUP, Oxford European Union Law Library; WYMEERSCH, E., HOPT, K. J. and FERRANINI, G. (eds) (2012) *Financial Regulation and Supervision: A Post-crisis Analysis*, Oxford: OUP; GORTSOS, C. (2013) 'The "single supervisory mechanism": a major building block towards a European Banking Union (the full Europeanisation of the "bank safety net")', *Hrematopistotiko Dikaio*, vol. 1, p. 5, and *ECEFIL Working Paper Series* No. 2013/8; TRIDIMAS, T. (2011) 'EU Financial Regulation: Federalization, Crisis Management, and Law Reform' in CRAIG, P. and De BÚRCA, G. (2011) *The Evolution of EU Law*, 2nd edition, Oxford: OUP, pp. 783–804.

91 OJ L 331/1 (the ESFS Regulation).

92 Ibid., Preamble, recital 7.

Also, '[t]he ESRB should contribute, inter alia, towards implementing the recommendations of the IMF, the FSB and the Bank for International Settlements (BIS) to the G-20'.[93]

It emerges from these provisions, that the implication and effect of the initiatives of international *fora* and organisations in the area of financial regulation has become considerable, especially following the GFC, for the development of EU financial law.

The ESFS Regulation not only explicitly urges the ESRB to contribute to implement the recommendations of the IMF, the FSB and the BIS, but perhaps also expresses a concern for the 'voice of the Union' to be heard.

It is not clear, however, in our view that an EU agency, such as the ESRB, may have as mandate to contribute to the implementation of recommendations of the IMF, the FSB and the BIS to the G-20; despite the fact that the EU directly, and also through its Member States, participates in the workings of such international *fora* and organisations, the law producing mechanisms of the EU are distinct and based on the provisions of the Treaties only.

The transposition of binding EU instruments mainly in the form of Directives into the national legal orders of the Member States is a process provided for by the EU Treaties, to which Member States have become members according to the relevant treaties of accession, and by the national law of the Member States. Moreover, a direct or indirect transformation of recommendations by international organisations and *fora* into binding EU law, through EU agencies, on the basis of delegation of powers from EU institutions, raises important issues of constitutional order, relating to the principles of democratic accountability, institutional balance within the EU, transparency, as well as legal and institutional relations between the EU and its Member States.[94]

The European System of Financial Supervision (ESFS)

The ESFS comprises the ESRB, the EBA, the EIOPA, the ESMA, the Joint Committee of the ESAs, and the competent or supervisory authorities of the Member States, as specified in applicable EU law.[95]

According to the ESFS Regulation, it is responsible for the macro-prudential oversight of the financial system within the EU in order to contribute to the prevention or mitigation of systemic risk, inter alia by determining, collecting and analysing information, identifying and prioritising systemic risks, issuing warnings and recommendations for remedial action, issuing confidential warnings addressed to the Council under conditions specified and providing the Council with an assessment of the situation, cooperating closely with all other parties to the

93 Ibid., Preamble, recital 8. Cf. ibid., Article 3.

94 See, in general, CRAIG, P. (2011) 'Integration, Democracy and Legitimacy' in CRAIG, P., De BÚRCA, G. (2011) The Evolution of EU Law, 2nd edition, Oxford: OUP, pp. 13–41; *idem* (2011) 'Institutions, Power, and Institutional Balance' in CRAIG, P., De BÚRCA, G. (2011) *The Evolution of EU Law*, 2nd edition, Oxford: OUP, pp. 41–85.

95 ESFS Regulation, Article 3(1).

European Financial Stability Facility (EFSF),[96] and coordinating its actions with those of international financial organisations, in particular the IMF and the FSB.[97]

The European Banking Authority (EBA)

The EBA Regulation[98] establishing the EBA states in relation to its objectives that it should act with a view to 'improving the functioning of the internal market, in particular by ensuring a high, effective and consistent level of regulation and supervision taking account of the varying interests of all [Member States] and the different nature of financial institutions'.[99]

It also states that it 'should protect public values such as the stability of the financial system, the transparency of markets and financial products, and the protection of depositors and investors'.[100]

It further provides that the EBA shall act with regard to both credit and other FIs[101] and the competent authorities that supervise them, in relation to prudential requirements and prudential supervision, within EU secondary law, and also in the fields of activities of FIs, including payment and e-money institutions in relation to matters not directly covered by said acts in order to ensure their effective and consistent application.[102]

According to the EBA Regulation, '[t]he objective of the [EBA] shall be to protect the public interest by contributing to the short, medium and long-term stability and effectiveness of the financial system, for the Union economy, its citizens and businesses',[103] and that in carrying out its tasks, the EBA 'shall act independently, objectively and in a non-discriminatory manner, in the interests of the Union as a whole',[104] while enhancing 'customer protection'.[105]

The EBA is established as an EU body with legal personality, enjoying the most extensive legal capacity under Member State law.[106]

Its tasks include inter alia contributing to the establishment of high-quality

96 See ECJ decision of 27.11.2012 in Case C-370/12, *Thomas Pringle v Government of Ireland, Ireland and The Attorney General*, ECLI:EU:C:2012:756.

97 ESFS Regulation, Article 3.

98 Regulation (EU) No. 1093/2010, OJ L 331/12, 15.12.2010 (the EBA Regulation). The EBA was established on 01.01.2011; ibid., Article 82. See, generally, GORTSOS, C. (2011) 'The European Banking Authority within the "European System of Financial Supervision"', *Hrematopistotiko Dikaio*, vol. 1, p. 56, and *ECEFIL Working Paper Series* No. 2011/1.

99 Ibid., Preamble, recital 11.

100 Ibid.

101 Ibid., Article 4: 'financial institutions' for its purposes means 'credit institutions', 'investment firms', and 'financial conglomerates' as defined in relevant stated Directives.

102 Ibid., Article 1(2) and (3).

103 Ibid., Article 1(5).

104 Ibid., Article 1(5), as amended by Regulation (EU) No. 1022/2013, OJ L 287/5, 29.10.2013. In its initial form, the same indent provided that the EBA 'shall act independently and objectively and in the interest of the Union alone'. In relation to independence, cf. EBA Regulation, Articles 42, 46, 49, 52 and 59.

105 Ibid., Article 1(5), indent (f).

106 Ibid., Article 5.

common regulatory and supervisory standards and practices, maintaining a European supervisory handbook, contributing to the consistent application of legally binding EU acts, preventing regulatory arbitrage, mediating and settling disagreements between competent authorities, ensuring effective and consistent supervision of FIs, ensuring a coherent functioning of colleges of supervisors and taking actions in emergency situations.[107]

Among its tasks is 'to foster depositor and investor protection',[108] and to 'promote ... monitoring, assessment and measurement of systemic risk, the development and coordination of recovery and resolution plans, providing a high level of protection to depositors and investors throughout the Union and developing methods for the resolution of failing [FIs] and an assessment of the need for appropriate financing instruments ...'[109]

Control of systemic risk is the fundamental aim of the EBA;[110] in order to effectively pursue this aim, the EBA may conduct an inquiry into a particular type of FI or type of product or conduct in order to assess potential threats to the stability of the financial system and make appropriate recommendations for action to the competent authorities concerned.[111] FIs that may pose a systemic risk shall be subject to strengthened supervision, and, where necessary, to recovery and resolution procedures.[112]

Furthermore, in developing the criteria for the identification and measurement of systemic risk posed by FIs, the EBA has to take into account the criteria established by the FSB, the IMF and the BIS (BCBS).[113]

The EBA Regulation provides a detailed system of rules regarding the development of draft regulatory technical standards by the EBA, to be submitted to the Commission (where the European Parliament and the Council have delegated power to the Commission to adopt regulatory technical standards);[114] the EBA may develop the implementation of technical standards by implementing acts.[115]

Important powers are conferred on the EBA in relation to exercising prudential supervision, where there are indications that Member State competent authorities are acting in breach or in non-application of EU law, in particular by failing to ensure that FIs satisfy the requirements laid down by applicable EU law.[116]

Following a structured procedure, involving the addressing of a recommendation by the EBA and the initiation of infringement proceedings by the Commission,[117] the EBA may adopt a directly applicable individual decision addressed to the

107 Ibid., Article 8(1).
108 Ibid., Article 1(5), indent (h).
109 Ibid., Article 1(5), indent (i).
110 Ibid., Articles 22–24.
111 Ibid., Article 22(4).
112 Ibid., Articles 23(1), 25 and 27.
113 Ibid., Article 23(2).
114 Ibid., Articles 10–14; TFEU, Article 290.
115 EBA Regulation, Article 15; TFEU, Article 291.
116 EBA Regulation, Article 17(1).
117 TFEU, Article 258.

FI concerned, requesting it to take any necessary action (including cessation of any practice), such an individual decision prevailing over any previous decision adopted by the national competent authorities on the same matter.[118]

Equally important, in case of systemic risk owing to adverse developments in financial markets, the EBA is to facilitate and coordinate necessary actions by Member State competent authorities.

In emergency situations, determined by a decision of the Council (following the relevant procedure involving the Commission, the ESRB, and the ESAs), the EBA may adopt, where coordinated action of Member State competent authorities is necessary, and according to procedurally lax rules, individual decisions addressed to the Member State competent authorities. If a Member State competent authority does not comply with the EBA decision within the relevant time limit, the EBA may adopt an individual decision addressed to the FI concerned, such an EBA decision prevailing over previous decisions of Member State competent authorities on the matter.[119]

Rules on hearing of the addressee of EBA decisions and on the reasoning and publication of such decisions are also provided.[120]

By this system of direct supervision, the EBA is allowed, in close cooperation with the Commission, to issue orders to Member State competent authorities and to ensure compliance by FIs with their obligations under EU law, even where Member State competent authorities are not cooperating with the EBA for any reason.

A system for settlement of disagreements between competent authorities in cross-border situations,[121] as well as a system for settlement of disagreements between competent authorities across sectors,[122] is also provided.

The EBA is also charged to ensure the correct application of EU law on DGSs, with the aim of ensuring that national DGSs are adequately funded, and to provide 'a high level of protection to all depositors in a harmonised framework throughout the Union, which leaves the stabilising safeguard role of mutual guarantee schemes intact, provided they comply with Union legislation'.[123]

A system of remedies is provided by the EBA Regulation for filing appeals against EBA decisions,[124] and for bringing proceedings before the ECJ against its decisions (following the stage of appeal, where applicable).[125]

Locus standi of individuals, natural or legal persons, for filing of appeals before the EBA Board of Appeal is allowed upon condition of showing direct and individual concern.[126] However, lodging an appeal does not have suspensive effect;

118 EBA Regulation, Article 17(7).
119 Ibid., Article 18.
120 Ibid., Article 39.
121 Ibid., Article 19.
122 Ibid., Article 20.
123 Ibid., Article 26(1).
124 Ibid., Article 60.
125 Ibid., Article 61.
126 Ibid., Article 60(1). Regarding the discretion of the EBA to initiate investigations pursuant to

but the decision may be suspended if the Board of Appeals considers that the circumstances so require.[127]

In particular in relation to individual redress, it appears that the EBA, which has been established to operate in the public interest, has not been awarded total immunity nor has it been exempted from non-contractual liability; according to the EBA Regulation, '[i]n the case of non-contractual liability, the [EBA] shall, in accordance with the general principles common to the laws of the [Member States], make good any damage caused by it or by its staff in the performance of their duties. The Court of Justice of the European Union shall have jurisdiction in any dispute over the remedying of such damage'.[128]

The new structure of EU financial supervisory architecture in the case of the EBA, and the particularly important powers conferred to the EBA, signify that the role of EU authorities in overseeing only in a wide sense the workings of Member State financial markets, and that only with a view to establish an internal EU financial market, has passed: in the face of systemic danger, directly applicable EU law in the form of the EBA Regulation, allows for the EBA to take control of the situation and adopt a wide array of measures directly applicable to individuals, namely the FIs concerned.

EU financial law, moving into this new stage of market regulation, opts for centralisation of power, at the EU level, and neutralisation or at least circumvention of non-responding Member State competent authorities.

At the same time, questions are raised if these developments are in line with EU and Member State rules of constitutional order, which affect also the position of financial consumers as citizens of the EU, financial market participants and potentially directly affected individuals.

This problematic was considered by the ECJ in the *Short Selling* case, in the context of the ESMA Regulation, whose structure and normative content corresponds to that of the EBA, and which also merits examination.

The European Securities and Markets Authority (ESMA)

The ESMA was also established in 2010, by the ESMA Regulation,[129] having as its objective (as in the case of the EBA) the protection of public interest, 'by

Article 17 of the EBA Regulation, rights of individuals in this regard and *locus standi* before its Board of Appeals, see General Court (Third Chamber) decision of 09.09.2015 in Case T-660/14, *SV Capital OÜ v EBA*, ECLI: EU: T: 2015: 608.

127 Ibid., Article 60(3).

128 Ibid., Article 69(1).

129 Regulation (EU) No. 1095/2010, OJ L 331/84, 15.12.2010 (the ESMA Regulation). For analysis, see TRIDIMAS, T. (2012) 'Financial Supervision and Agency Power: Reflections on ESMA' in SHUIBHNE, N. and GORMLEY, L. (eds) *From Single Market to Economic Union: Essays in Memory of John A. Usher*, Oxford: OUP, pp. 55–83; MOLONEY, N. (2011) 'The European Securities and Markets Authority and institutional design for the EU financial market: a tale of two competences: part (1) rule-making', *European Business Organization Law Review*, vol. 12, no. 1, pp. 41–86; *idem* (2011) 'The European Securities and Markets Authority and Institutional Design for the EU Financial Market – A tale of two competences: part (2) rules in action', *European Business Organization*

contributing to the short, medium and long-term stability and effectiveness of the financial system, for the Union economy, its citizens and businesses',[130] inter alia contributing to 'enhancing customer protection'.[131]

The ESMA has to act within the scope of relevant investment services Directives, including the ICSD, and without prejudice to the competence of the EBA in terms of prudential supervision; it also acts with regard to activities of financial market participants not directly covered by such EU law acts.[132]

The normative structure of the ESMA Regulation, its legal status, organisation and operation, competences and powers, liability and all other matters correspond *mutatis mutandis* to the relevant norms of the EBA Regulation.[133]

It is interesting to note, however, that the repetition in the ESMA Regulation of rules on systemic risk, as defined in the ESFS Regulation, and as addressed by the EBA Regulation, confirms the new position of international financial regulation in relation to systemic risk, i.e. that it is not generated only by the traditional banking sector, owing to the globalised and interconnected nature of financial activities.[134]

Indeed, the ESMA is obliged under its founding Regulation to develop criteria for the identification and measurement of systemic risk,[135] and is also obliged, as is the EBA, to be able to respond effectively to the materialisation of systemic risks, being able to ensure coherent and coordinated crisis management and resolution acts.[136]

Moreover, it has to contribute to strengthening the European system of ICSs, ensuring correct application of the ICSD, and 'provide a high level of protection to all investors in a harmonized framework throughout the Union'.[137]

It emerges, in our view, that EU law has taken a clear stance in relation to the eventuality of Member State competent authorities exercising their duties ineffectively and thus failing to protect the EU financial market – the ESAs are to take direct control of the situation and exercise directly, if need be, supervisory powers on individual FIs.

Beyond a sense of mistrust as to the efficiency – or to the willingness – of Member State competent authorities that emerges from the new EU financial law framework, concerning the aim and powers of the EBA and the ESMA, constitutional and institutional issues are also raised in relation to this new federalised normative structure.

Moreover, while the new centralised structure for the exercise of prudential

Law Review, vol. 12, no. 2, pp. 177–225; SCHAMMO, P. (2011) 'The European Securities and Markets Authority: Lifting the Veil on the Allocation of Powers', *Common Market Law Review*, 48, pp. 1879–914.

130 Ibid., Article 1(5).

131 Ibid., Article 1(5)(f).

132 Ibid., Article 1(2) and (3).

133 Therefore, and in order to avoid repetition, the comments made regarding the EBA Regulation apply equally to the ESMA Regulation.

134 Ibid., Article 22.

135 Ibid., Article 23.

136 Ibid., Articles 23–25 and 27.

137 Ibid., Article 26(1).

supervision in the EU appears to be allowing, in respect of EU *acquis*, or even as a counterweight to enhanced centralised competence and powers of ESAs, for the non-contractual liability of the latter, the application of such rules may prove difficult in practice.[138]

In our view, it is possible that causality issues will become even more complicated and difficult to prove, especially for financial consumers, since the factors of an eventual failure of an FI in relation to regulatory and supervisory acts and omissions will be multiplied and causes may be further distanced from effects.

Moreover, the EBA and the ESMA Regulations do not provide rules in relation to the situation where Member State competent authorities may be found liable according to national law to compensate individuals, such as financial consumers, but also FIs, for damage caused in breach of EU law, as a result of instructions provided to Member State competent authorities by ESAs.[139]

A major source of potential litigation, involving also financial consumer actions, may be provided by the very wide discretionary powers provided by the founding Regulation to the ESAs, which may be challenged before courts.

In this direction, it is necessary to take into account the recent decision of the ECJ in the *Short Selling* case.

The ECJ decision in the Short Selling *case*

In the *Short Selling* case,[140] the ECJ (Grand Chamber) was called to decide on an action under TFEU Article 263 brought by the United Kingdom against the European Parliament and the Council for the annulment of Article 28 of Regulation (EU) No. 236/2012 on short selling and certain aspects of credit

138 See in general ATHANASSIOU, P. (2011) 'Financial Sector Supervisors' Accountability: A European Perspective',. ECB Legal Working Paper Series, No. 12.

139 Cf. relevant provisions under the SRM Regulation; see Ch. 8.2.

140 See ECJ decision of 22.01.2014 in Case C-270/12, *United Kingdom v European Parliament and Council*, ECLI:EU:C:2014:18. For discussion see ALEXANDER, K. (2015) 'European Banking Union: A Legal and Institutional Analysis of the Single Supervisory Mechanism and the Single Resolution Mechanism', *ELRev*, 40(2), pp. 154–87, at p. 181; BERGSTRÖM, C. F. (2015) 'Shaping the New System of Delegation of Powers to EU Agencies: United Kingdom v European Parliament and Council (Short Selling)', *CMLRev.*, pp. 219–42; DENYS, S. (2014) 'Délégation de compétences à l'Autorité européenne des marches financiers', *Europe*, Mars Comm. No. 3, pp. 14–15; DI NOIA, C. and GARGANTINI, M. (2014) 'Unleashing the European Securities and Markets Authority: Governance and Accountability after the ECJ Decision on the Short Selling Regulation (Case C-270/12)', *European Business Organization Law Review*, vol. 15, no. 1, pp. 1–57; Van GESTEL, R. (2014) 'European Regulatory Agencies Adrift?', *Maastricht Journal of European and Comparative Law*, pp. 188–96; CHAMON, M. (2014) 'The Empowerment of Agencies under the Meroni Doctrine and Article 114 TFEU: Comment on United Kingdom v Parliament and Council (Short-selling) and the Proposed Single Resolution Mechanism', *ELRev*, pp. 380–403; HOWELL, E. (2014) 'The European Court of Justice: Selling us Short?', *European Company and Financial Law Review*, vol. 11, no. 3, pp. 457–77; ADAMSKI, D. (2014) 'The ESMA Doctrine: a Constitutional Revolution and the Economics of Delegation', *ELRev*, pp. 812–34; MALETIC, I. (2014) 'Delegating Harmonization of the Internal Market: the Ruling in Case C-270/12', *YEL*, pp. 501–17.

default swaps (the Short Selling Regulation),[141] which was adopted on the basis of TFEU Article 114. Spain, France, Italy and the Commission intervened in the proceedings before the ECJ in support of the defendants, the European Parliament and Council.

Article 28 of the Short Selling Regulation entitles the ESMA, in accordance with Article 9(5) of the ESMA Regulation, among other measures:

> [t]o prohibit or impose conditions on the entry by natural or legal persons into a short sale or a transaction which creates, or relates to, a financial instrument … where the effect or one of the effects of the transaction is to confer a financial advantage on such person in the event of a decrease in the price or value of another financial instrument.[142]

Further, the Short Selling Regulation provides certain conditions under which ESMA may take such a decision prohibiting or imposing conditions on short selling, i.e. (a) that such measures 'address a threat to the orderly functioning and integrity of financial markets or to the stability of the whole or part of the financial system in the Union and there are cross-border implications' and (b) that 'no competent authority has taken measures to address the threat or one or more of the competent authorities have taken measures that do not adequately address the threat'.[143] In taking such measures, the ESMA has to take into account the impact of it on financial markets and participants,[144] and before imposing such measures ESMA has to consult the ESRB and other relevant authorities.[145]

Furthermore, the Short Selling Regulation empowers the Commission to adopt delegated acts specifying criteria and factors for the ESMA to determine the threats referred to in Article 28(2)(a) of the Regulation.[146] On this basis, the Delegated Regulation (EU) No. 918/2012[147] and the Implementing Regulation (EU) No. 827/2012[148] were issued by the Commission.

In its action for annulment the United Kingdom claimed that Article 28 of the Short Selling Regulation should be annulled for four main reasons.

In its first plea in law, the United Kingdom claimed that Article 28 was not compatible with the principles relating to the delegation of powers laid down in *Meroni*: (a) because the criteria set out in Article 28(2) of the Regulation entails a very

141 OJ 2012 L86/12, 24.03.2012. According to Article 2(1) b of this Regulation, 'short sale' in relation to a share or debt instrument is defined as 'any sale of the share or debt instrument which the seller does not own at the time of entering into the agreement to sell including such a sale where at the time of entering into the agreement to sell the seller has borrowed or agreed to borrow the share or debt instrument for delivery at settlement'.

142 Ibid., Article 28(1).

143 Ibid., Article 28(2).

144 See ibid., Article 28(3).

145 See ibid., Article 28(4).

146 See ibid., Articles 30 and 42.

147 OJ 2012 L274/1, 09.10.2012.

148 OJ 2012 L251/11, 19.08.2012.

large measure of discretion and a highly subjective judgment as to the existence of a threat to the financial system; (b) because ESMA has a wide range of choices as to which measure or measures to impose and as to any exceptions that may be specified, under Article 28(1) of the Regulation and 'extremely wide-ranging discretion' when deciding how to take account of the factors set out in Article 28(3) of the Regulation; (c) because in deciding which measures to impose, ESMA must be guided by the factors set out in Article 28(3) of the Regulation, which, however, encompass tests that are 'highly subjective'; (d) because whilst measures adopted by ESMA are theoretically temporary, the principles established in *Meroni* apply to temporary measures as much as to permanent measures; and (e) because even if Article 28 of the Regulation were to be interpreted as not involving ESMA in making policy choices in the form of decisions on macroeconomic policy, it would still be bound by the *Meroni* principle.[149]

In his Opinion of 12.09.2013 in the *Short Selling* case,[150] AG Jääskinen, after an analysis of the ECJ case law concerning the delegation of powers by EU institutions to EU agencies under the light of the EU Treaties, concluded that in his view the *Meroni* and *Romano* principles had not been breached by Article 82 of the Short Selling Regulation.[151]

The ECJ dismissed the action for annulment considering that the *Meroni* principles had not been violated.[152]

Proceeding to distinguish the legal context of *Meroni* from those of the competences of ESMA under the Short Selling Regulation, the ECJ noted that in *Meroni* the entities in question were of private law whereas ESMA is an EU agency,[153] and that Article 28 of the Regulation does not confer to ESMA any autonomous power that goes beyond the bounds of the regulatory framework established by the ESMA Regulation.[154] Also, that unlike the case in *Meroni*, the exercise of the powers under Article 28 of the Short Selling Regulation is circumscribed 'by various conditions and criteria which limit ESMA's discretion',[155] proceeding to examine such conditions and criteria under Article 28 of the Regulation.[156] Thus, the Court concluded that: 'the powers available to ESMA under Article 28 of [the Short Selling Regulation] are precisely delineated and amenable to judicial review in the light of the objectives established by the delegating authority', and so were in accordance with the requirements laid down in *Meroni*.[157]

149 *Short Selling* Case, paras 27–34.

150 ECLI:EU:C:2013:562.

151 As the AG noted, 'the evolution in the EU constitutional law that occurred under the Lisbon Treaty has indeed accommodated the pivotal concerns with which the Court had to deal in *Meroni* and *Romano*; namely, the absence of Treaty-based criteria for the conferral and delegation of powers so as to ensure respect for institutional balance, and the vacuum in terms of judicial review of legally binding acts of agencies'; ibid., point 72.

152 Ibid., paras 41–42.

153 Ibid., para. 43.

154 Ibid., para. 44.

155 Ibid., para. 45.

156 Ibid., paras 46–52.

157 Ibid., para. 53.

In a similar line of reasoning, the ECJ rejected the other arguments of the applicant.

The Court held that: 'With regard to second plea in law, that the principle established in *Romano*[158] was also breached, as Article 28 of the Short Selling Regulation authorises ESMA to adopt quasi-legislative measures of general application because the power of ESMA to prohibit short-selling under this provision amounts to a 'measure of general application having the force of law',[159] and noted that: 'it cannot be inferred from *Romano* that the delegation of powers to a body such as ESMA is governed by conditions other than those set out in *Meroni*'.[160]

With regard to the third plea in law alleging incompatibility of the delegation of powers with TFEU Articles 290 and 291, on the ground that any prohibition on short sales by the ESMA under Article 28(1) of the Regulation is a measure of general application, which cannot be entrusted to such an agency,[161] the ECJ, noting that Article 28 delegates powers not to the Commission but to a Union body, office or agency,[162] considered that it was called upon to adjudicate on whether under these Treaty provisions delegated and executive powers may be attributed solely to the Commission.[163]

In examining this issue, the ECJ took into account that the legal framework of Article 28 of the Short Selling Regulation is established, inter alia, by the ESFS Regulation, the ESMA Regulation and the Short Selling Regulation, which form part of a series of regulatory instruments adopted by the EU legislature 'so that the Union may, in view of the integration of international financial markets and the contagion risk of financial crises, endeavour to promote international financial stability',[164] which entails that Article 28 cannot be considered in isolation. From this finding, the Court was led to the conclusion that Article 28, 'read in conjunction with the other regulatory instruments adopted in that field identified above, cannot be regarded as undermining the rules governing the delegation of powers laid down in Articles 290 TFEU and 291 TFEU'.[165]

Moreover, with regard to the fourth plea in law, the ECJ dismissed the argument that Article 28 is ultra vires Article 114 TFEU, since individual decisions by ESMA under Article 28 constitute direct regulatory measures by an EU agency directed at individuals in Member States, whereas Article 114 TFEU does not empower the EU legislature to take individual decisions that are not of general application or to delegate to the Commission or a Union agency the power to adopt such decisions.[166]

AG Jääskinen had found merit in the plea in law concerning the legal basis

158 ECJ decision of 14.05.1981 in Case 98/80 *Romano* (n. 83).
159 *Short Selling* case, paras 56 and 57.
160 Ibid., para. 66.
161 Ibid., para. 70.
162 Ibid., para. 71.
163 Ibid., para. 78.
164 Ibid., para. 84.
165 Ibid., para. 86.
166 Ibid., para. 88–90.

of the Short Selling Regulation, as in his view Article 114 of the TFEU was not an appropriate legal basis for the adoption of Article 28 of the Regulation. AG Jääskinen considered that Article 28 of the Short Selling Regulation does not entail a delegation of authority by either of the EU executive institutions to an agency, but relates to a direct conferral of power to an agency by the legislature pursuant to an Article 289(3) TFEU legislative act.[167]

The AG supported that Article 28 of the Short Selling Regulation should have as legal basis Article 352 of the TFEU, and not Article 114 of the TFEU, noting inter alia that:

> [a] centralised emergency decision making process that replaces the decision of the competent [Member State] authority, without its consent, or which provides a substitution for the absence of one, cannot be considered to be encompassed by the concept of 'approximation of the provisions laid down by law, regulation or administrative action' in [Member States] under Article 114 TFEU.[168]

The Court considered in this regard that the question posed was whether the system of intervention established by Article 28 may fall within the scope of TFEU Article 114.[169]

Reviewing its case law with regard to the scope of TFEU Article 114, the Court recalled that 'the concept of 'measures for the approximation' of legislation must be interpreted as encompassing the EU legislature's power to lay down measures relating to a specific product or class of products as well as, if necessary, individual measures concerning those products',[170] and taking into account that the purpose of the powers provided for in Article 28 is to improve the conditions for the establishment and functioning of the internal market in the financial field, it found Article 28 to be in conformity with TFEU Article 114, which it considered to constitute an appropriate legal basis for the adoption of Article 28.[171]

The decision of the ECJ in the *Short Selling* case cannot be considered, in our view, as satisfactory in terms of reasoning. Even if the developments in the EU constitutional order since the issuing of the *Meroni* and *Romano* rulings entail that conferral of powers to EU regulatory agencies may be easier to accommodate under conditions, the reasoning in the *Short Selling* case, in particular with

167 Ibid., point 6.

168 Ibid., point 54.

169 Ibid., para. 99.

170 Ibid., para. 106, referring to the decision of the ECJ of 09.08.1994 in Case C-359/92 *Germany v Council* [1994] ECR I-3681, para. 37.

171 Ibid., para. 117. In considering the issue relating to Article 114 of the TFEU as legal basis of Article 28 of the Short Selling Regulation, the ECJ also took into consideration its decision of 06.12.2005 in Case C-66/04 *United Kingdom v Parliament and Council* [2005] ECR I-10553, ECLI:EU:C:2005:743 (*Smoke Flavourings* case), and its decision of 02.05.2006 in Case C-217/04 *United Kingdom v Parliament and Council* [2006] ECR I-3771, ECLI:EU:C:2006:279 (*ENISA* case).

<table>
<tr><td colspan="2">Supervision and regulation of financial institutions</td><td colspan="2">Deposit guarantee and investor compensation</td><td colspan="2">Recovery and resolution</td><td>Insolvency and liquidation</td></tr>
<tr><td colspan="7">EUROPEAN COURT OF JUSTICE</td></tr>
<tr><td colspan="7">EU LAW</td></tr>
<tr><td>ESFS</td><td>SSM</td><td colspan="2">EDIS</td><td colspan="2">SRM</td><td></td></tr>
<tr><td colspan="7">EU FINANCIAL MARKET AUTHORITIES</td></tr>
<tr><td>ESAs (EBA – ESMA)</td><td>ECB</td><td>[SRDI Board]</td><td>[DIF]</td><td>SRB</td><td>[SRF]</td><td></td></tr>
<tr><td colspan="7">EU FINANCIAL LAW INSTRUMENTS</td></tr>
<tr><td colspan="2">CRR</td><td colspan="2">[Proposal for EDIS]</td><td colspan="2">SRM Regulation</td><td></td></tr>
<tr><td colspan="2">CRDIV</td><td>DGDS (recast)</td><td>DGSs</td><td colspan="2">BRRD</td><td></td></tr>
<tr><td colspan="2"></td><td>ICSD</td><td>ICSs</td><td colspan="2"></td><td></td></tr>
</table>

<table>
<tr><td>NATIONAL FINANCIAL MARKET AUTHORITIES</td></tr>
</table>

<table>
<tr><td>NATIONAL LAW OF EU ORIGIN AND OF NON-EU ORIGIN</td></tr>
<tr><td>NATIONAL COURTS OF JUSTICE</td></tr>
</table>

Figure 2 Basic areas of financial institution regulation relating to the risk of failure: prudential supervision and regulation, deposit guarantee and investor compensation, recovery and resolution, and insolvency and liquidation. In grey colour demarcation of areas without (significant) regulation by EU law (as in December 2015).

regard to the use of Article 114 of the TFEU, does not appear to be promoting legal certainty and predictability, institutional balance within the EU, democratic accountability and judicial review of EU regulatory agencies' decisions.

As the Short Selling ruling will be applicable in the wider area of delegation of power to EU regulatory agencies, it appears in our view that the necessity to control systemic risk in financial markets through professionally expert regulatory agencies at the EU level may entail negative consequences at the level of individual protection and perhaps at the level of EU – Member State relations.

The new Single Supervisory Mechanism (SSM)

As the GFC in the EU deepened and took menacing proportions, it became evident that prudential supervision of systemically important FIs only at the Member State level was not effective in addressing systemic risk on a European level, so as to protect also the single currency and the financial markets, in particular of the Euro area.[172]

In this context, the Commission proposed in 2012 to adopt an SSM Regulation,[173] in order to provide the ECB with specific competences to prudentially supervise SIFIs, and to utilise TFEU Article 127(6) as the legal basis for its adoption.[174]

Following a political debate on the extent and organisation of the new ECB competences,[175] the SSM Regulation was adopted in October 2013.[176]

The SSM Regulation

> confers on the ECB specific tasks concerning policies relating to the prudential supervision of credit institutions, with a view to contributing to the safety and soundness of credit institutions and the stability of the financial system within the Union and each Member State, with full regard and duty of care for the unity and integrity of the internal market based on equal treatment of credit institutions with a view to preventing regulatory arbitrage'.[177]

While the SSM Regulation stresses that only supervisory competences attributed specifically to the ECB shall be exercised by it,[178] its function as bank

172 For earlier proposals by the European Parliament to transfer certain supervisory powers on the EU level, see European Parliament resolutions of 13.04.2000, OJ C40/453, 07.02.2001, and of 21.11.2002, OJ C35E/394, 29.01.2004.

173 COM(2012) 511 final. The Commission noted inter alia that: 'supervision of banks remains to a large extent within national boundaries and thereby fails to keep up with integrated banking markets. Supervisory failings have, since the onset of the banking crisis, significantly eroded confidence in the EU banking sector and contributed to an aggravation of tensions in euro area sovereign debt markets'; ibid., p. 2.

174 TFEU Article 127(6) provides that: 'The Council, acting by means of regulations in accordance with a special legislative procedure, may unanimously, and after consulting the European Parliament and the European Central Bank, confer specific tasks upon the European Central Bank concerning policies relating to the prudential supervision of credit institutions and other financial institutions with the exception of insurance undertakings'. It is not clear whether this 'enabling clause' of the TFEU forms adequate legal basis for the provision of extensive supervisory competence to the ECB, in view of the specific powers conferred to it by the TFEU in the context of ECBS: see TFEU, Articles 271(1), 129(1), 130, 132, 282–84 and Protocol (No. 4) to the Treaties. For a critical analysis, see ALEXANDER, K. (2015) 'European Banking Union: A Legal and Institutional Analysis of the Single Supervisory Mechanism and the Single Resolution Mechanism', *ELRev* 40(2), pp. 154–87.

175 See European Parliament Opinion on 1st Reading, OJ C55/157, 12.2.2016.

176 Council Regulation (EU) No. 1024/2013 of 15 October 2013 conferring specific tasks on the European Central Bank concerning policies relating to the prudential supervision of credit institutions, OJ L 287/63, 29.10.2013.

177 SSM Regulation, Article 1, first para.

178 Ibid., second para.; also ibid., Articles 4(1) and 6, and Preamble, indents 15 and 28.

supervisor reflects financial market stability[179] as well as perhaps single market considerations,[180] but it is doubtful – taking into account also the ECB according to the Treaties – that it includes financial consumer[181] or even depositor protection.[182]

The ECB, acting as bank supervisor, together with national competent authorities of participating Member States, form the system of financial supervision defined as the SSM.[183] The SSM Regulation provides rules for the cooperation of the ECB with the ESAs, the ESRB and other authorities of the EFSF, competent authorities of Member States, as well as the ESM.[184]

The SSM Regulation confers on the ECB a wide array of prudential supervision tasks in relation to all credit institutions established in participating Member States, including authorisation and withdrawal of authorisation, exercise of the competences of a home Member State competent authority with regard to the establishment of branches or the provision of cross-border services in a non-participating Member State, assessment of notifications of the acquisition and disposal of qualifying holdings (except in case of resolution), ensuring compliance with prudential requirements in the areas of own funds, securitisation, large exposure limits, liquidity, leverage, reporting and public disclosure on those matters, ensuring compliance with governance requirements ('fit and proper' requirements, risk management, internal control and others), carrying out supervisory reviews and stress tests and imposing additional own funds requirements, carrying out supervision on a consolidated basis, participating in supplementary supervision of financial conglomerates, and carrying out supervisory tasks in relation to recovery plans and early intervention measures (excluding resolution powers).[185]

It is interesting to note that, according to the SSM Regulation, for the purpose of carrying out those tasks the ECB shall apply not only relevant EU law but also, where relevant EU law is composed of Directives, the ECB shall also apply the Member State legislation transposing the Directives; and when the relevant EU law is composed of Regulations granting options to Member States, the ECB shall apply also the Member State legislation exercising those options.[186]

179 Ibid., Articles 1 and 15; Preamble, recitals 2, 5, 6, 13, 16, 30, 42, 44, 55, 56, 65.

180 Ibid., Article 1; Preamble, recitals 2, 3, 10, 11, 12, 30, 42.

181 Ibid., Preamble, recital 28.

182 See ibid., recital 30, where it is mentioned that the ECB should exercise its supervisory competence in the context of the SSM to ensure the safety and soundness of credit institutions and the stability of the EU and Member States' financial system and the unity and integrity of the internal market 'thereby ensuring also the protection of depositors …'; thus depositor protection emerges as a beneficial result of the function of the ECB as bank supervisor rather than as a direct aim of it.

183 Ibid., Article 2, point 9.

184 Ibid., Articles 3, 6, 7. See also Regulation (EU) No. 468/2014 of the ECB of 16.04.2014 establishing the framework for cooperation within the SSM between the ECB and the national competent authorities and with national designated authorities (the SSM Framework Regulation), OJ L 141/1, 14.05.2014.

185 SSM Regulation, Article 4(1).

186 Ibid., Article 4(3).

In the context of the exclusive supervisory powers of the ECB under the SSM Regulation, the ECB and the national competent authorities are under a duty of cooperation in good faith;[187] when the ECB is exercising its exclusive supervisory powers, national competent authorities are obliged to follow its instructions.[188] The ECB may further, if deemed necessary, apply macro-prudential tasks and tools and in particular apply higher requirements for capital buffers than applied by Member State authorities.[189]

Furthermore, the SSM Regulation provides for the exemption of certain less systemically significant credit institutions from the exclusive prudential supervision of the ECB (except for authorisation, withdrawal of authorisation, and assessment of notifications of acquisition and disposal of qualifying holdings), so that they remain under the responsibility of national competent authorities;[190] however, the relevant criteria set by the SSM Regulation are rather vague.[191] For the exercise of its supervisory competence, extensive powers are conferred by the SSM Regulation to the ECB, including investigatory powers, 'specific supervisory powers' (in relation to authorisation and assessment of acquisition of qualified holdings), and other supervisory powers including the imposition of administrative penalties.[192]

The SSM Regulation provides for the independence of the ECB and national competent authorities acting within the SSM;[193] furthermore, it provides for the (functional) separation of ECB organs acting in the context of the SSM from those acting in the context of the European monetary policy.[194] However, this separation relies only on internal organisation measures; the single Supervisory board (SSB), the internal body of the ECB established by the SSM Regulation for the planning

187 Ibid., Article 6(2).
188 Ibid., Article 6(3).
189 Ibid., Article 5(2).
190 Ibid., Article 6(4)–(7).
191 Ibid., Article 6(4).
192 Ibid., Articles 9–18. In case authorisation by a judicial authority is required by national law for the execution of investigation, the SSM Regulation provides that 'the national judicial authority shall control that the decision of the ECB is authentic and that the coercive measures envisaged are neither arbitrary nor excessive having regard to the subject matter of the inspection'; ibid., Article 13(2). However, it also provides that 'the national judicial authority shall not review the necessity for the inspection or demand to be provided with the information on the ECB's file. The lawfulness of the ECB's decision shall be subject to review only by the ECJ. Beyond evident considerations in relation to the procedural autonomy of Member States, and more generally with regard to national sovereignty in the administration of justice, this provision causes further concerns in particular when examined in conjunction with the provision of Article 4(3) of the SSM Regulation according to which in certain cases the ECB will be applying also national law.
193 Ibid., Article 19.
194 Ibid., Article 25. In this regard, the SSM Regulation provides that the ECB staff involved in carrying out the tasks of the ECB in the context of the SSM 'shall be organisationally separated from, and subject to, separate reporting lines from the staff involved in carrying out other tasks conferred on the ECB'; ibid., Article 25(2).

and execution of the SSM tasks conferred to the ECB,[195] does not constitute an EU agency with autonomous legal personality.

The SSM Regulation further provides for accountability of the ECB in the context of the SSM, including reporting obligations of the ECB to the European Parliament and national parliaments,[196] for procedural safeguards relating to due process for adopting supervisory decisions,[197] and for an internal review procedure by an Administrative Board of Review without prejudice to the right to bring proceedings before the ECJ.[198]

In particular, with regard to extra-contractual liability of the ECB in the exercise of its powers in the context of the SSM, the SSM Regulation does not set particular rules; however, it refers to the relevant general provisions of the Treaty as also applicable in this context.[199]

It emerges that very extensive powers have been conferred to the ECB, to act as prudential supervisor of SIFIs in the EU. It is questionable, however, that the legal basis for the relevant conferral is adequate. In this regard, the ruling of the General Court in Case T-496/11, *United Kingdom v ECB*, needs to be taken into account.

The General Court decision in **United Kingdom v ECB**

The extent of competences of the ECB under the TFEU was examined by the General Court in Case T-496/11, *United Kingdom v ECB*.[200] In this case, relating to the activity of securities clearing systems, the ECB relying on Article 127(1) and (2) of the TFEU and Articles 3.1 and 22 of Protocol (No4) to the TFEU on the Statute of the ESBC and the ECB had published in 2011 on its website the 'Eurosystem Oversight Policy Framework', referring inter alia to a requirement for CCPs and securities clearing systems to be located in the Euro area.

The Court, finding that the Policy Framework was intended to impose compliance with a location requirement, had legal consequences and was thus challengeable under Article 263 of the TFEU.

195 Ibid., Article 26. The SSB consists of its Chair, Vice Chair, four representatives of the ECB and one representative of the national competent authority in each participating Member State; ibid, Article 26(1). The Chair and Vice Chair are appointed by the Council following proposal by the ECB and approval by the European Parliament; ibid., Article 26(3). The SSB decides mainly by simple majority of its members; ibid., Article 26(6)–(8), while its steering committee has no decision-making powers; ibid., Article 26(10). The members of the SSB, as well as any staff of the ECB and staff seconded by Member States, are under professional secrecy obligations; ibid., Article 27.

196 Ibid., Articles 20 and 21.

197 Ibid., Article 22.

198 Ibid., Article 24. These provisions reflect the normative content of the relevant provisions in the SRM Regulation, Ch. 8.2, so that the comments to the latter apply *mutatis mutandis* also in the context of the SSM Regulation.

199 See SSM Regulation, Preamble, indent 61, referring to Article 340 of the TFEU.

200 General Court (Fourth Chamber) decision of 04.03.2015 in Case T-496/11, *United Kingdom v ECB*, ECLI:EU:T:2015:133.

Examining the substance of the case, the Court noted that:

> [t]he matter at issue is the ECB's competence to impose, on behalf of the Eurosystem, a requirement to be located within the euro area that is applicable to CCPs providing clearing services for euro-denominated securities beyond certain thresholds. It is clear that creation of such a requirement goes beyond mere oversight of the infrastructures of securities clearing systems, and partakes of regulation of their activity.[201]

Accepting that Article 127(1) and (2) of the TFEU and Articles 3.1 and 22 of the ECSB and ECB Statute have a complementary relationship as legal bases,[202] and acknowledging that 'powers not expressly provided for by the provisions of the Treaties may be used if they are necessary to achieve the objectives set by the Treaties',[203] the Court stressed that: '[n]evertheless, the existence of an implicit regulatory power, which constitutes a derogation from the principle of conferral laid down by Article 13(2) TEU, must be appraised strictly'.[204]

Thus, the Court concluded that 'the ECB does not have the competence necessary to regulate the activity of securities clearing systems',[205] and noted that it would be for the ECB to request the EU legislature to amend Article 22 of the Statute, by the addition of an explicit reference to securities clearing systems.[206]

Interim concluding remarks

The GFC led to the emergence of a new EU financial supervisory architecture, and the adoption of single rulebooks for FIs.

At the institutional level, the new EU law is characterised by centralisation of authority at the EU level, in the context of which the sectoral approach to financial market regulation has been maintained, but placed in a hierarchical structure of financial supervision focusing on systemic risk prevention and control.

In this new system, Member State competent authorities may be circumvented by the new EU supervisors imposing measures directly on FIs, while there is minimum participation by other EU institutions except for the Commission and almost no participation by the national authorities.

Beyond considerations of constitutional and institutional order, the new EU framework providing for the exercise of supervision and enforcement directly by the ESAs necessarily leaves unregulated the area of competence of national competent authorities exercised pursuant to applicable national law only. While national authorities can – and have an obligation – to apply both EU law (if it is directly applicable or else to act in conformity with it) and national law (as a system

201 Ibid., para. 84.
202 Ibid., para. 89.
203 Ibid., para. 104.
204 Ibid., para. 105.
205 Ibid., para. 110.
206 Ibid., para. 109.

of rules, which may be of EU origin as in the case of transposition of Directives or of only national origin), this does not apply vice versa, as EU law is not a complete system of law: EU law is necessarily partial, covering only the areas where the EU has sole or concurrent competence. In this regard, it is questionable whether the new EU supervisory framework may function effectively, protecting both market stability and financial consumers and in particular in a crisis situation.

At the substantive level, the adoption of new EU rulebooks for FIs, building on the experience of the GFC, aims to enhance and update prudential requirements and authorisation and operation rules for FIs. Representing an important effort to follow the development of financial instruments and markets, the new rulebook attempts to balance legal certainty and predictability with flexibility and a functional approach so as not to allow for inconsistencies, gaps or regulatory arbitrage. In this respect, however, the differentiation in legal treatment of retail depositors vis-à-vis retail investors, according to the traditional sectoral approach, appears all the more difficult to uphold when examined under the scope of FI failure risk.

More generally, two main conclusions may be drawn with regard to the emergence of the new structures and norms of EU financial law after the GFC.

First, in relation to the production of EU rules, a dimension appears as to the role of international *fora* and organisations in the promulgation of EU law. While there has always been an important interplay between international initiatives and proposals for the formation of new financial law, following the GFC there appears to be a stronger influence on the EU legal order by international *fora* and organisations, and in particular by the IMF, the FSB and the BIS. Beyond the possible political and practical merits of such cooperation, important questions are raised from a constitutional and institutional point of view.

Moreover, this question is complicated by the highly technical nature of many areas of financial regulation, which has led to the provision of extensive delegated powers to EU institutions and agencies, such as the Commission or the EBA, with minimum control by the European Parliament.

Thus, the political and law-making role of the European Parliament in the new legislative procedures appears to have been diminished, either owing to the incorporation into the EU legal order of structures and norms discussed and proposed at the international level, or as a consequence of the highly technical nature of rules entailing conferral of powers to EU institutions and agencies with professional expertise.

In this respect, it appears as though – as with the swing of a pendulum – EU financial law, which until the GFC opted for minimum harmonisation forming a basis for Member State regulation and supervision of FIs and markets, has moved from this extreme to the opposite extreme, where not only generally applicable rules but even individual decisions may be taken and enforced according to a centralised mechanism by EU institutions and agencies of the executive, with minimum involvement of EU political authorities and with minimum or even no participation of Member State institutions and authorities.

It is as if the process, which in times of growing prosperity and optimism gradually led to the acceptance of individual protection considerations and the empowerment of the European Parliament through initially the creative case law of the ECJ and then by the SEA and the new EU treaties that followed, is being reversed at these times of crisis and scepticism and the European Parliament – and also the other EU and Member State political institutions – are being alienated from their central role in decision-making.

As a result, both at the level of new financial architecture and at the level of rules on regulation and supervision of FIs and markets by EU institutions, the financial consumer may be considered secluded: at the political level, by the distancing of law-making and decision-taking from both EU and Member State parliamentary bodies and administrative authorities; and at the legal level, by the lack of preventive remedies and by the distancing between acts (of institutions and agencies at the EU level) and effects (at the Member State or individual levels).

Beyond merits at the financial level, from a technical point of view regarding the prevention and control of systemic risk, this emerging status of the EU financial law cannot be considered as satisfactory in constitutional terms, relating also to the effective protection of financial consumers as individuals participating in the financial market.

Part II

Delineating financial consumer protection under EU law in the event of financial institution failure

Having examined the general development of EU financial law under the influence of international developments and initiatives, and with regard primarily to the *ratio* of EU financial law as concerns financial consumer protection, it is now necessary to examine more specifically the protection awarded by EU law to financial consumers in the event of FI failure, as delimitated by the *ex lege* compensation regime, pre- and post- the global financial crisis, and as affected by the new resolution regime, also taking into account judicial protection considerations.

6 EU law on financial consumer minimum protection in the event of financial institution failure prior to the GFC

Depositors as savers

Introductory note

The introduction of the Deposit Guarantee Schemes Directive (DGSD) for the minimum protection of (retail) depositors and of the Investor Compensation Schemes Directive (ICSD) for the minimum protection of (retail) investors followed the sectoral distinction of EU financial law, according to a criterion of presumed sector-based risk.

For systematic reasons, it will be useful to analyse each of these EU law instruments per se, and in relation to each other, before examining the effect of the new rules and proposed reforms as a result of the global financial crisis (GFC).

6.1 The Deposit Guarantee Schemes Directive (DGSD)

EU law regulated minimum protection guaranteed to depositors only in 1994, by the introduction of the DGSD.[1]

Ratio and scope of the DGSD

The DGSD was adopted as a minimum harmonisation measure[2] with a view to address competition issues between credit institutions, caused by the disparity of deposit guarantee protection awarded to their clients before harmonisation,[3] to protect depositor confidence in the soundness of the banking system,[4] and thus to protect savers.[5]

1 Directive 94/19/EC, OJ L 135/5, 31.05.1994; now replaced by Directive 2014/49/EU (recast), OJ L 173/149, 12.06.2014 (DGSD Recast). The legal basis for the adoption of the DGSD was EC Treaty, Article 57(2), as a market integration measure. For the relevant legislative procedure, see Commission Recommendation [1987] OJ L 33/16; Commission Proposal [1992] OJ C 163/6; Commission Proposal [1993] OJ C 115/91; Commission Amended Proposal [1993] OJ C 178/14; Decision of the Common Position [1994] OJ C 91/85. For analysis of relevant ECJ case law, see Ch. 8.

2 DGSD, Preamble, recital 8.

3 Ibid., recitals 2 and 3.

4 Ibid., recitals 4 and 21.

5 Ibid., recital 1. Cf. recital 15. See in this regard the ECJ decision of 02.09.2015 in Case C-127/14,

The *ratio* of the DGSD was to provide depositors access to funds as soon as a credit institution was unable to repay them;[6] and while deposits made by credit institutions on their own behalf and for their own account were not protected by the DGSD, it provided that national DGSs could take measures necessary for the rescue of a credit institution in difficulty.[7]

The scope of the DGSD encompassed deposits in credit institutions established in Member States, deposits being defined as 'any credit balance which results from funds left in an account or from temporary situations deriving from normal banking transactions and which a credit institution must repay under the legal and contractual conditions applicable, and any debt evinced by a certificate issued by a credit institution',[8] while credit institutions were defined as in the relevant banking Directives.[9]

Except for a limited number of exclusions (deposits from credit institutions on their own account, instruments constituting own funds, deposits arising out of transactions in connection to which there has been a criminal conviction for money laundering),[10] all other deposits were *a priori* covered by the DGSD, while Member States were allowed to provide that certain depositors or deposits would be excluded from guarantee or would be granted a lower level of guarantee – such optional exclusions being also *numerus clausus*.[11] Deposits held by a credit institution at the time of withdrawal of its authorisation were also covered by the DGSD.[12]

It is interesting to note that questions regarding the notion of 'deposit' under the DGSD were brought before the EFTA Court in Case E-17/11, for an advisory opinion.[13]

The EFTA Court decision in Case E-17/11

The questions in Case E-17/11 related to whether interbank loans could be considered as deposits for the purposes of the DGSD, and whether deposits of credit institutions with other credit institutions could be protected under the DGSD.

In particular, the first question submitted to the EFTA Court asked, as rearticulated by said court, whether loans made by one credit institution to another 'are to

Andrejs Surmačs v Finanšu un kapitāla tirgus komisija, ECLI:EU:C:2015:522, in which the Court considered that 'it is clear from the first recital in the preamble to Directive 94/19 that it has the dual objective of protecting savers in the event of the unavailability of deposits made in credit institutions and of increasing the stability of the banking system' (ibid., para. 19).

6 Ibid., 9th recital.

7 Ibid., 10th recital. However, the DGSD did not provide any directions as to how this option could be exercised by Member States.

8 Ibid., Article 1(1), point 1.

9 Ibid., Article 1(1), point 4.

10 Ibid., Article 2.

11 Ibid., Article 7(2) and Annex I.

12 Ibid., Article 5.

13 EFTA Court decision of 22.11.2012 in Case E-17/11, *Aresbank SA and Landsbankinn hf., Fjármálaeftirlitið (the Financial Supervisory Authority) and the Icelandic State* [2012] EFTA Court Reports 918.

be considered deposits within the meaning of Article 1(1) of DGSD, even though (i) the funds were not entered as deposits in the borrower bank's books; (ii) nor were they placed in a special account in the lender bank's name; (iii) no special documents recording the receipt of the funds were issued; and (iv) no premiums to the [national deposit and investor guarantee scheme] were paid in respect of the funds'.[14]

The EFTA Court answered the question in the affirmative,[15] noting that while such deposits fall within the notion of deposit under the DGSD, they do not constitute covered deposits.[16] The EFTA Court took into account inter alia that the requirements for funds to be treated as deposits under Article 1(1) of the DGSD are not cumulative, and that the concept of 'credit balance' is not explained in the DGSD.

In this regard, the EFTA Court noted that 'it can be of no relevance that the funds have not been entered as a deposit in the borrowing bank's books. It would be contrary to the purpose of [the DGSD] if protection were to be dependent on the characterisation given by the credit institution receiving the funds'.[17]

Furthermore, the EFTA Court, concurring with the position of the Commission which submitted written observations,[18] proposed a distinction between a 'functional' definition of eligible deposits under the DGSD and a 'technical' definition also including deposits not covered by said Directive for repayment.[19]

Thus, the EFTA Court, in our view, held that the effectiveness of the protection in principle awarded by the DGSD should not depend on the characterisation of a transaction by the interested parties or on their behaviour (as in the case of not entering it in the relevant books and records).

Moreover, in its recent ruling of 2 September 2015 in Case C-127/14,[20] the ECJ referred to (retail) depositors meriting protection by the legal order, and introduced a functional criterion as to the classification of depositors.

The ECJ decision in Case C-127/14

In Case C-127/14, the ECJ considered a definition of depositors falling within the protective ambit of DGSD, taking into account – in absence of a definition in the Directive – its Preamble and the relevant Commission proposal.[21]

The Court considered with regard to the objectives of DGSD, that 'that legislation seeks, in particular, according to its first recital, to protect savers in their legal relationships with credit institutions. Not having, in most cases, the information

14 Ibid., para. 47.
15 Ibid., para. 63.
16 Ibid., para. 64.
17 Ibid., para. 56.
18 Ibid., para. 49.
19 Ibid., para. 64.
20 ECJ decision in Case C-127/14 (n. 5).
21 Ibid., paras. 30–34.

or the expertise required to assess the actual financial situation of the credit institution with which they deal, savers are unable to assess the risks of insolvency of those institutions'.[22]

The ECJ continued to note that '[i]n that regard, the 18th recital in the preamble to Directive 94/19 states that only savers who do not 'need special protection' may be excluded from the guarantee by the Member States'.[23]

Obligations under the DGSD

The main obligation of Member States emanating from the DGSD was to ensure that within their territory one or more DGSs are introduced and officially recognised, while credit institutions authorised in Member States may not take deposits unless they are members of a DGS.[24]

The DGSD provided minimum rules regarding the relation between the national DGS(s) and the competent national authorities for the supervision and regulation of financial markets. Relevant rules regulated the initiation of depositor payment proceedings by national deposit guarantee schemes, following determination of unavailability of deposits by a credit institution,[25] the obligation of national competent authorities to prohibit taking of deposits by credit institutions that are not members of a DGS[26] and to impose sanctions on credit institutions which do not comply with obligations regarding membership deposit guarantee scheme,[27] and the discretionary power of national competent authorities to provide extension of the time limit for a national DGS to pay depositor claims.[28]

The DGSD provided for a minimum amount of deposits to be protected per depositor per credit institution,[29] while Member States could limit the protection, for moral hazard reasons,[30] but not to less than 90 per cent of the protected amount of (aggregate) deposits per depositor per credit institution ('co-insurance').[31]

Further, the DGSD provided that (national) DGSs had to be in a position to pay duly verified claims by depositors within 20 working days of the date on which the competent authorities determine the unavailability of deposits.[32] Under exceptional circumstances, a short extension of the time limit could be approved by the competent authorities.[33]

No further substantive or procedural rules were provided by the DGSD in

22 Ibid., para. 30.
23 Ibid., para. 31.
24 DGSD, Article 3.
25 Ibid., Article 1(3).
26 Ibid., Article 3(1).
27 Ibid., Articles 3(2) and 4(4).
28 Ibid., Article 10(1).
29 Ibid., Article 7(1a), after 01.01.2011, as the relevant provision was introduced by Directive 2009/14/EC [2009] OJ L 68/3.
30 DGSD, Article 7(1) and (3).
31 Ibid., Article 7(4).
32 Ibid., Article 10(1), as amended by Directive 2009/14/EC. The initial time limit was three months.
33 Ibid.

relation to the conditions for payment to be made by national DGSs to depositors, including rules on claim verification. The DGSD provided in this direction only that 'the documents relating to the conditions to be fulfilled and the formalities to be completed to be eligible for a payment under the guarantee ... shall be drawn up in detail in the manner prescribed by national law in the official language or languages of the [Member State] in which the guaranteed deposit is located'.[34]

Following the amendments introduced by Directive 2009/14/EC, it was provided that the time limit for payment of covered depositor claims (i.e. 20 working days) included 'the collection and transmission of the accurate data on depositors and deposits, which are necessary for the verification of claims'.[35] However, such time limits could not be invoked by the DGS against a depositor who had been unable to assert his claim in time.[36]

The European deposit guarantee system as designed at the time of introduction of the DGSD remained unaltered in its substance for almost two decades, and remained unchanged through most of the GFC.

When the financial crisis had reached Europe, it was urgently modified by Directive 2009/14/EC, but only in relation to technical features such as coverage level and pay-out delay. Later, in the context of the wider reform of EU financial law, it was replaced by Directive 2014/49/EU, the new DGSD (Recast).[37]

Taking into account the gradual development of deposit protection in the EU legal order in the event of financial institution (FI) failure prior to the GFC, it appears that the normative formation of the DGSD may be attributed, in our view, to three main factors.

First, the need to protect the stability of the financial system which would be endangered in case of loss of depositor confidence (mainly to avoid 'bank runs' which cause systemic risk).

Secondly, the need to achieve minimum harmonisation in deposit insurance regimes between Member States, a factor connected to intra-bank competition.

Thirdly, it may be argued that the gradual enhancement of the powers of the European Parliament, on the basis of democratic accountability and institutional balance considerations,[38] in particular since the SEA of 1986, and relevant national considerations, built political impetus for protecting financial consumers, such as retail depositors.

Depositor protection was thus an element of European policy in the banking sector, aiming primarily at avoidance of systemic danger by enhancing confidence in order to achieve market stability.

34 Ibid., Article 10(4).

35 Ibid., Article 10(1), as amended by Directive 2009/14/EC.

36 Ibid., Article 10(3).

37 See Ch. 7.1.

38 For a reflection of considerations relevant to democratic accountability and institutional balance in the ECJ case law during this period see, generally, ECJ decision in Case C138/79 *Roquette Frères v Council* [1980] ECR 3333, ECLI:EU:C:1980:249; ECJ decision of in Case 294/83 *Les Verts v Parliament* [1986] ECR 1339, ECLI:EU:C:1986:166; ECJ decision in Case C70/88 *Parliament v Council* [1990] ECR I2041, ECLI:EU:C:1990:217 (the 'titanium dioxide' case).

In this sense, depositor protection per se has been an for EU law economic 'externality' which was treated by legal means mainly for systemic protection reasons, on the basis of a minimum harmonisation approach.

6.2 The Investor Compensation Schemes Directive (ICSD)

The ICSD[39] has been characterised as 'one of the pillars of the European Framework for a Single Market in the financial services field'.[40]

Ratio and scope of the ICSD

As with the DGSD, it is also an instrument of minimum harmonisation of national compensation systems, its adoption necessitated by the introduction of the single European license of investment firms by the ISD.[41]

As opposed to the (initial) DGSD, the ICSD continues to be in force, in essence as originally adopted in 1997, since there has not yet been political agreement on its proposed modification.[42]

The aim of the ICSD, as announced in its Preamble, is the 'protection of investors and the maintenance of confidence in the financial system'[43] as an 'important aspect of the completion and proper functioning of the internal market',[44] especially taking into account that 'no system of supervision can provide complete protection, particularly where acts of fraud are committed'.[45]

Thus, it was deemed 'essential that each [Member State] should have an [ICS] that guarantees a harmonized minimum level of protection at least for the small investor in the event of an investment firm being unable to meet its obligations to its investor clients'.[46]

An important question that arises is whether the protection of the 'small investors' is considered an essential aim: (a) to the protection of 'small investors' per se, as an autonomous aim of EU law, (b) to the protection of participants' confidence in the financial market, as a mechanism to protect the stability of financial markets, or (c) a combination of the two.[47]

39 Its legal basis is EC Treaty, (ex) Article 47(2) and it was issued on the co-decision procedure of EC Treaty, (ex) Article 251. For the legislative procedure leading to its adoption, see EP opinion [1994] OJ C 128/85, Council common position [1995] OJ C 320/9, EP Decision [1996] OJ C 96/28, Decision of the Council and of the EP [1997] OJ C 85.

40 See Commission report on the application of the export prohibition clause: COM(2000) 0081 final, 3.

41 See ISD, Article 12; Preamble, recitals 1 and 2.

42 For the proposed reform of ICSD, see Ch. 7.3.

43 ICSD, Preamble, recital 3.

44 Ibid., recital 3.

45 Ibid., recital 4.

46 Ibid., recital 4. The reference to 'small investors' in recital 4, as well as in recitals 5 and 11, is not repeated in the provisions of the ICSD; nor does it correspond to any definition provided by the ISD or any other Directive.

47 This problematic is similar to that in Case C-233/94 *Germany v European Parliament and Council*

The Preamble of the ICSD appears to attach importance mainly to competition issues and to the protection of small-investor confidence in the market.

Indeed, it states that minimum harmonisation of ICSs will entail that 'small investors will … be able to purchase investment services from branches of Community investment firms or on the basis of the cross-border provision of services as confidently as from domestic investment firms',[48] while 'in the absence of such minimum harmonization, a host [Member State] might consider itself justified, by considerations of investor protection, in requiring membership of its compensation scheme'[49] by an investment firm established and licensed by another Member State, 'whereas such a requirement might prejudice the operation of the internal market'.[50]

Thus, the imposition of restrictive measures on investment firms licensed in another Member State, by invoking reasons of general interest relevant to the protection of investors in the event of investment firm failure, has been perceived as a potential impediment to the completion of the internal financial market necessitating harmonisation of protective measures at the EU level.

Further, the disparity of national investor compensation schemes might lead 'to disparities in competition and unequal conditions of competition between national investment firms and branches of firms from other [Member States]'[51] and 'market disturbances',[52] necessitating the introduction of specific provisions in relation to branch participation in host Member State ICSs, since 'it is not appropriate that the level or scope of cover offered by compensation schemes should become an instrument of competition'.[53] In this regard, the ICSD was introduced as an instrument to achieve equal access to the market for competing financial firms, as also confirmed by its legal basis.

The field of application of the ICSD encompasses a wide range of investment services offered by investment firms to retail investors, leaving however the exact delimitation of its scope to the Member States.

Specifically, the definition of 'investment firm' for the purposes of the ICSD encompasses investment firms as defined in the MiFID which were authorised in accordance with the ISD and then the MiFID (cf. MiFID II) or authorised as credit institutions[54] the authorisation of which covers one or more of the

(Ch. 4, n. 8), where the question of whether depositor (consumer) protection was an aim of the DGSD, and of what nature, was considered by the ECJ and by AG Léger in Case C-222/02, *Peter Paul*. For discussion see Ch. 9.2.

48 ICSD, Preamble, recital 5; cf. ibid., recital 21.

49 Ibid., recital 6.

50 Ibid., recital 6; cf. ibid., recital 25.

51 Ibid., recital 15.

52 Ibid., recital 16.

53 Ibid.

54 ICSD, Article 1(1) in its original form; this article referred to the relevant provisions of the ISD, i.e. Articles 1(2) and (2), which were replaced and repealed by the MiFID (see MiFID, Article 69) and further replaced and repealed by the MiFID II (see MiFID II, Article 94 and Annex IV).

investment services (or activities) listed in Section A of Annex I relating to any of the instruments listed in Section C of Annex I of the MiFID.[55]

Further, the ICSD defines 'investor', for the purposes of its application, as 'any person who has entrusted money or instruments to an investment firm in connection with investment business'.[56]

Furthermore, it defines 'investment business' as any investment service as defined in the MiFID[57] plus 'safekeeping and administration' in relation to one or more of the financial instruments listed in Section C of the MiFID.[58]

Apart from the general differences between the scope and definitions of the ICSD, owing to the corresponding differences of the MiFID in relation to the ISD, it is important to note what appears to be a crucial element in the definition of 'investor' for the purposes of the ICSD: 'investor' is defined by the ICSD as a person who has entrusted money or instruments to an investment firm 'in connection' with investment business.[59]

The wording 'in connection' appears to be implying, in our view, the general context of the relation of the 'investor' with the investment firm, covering all stages of the relation between a person interested in investing and the investment firm. If this is correct, it may imply a wider field of application of the ICSD than in relation only to financial transactions that had already been entered into or executed at the time of the occurrence of unavailability of funds or instruments by the financial intermediary, covering both '*stricto sensu* investors' and '*lato sensu* investors'. It is necessary then to explore whether such an interpretation may be valid.

Literal interpretation of the provision in other official languages of the EU appears to be confirming the above observation regarding the term 'in connection'.[60]

55 MiFID, Article 4(1), point 2, and the same in the MiFID II; the original reference by the ICSD was to investments services listed in ISD, Annex, Section A.

56 ICSD, Article 1(4) referring to MiFID, Article 4(1), point 2 (the same as in the MiFID II).

57 ICSD, Article 1; reference in the text of the Directive is to the relevant provisions of ISD, Article 1(1), and Annex, Section C, point 1, replaced by the MiFID and now by the MiFID II; see n. 54.

58 Ibid.; reference in the text of the Directive is to ISD, Section B replaced by MiFID, Section C, now MiFID II, Section C; see n. 54.

59 Cf. ICSD, Preamble, recital 8: 'each scheme must cover money and instruments held by an investment firm in connection with an investor's investment operations which, where an investment firm is unable to meet its obligations to its investor clients, cannot be returned to the investor'. Further, according to ICSD, Article 2(2), '[c]over shall be provided for claims arising out of an investment firm's inability to … repay money owed to or belonging to investors and held on their behalf in connection with investment business, or … return to investors any instruments belonging to them and held, administered or managed on their behalf in connection with investment business, in accordance with the legal and contractual conditions applicable'.

60 In the French version of the provision, *'dans le cadre d'opérations d'investissement'*; in the Spanish version, *'en el marco des operaciones de inversión'*; in the Italian version, *'nell'ambito di operazioni d'investimento'*; in the Hellenic version, '[in the context of investment services transactions]'. According to settled case law of the ECJ, the various language versions of a text of EU law must be given a uniform interpretation and hence, in the case of divergence between the language versions, the provision in question must be interpreted by reference to the purpose and general scheme of the rules of which it forms a part; see e.g. ECJ decision of 28.06.2012 in Case C-19/11, *Markus Geltl v Daimler AG* ECLI: EU: C: 2012: 397, para. 43 and case law cited therein.

Furthermore, this interpretation, based on the wording of the provision under examination,[61] appears to be in harmony with the generally stated obligation of Member States to have in operation an ICS compensating investors where a decision or ruling has been issued 'which has the effect of suspending investors' ability to make claims against [the investment firm]'.[62] The reference of the latter provision to 'investors' ability to make claims' does not specify the cause of the claims, i.e. whether it is outstanding obligations on the basis of executed transactions in the financial market or whether it can also be the deposit of funds and/or instruments with the intention to enter into transactions in the financial market.

Thus, literal interpretation does not resolve the issue of whether depositing of funds or instruments with an investment firm falls per se within the ambit of the ICSD, and two different interpretations are *a priori* possible: (a) that only *stricto sensu* investors are covered by the ICSD, or (b) that also *lato sensu* investors may be covered by it.

The exclusion of *lato sensu* investors from the protective field of application of the ICSD would have important legal consequences, as this category of market participants might fall out of the scope of the DGSD as well, revealing an important *lacuna* in the ambit of protection offered by EU law. *Lato sensu* investors would be left totally unprotected, in particular in case of fraud perpetrated against them by the failing investment firm, a result which, in our view, manifestly ultimately contravenes the *ratio* of the ICSD – which is stated to protect investors especially in cases of fraud.[63]

In this direction, the teleological interpretation that *lato sensu* investors are also covered by the ICSD appears *de lege lata* to be in accordance with the aim of the latter to provide protection also in cases where (prudential) supervision has failed and damage is incurred by the retail investor as a result of an act that is *a priori* extraneous to the operation of the financial market in normal conditions, such as and particularly 'where acts of fraud are committed'[64] – i.e. in the case of an externality to (normal) financial market operations.

Indeed, it is not necessary that an act of fraud against the *lato sensu* investor will be committed at a specific point in time; on the contrary, an act of fraud may be committed at any time.

Although this is evident, the ICSD does not provide any rule clearly differentiating the case of unavailability of funds or instruments occurring after or in connection to the execution of transactions from the case of such unavailability occurring before or independently of the execution of transactions.[65]

The absence of any such clear rule advocates for the treatment of both cases as equivalent by the ICSD; this would entail that both cases fall within its field of

61 I.e. ICSD, Article 4(1) 1.

62 ICSD, Article 2(2).

63 Ibid., Preamble, recital 3.

64 Ibid.

65 See, however, ICSD, Article 6.

application also on the basis of an argument *a majore ad minus*, since the first case, of *stricto sensu* investors, certainly falls within its field of application.

Furthermore, an argument in support of the interpretation that the field of application of the ICSD encompasses not only *stricto sensu* investors but also *lato sensu* investors persons may be derived from the rule of the ICSD, providing that:

> [a] [Member State] may ... exempt a credit institution to which this Directive applies from the obligation to belong to an investor-compensation scheme where that credit institution is already exempt under Article 3 (1) of [the DGSD] from the obligation to belong to a deposit-guarantee scheme, provided that the protection and information given to depositors are also given to investors on the same terms and investors thus enjoy protection at least equivalent to that afforded by an investor-compensation scheme.[66]

The condition that the protection awarded to depositors is provided to investors on the same terms may be interpreted as including the case of funds deposited by a person with a financial conglomerate with a view to conduct transactions in the financial market.

This assumption is reinforced by the rule of the ICSD that '[a]ny claim ... on a credit institution which, in a given [Member State], would be subject both to this Directive and to [the DGSD] shall be directed by that [Member State] to a scheme under one or other of those Directives as that [Member State] shall consider appropriate',[67] and that 'no claim shall be eligible for compensation more than once under those Directives'.[68]

For a claim to be eligible under the DGSD, it must be: (a) a duly verified claim by a depositor in respect of unavailable deposit and (b) not a claim exempted from the field of application of said Directive, according to either EU law or national law. Thus, if a person who had deposited funds with a financial conglomerate would be protected on the same terms by a national DGS or a national ICS, then the simple depositing of funds with an FI with a view to proceed to transactions in the financial market should be covered by the ICSD.[69] However, *de lege lata* the answer is not clear.

Another argument in the same direction may be derived from the rule of the ICSD that an Member State may limit the cover provided to a specified percentage of an investor's claim, in order 'to encourage investors to take due care in their choice of investment firms'.[70]

This option of Member States may be interpreted as leading to two (concurrent) conclusions: (a) that ICSD law is compatible with national measures designed to

66 ICSD, Article 2(1).

67 Ibid., Article 2(3).

68 Ibid.

69 Cf. ICSD, Preamble, recital 9 stating that 'in the case of investment firms which are credit institutions it may in certain cases be difficult to distinguish between deposits covered by [the DGSD] and money held in connection with investment business; ... [Member States] should be allowed to determine which Directive shall apply to such claims'.

70 ICSD, Preamble, recital 13; Cf. DGSD, Preamble, recital 19.

prevent or reduce moral hazard, providing incentives to retail investors to make careful and informed choices of investment firms as financial intermediaries; however, there is no indication as to how retail investors are to evaluate and select investment firms to enter into contract with; (b) that the ICSD does not allow for total transfer of risk (market, counterparty, etc.) to retail investors, in particular in the case of FI failure, but only to a very small degree and in specific conditions, in order to satisfy moral hazard considerations. Member States are *a priori* not allowed to provide that no compensation at all will be paid to retail investors, which would imply that counterparty risk is borne by the latter.[71]

This implies that *a priori* the ICSD does not allow for a national system of law transferring the risk of FI failure to retail investors, especially in case where failure occurs as a result of fraud.[72]

According to the wording and the spirit of the ICSD, *stricto sensu* investors may be compensated by national ICSs even in the case of investors' unwise or uninformed decisions regarding the choice of FI.

However, the reasoning leading to the conclusion that *lato sensu* investors are protected under the ICSD is not unquestionable. There are certain indications that the opposite conclusion might as well be sound, for different reasons.

Indeed, the above initial conclusion appears incompatible the ICSD rule providing that '[a]fter the withdrawal of an investment firm's authorization, cover … shall continue to be provided in respect of investment business transacted up to the time of that withdrawal'.[73]

The reference to transactions concluded up to the time of the withdrawal of an investment firm's authorisation – and which would be connected to the unavailability of investors' funds and/or instruments – may provide an argument to the direction that only obligations outstanding at the time of investment firm failure as a result of investment services transactions are covered by the ICSD, thus excluding the simple deposit of funds and/or instruments from its field of application.[74]

71 The discretion of Member States to exclude retail investors from compensation schemes or to grant a lower level of cover than that provided by ICSD is strictly delimited; see ICSD, Article 4(2; Annex I. Cf. however ICSD, Article 8(1). In relation to retail investors not connected to the failing investment firm (see categories of connected persons in ICSD, Annex I, points 4 and 5), Member States are allowed to exclude or grant smaller compensation only to '[i]nvestors who have any responsibility for or have taken advantage of certain facts relating to an investment firm which gave rise to the firm's financial difficulties or contributed to the deterioration of its financial situation' or claims connected to money laundering (ICSD, Annex I, point 7); these exceptions from protection being specific and *numerus clausus*, they must be interpreted strictly. For the established case law of the ECJ regarding strict interpretation of exclusions, see e.g. ECJ decision of 17.06.1981 in Case 113/80, *Commission v Ireland* [1981] ECR 1625, para. 7.

72 Under the DGSD (Recast), this form of co-insurance has been considered unfair to financial consumers and repealed.

73 ICSD, Article 6.

74 The same problem is posed by the ICSD rule, providing in relation to investment firm branch exclusion from the ICS of a host Member State inter alia that '[i]nvestment business transacted before the date of exclusion shall continue to be covered after that date by the compensation scheme of which the branch was a voluntary member'; ibid., Article 7(2), point 2. See also ICSD,

It emerges, in our opinion, that legal certainty and predictability are not achieved by the above ICSD rules, in particular when an investment firm fails as a result of fraud (or in connection to other tortuous behaviour); this in turn affects the effectiveness awarded by EU law to retail investors, and financial consumers as a whole.

Moreover, at least under the regime of (initial) DGSD, another aspect of this problematic could arise with regard to exclusions of certain instruments from the protective ambit of DGSD in conjunction with ICSD.

Such was the case brought before the ECJ in Case C-671/13 following reference for a preliminary ruling.[75]

The ECJ decision in Case C-671/13

The case before the referring national court of justice concerned a financial consumer who had concluded an agreement with a credit institution (bank *Snoras*) for the acquisition of an inflation-linked certificate of deposit, and had concluded relevant bond subscription agreements with the bank, when its business activities were suspended in 2011 and entered into insolvency proceedings.[76]

The ECJ, considering EU law on depositor protection, and taking into account the definition of covered deposits,[77] first considered that 'neither Article 7(2) of [DGSD] nor point 12 of Annex I to that directive provides, for the purposes of the exclusion of the deposit guarantee, that the instruments in question must have all the characteristics of a financial instrument within the meaning of [MiFID]',[78] and that it is necessary though 'in view of the requirements of [DGSD], that the instruments covered by the exclusion which the [Member States] apply be amongst those which fall within the scope of [DGSD]'.[79]

Examining the particular definition of 'deposit' for the purposes of the DGSD, it noted that it is clear that the concept of 'deposit', for the purposes of DGSD, 'is not defined by reference to the characteristics of a financial instrument within the meaning of [MiFID]'.[80]

Thus, the ECJ concluded that Member States may exclude negotiable debt securities (certificates of deposit) issued by credit institutions that may be excluded from deposit guarantee, without the need for such certificates to have all the characteristics of a financial instrument within the meaning of the MiFID.[81]

Article 5(2), regarding transactions while there has been notice to the investment firm of excluding it from membership of the scheme.

75 See ECJ decision of 25.06.2015 in Case C-671/13, '*Indėlių ir investicijų draudimas*' *VĮ*, *Virgilijus Vidutis Nemaniūnas*, ECLI:EU:C:2015:418.

76 Ibid., paras 19–21.

77 The ECJ considered in particular Article 20(1) of Directive 86/635/EEC (regarding debts evidenced by certificates), recitals 16, 17 in the Preamble to DGSD, Articles 1 point 1, 3(1), 7(1) and (2) and Annex I of the DGSD; ibid., paras 3–8. It also took into account the Commission proposal for the DGSD; ibid., para. 37.

78 Ibid., para. 33.

79 Ibid, para. 34.

80 Ibid., para. 36.

81 Ibid., para. 38.

Then, moving on to consider the protective regime under the ICSD, in conjunction also to the MiFID,[82] the ECJ noted that 'in view of the definitions of the concepts of 'deposit' and 'instrument' in [DGSD] and [ICSD] respectively, a single debt security may … be encompassed by both those concepts and therefore fall within the scope of both directives',[83] and that 'the guarantee schemes provided for by the two directives entail different conditions, in particular in terms of exclusion. Whilst Article 7(2) of [DGSD] and Annex I thereto allow for exclusions based on either the type of depositor or the type of deposit, Article 4(2) of [ICSD] provides for exclusions solely on the basis of the type of investor'.[84]

Thus, the ECJ concluded that DGSD and ICSD must be interpreted as meaning that:

> when claims against a credit institution are such as to be encompassed by both the concept of 'deposit' within the meaning of [DGSD] and that of 'instrument' within the meaning of [ICSD], and the national legislature has made use of the option … to exclude those claims from the protection scheme provided for by [DGSD], such an exclusion cannot result in those claims also being excluded from the protection scheme provided for by [ICSD], other than under the conditions mentioned in Article 4(2) of that directive.[85]

In this way, the ECJ considered the DGSD in conjunction with the ICSD through systemic and teleological interpretation, in a dynamic way that, taking into account the conditions for application of the two regimes, unifies in our view their protective ambit in a functional way in cases where financial consumers may be deprived in practice from effective protection for reasons connected to the classification of financial instruments.

Obligations under the ICSD

The ICSD provides clear, precise and unconditional rules on the conditions triggering the obligation of ICSs to pay compensation to retail investors, i.e. following decision by the competent authority or a judicial authority relevant to the inability of investors' claims to be met by an investment firm, and on the minimum amount of compensation payable and the relevant exclusions.[86]

However, the ICSD, as an instrument of minimum harmonisation, does not provide detailed rules on the structure and operation of national ICSs; it does, however, impose on Member States a series of minimum obligations,

82 The ECJ took in particular into account recital 9 to the Preamble to the ICSD, Articles 1 points 3 and 4, 2(2) and (3), 4(1) and (2) to the ICSD, Section C of Annex I to the MiFID, and Article 4(1) point 19 to the MiFID; ibid., paras 9–15.

83 Ibid., para. 43.

84 Ibid., para. 44.

85 Ibid., para. 47.

86 On the direct effect of ICSD Articles 2(2) and 4(2) see ECJ decision of 25.06.2015 in Case C-671/13 (n. 75) para. 58, and Opinion of AG Cruz Villalón in the same case, EC LI:EU:C:2015:129, points 86–87.

regarding inter alia the basic obligation of Member States is to ensure that one or more ICSs are introduced and officially recognised within their territory and to ensure that no investment firm authorised in their jurisdiction may provide investment services unless it belongs to an ICS.[87] However, the ICSD does not provide for the legal status of the ICSs, leaving this to the discretion of Member States.[88]

The obligation of Member States to have in place one or more ICSs (belonging to their public or private sector) appears to be an *obligation de résultat*, in the sense that this obligation of Member States would be void of meaning if national ICSs do not operate effectively; otherwise, the useful effect of the ICSD would be compromised.[89]

Furthermore, the ICSD provides rules for the relationship between ICSs and competent authorities of Member States for the supervision and regulation of financial markets only on specific issues.[90]

The role of ICSs as outlined by the ICSD is complementary to the role of supervisory authorities, as 'no system of supervision can provide complete protection, particularly where acts of fraud are committed'.[91]

In our view, since the introduction and operation of ICSs in Member States is considered essential for the single market in financial services, and especially since these schemes may not belong to the public sector of Member States, minimum rules on the regulation and supervision of ICSs by the competent national authorities should be provided at the EU level. However, no such rule has been provided by the ICSD.[92]

The above observations reveal a deficiency, in our view, in the normative structure of the ICSD: despite the minimum harmonisation approach adopted, the normative structure of the ICSD – examined per se – is unclear and ambiguous in terms of the relationship between national competent authorities and ICSs, thus leading to further uncertainty as to the respective obligations and possible liability of national competent authorities in case of deficient supervision of ICSs.

Moreover, while the basic obligation of ICSs as provided by the ICSD is to provide compensation for investors in the delay set by law following establishment

87 ICSD, Article 2(1); Preamble, recital 8.

88 ICSD, Preamble, recitals 7, 11, 14 and 18.

89 Cf. ibid., recital 24, providing that 'this Directive may not result in the Member States or their competent authorities being made liable in respect of investors if they have ensured that one or more schemes for the compensation or protection of investors under the conditions prescribed in this Directive have been introduced and officially recognized'. For discussion, see Ch. 9.2.

90 Such as the decision of the competent authorities that an investment firm is unable to meet its obligations arising out of investors' claims: ICSD, Article 2(2); the cooperation between the competent authorities and the ICS in case an investment firm does not meet its obligations as member of the scheme: ibid., Article 5; and the right of an ICS 'in wholly exceptional circumstances and in special cases' to apply to the competent authorities for an extension of the time limit to compensate investors: ibid., Article 9(1) and (2).

91 ICSD, Preamble, recital 3.

92 Rules in this area have been provided by the new EU financial architecture, establishing inter alia the ESMA.

of the eligibility and the amount of their claim,[93] the ICSD does not provide specific rules either for establishing the eligibility of the claim or for establishing the amount of the claim.[94]

More specifically, the ICSD provides that 'the amount of an investor's claim shall be calculated in accordance with the legal and contractual conditions, in particular those concerning set off and counterclaims, that are applicable to the assessment, on the date of the determination or ruling [on investment firm's inability to fulfil its obligations], of the amount of the money or the value, determined where possible by reference to the market value, of the instruments belonging to the investor which the investment firm is unable to repay or return', therefore in accordance with the applicable rules of the national legal order.[95]

However, this minimum harmonisation approach by the ICSD, in our view, leaves unregulated certain important issues, which affects in turn the effectiveness of protection awarded.

In the absence of harmonisation of insolvency law in the EU legal order, eligibility of an investor's claim under national law may be governed either by rules specific to ICSs and/or by general or special rules on insolvency and winding-up of FIs.

The risk of multiple verification procedures under national law and the ensuing legal uncertainty as well as the possibility of lengthy and inconclusive proceedings[96] may affect the useful effect of the ICSD.

Furthermore, it is for the Member State to choose the appropriate national measures to achieve fulfilment by the investor compensation scheme of its obligations, in light of their obligation to effectively transpose and apply the ICSD.

Thus, where national law provides for a complex system of investors' claim verification and calculation, it is for the Member States and the competent public authorities of the Member States to ensure effective application of the Directive, by interpreting and applying national law in conformity with the ICSD.[97]

93 Ibid., Article 2(2); Article 4(1); Article 9(2).

94 ICSD, Article 9(2); Cf. ibid., Preamble, recital 19.

95 Cf. ICSD, Preamble, recital 8, 'every [Member State] should be required to have an [ICS] or schemes to which every such investment firm would belong; each scheme must cover money and instruments held by an investment firm …; this is entirely without prejudice to the rules and procedures applicable in each [Member State] as regards the decisions to be taken in the event of the insolvency or winding-up of an investment firm'.

96 The ICSD provides that the ICS 'may fix a period during which investors shall be required to submit their claims'; ibid., Article 9. It does not provide whether the claims to be submitted during this period have to have already been verified and evaluated. Further, it provides that '[t]he fact that that period [i.e. the period fixed for submittal of claims] has expired may not, however, be invoked by the scheme to deny cover to an investor who has been unable to assert his right to compensation in time'; ibid. This reference may be understood as meaning that claim verification and calculation difficulties may not be invoked by the ICS against the investor. The resulting uncertainty is not resolved by the provision of the ICSD that '[Member States] shall ensure that an investor's right to compensation shall be the subject of an action by the investor against the compensation scheme'; ibid., Article 13.

97 See inter alia ECJ decision of 22.10.1998 in Cases C-10/97 to C-22/97, *Ministero delle Finanze v IN.CO.GE. '90 Srl, Idelgard Srl, Iris '90 Srl, Camed Srl, Pomezia Progetti Appalti Srl (PPA), Edilcam Srl, A.*

In this direction, and in order for the protection awarded to retail investors by Member States and national ICSs to be effective, Member States are required inter alia to regulate and ensure the payment of minimum compensation following prompt and simple claim verification and calculation procedures according to national law, covering not only *stricto sensu* investors but also *lato sensu* investors in case of investment firm failure as a result of fraud.

Interim concluding remarks

The DGSD and the ICSD, as originally adopted, reflected a concern to facilitate the creation of a level playing field for FIs across the EU, in order to create a single EU financial market, in an era where systemic risk was considered intrinsic to the banking sector, while securities markets considerations related mostly to financial market integrity.

In this context, and with a corresponding differentiation of the risk perceived to be accepted by retail depositors vis-à-vis retail investors, EU law provided for minimum harmonisation through the DGSD and the ICSD, and minimum *ex lege* protection in the form of compensation.

This dual mechanism of financial consumer protection, despite its inconsistencies and inefficiencies in certain areas, provided a basic framework which allowed financial markets and FIs to develop and expand over a long period, almost uninterrupted by considerations as to the *ratio* of EU financial law or as to the status of retail depositors vis-à-vis retail investors.

Despite the differences in the conditions for protection of retail depositors vis-à-vis retail investors under EU law prior to the GFC, and the disparities in the structure and normative content of DGDS and ICSD, before the GFC retail depositors were perceived as savers only, and not as investors. Indeed, there was perhaps little reason to consider that retail depositors could be making an investment decision when selecting a bank to trust their money with.

This was probably facilitated by the growth of Member State economies and the general positive developments which did not provide grounds for much concern, and by the rather discreet role of courts, at the national and the EU levels, which appeared hesitant to 'rock the boat' during times of prosperity.

However, the strength with which the GFC hit the European financial markets, Member State economies and legal constructions, led to the total reassessment of such issues and to the designing of a new EU financial regulatory architecture and law, which now merits examination.

Cecchini & C. Srl, EMO Srl, Emoda Srl, Sappesi Srl, Ing. Luigi Martini Srl, Giacomo Srl and Mafar Srl. [1998] ECR I-6307, para. 21; ECJ decision of 02.12.1997 in Case C-188/95, *Fantask A/S e.a. v Industriministeriet (Erhvervministeriet)* [1997] ECR I-6783, para. 12; ECJ decision of 15.12.1976 in Case 35/76, *Amministrazione delle Finanze dello Stato v Simmenthal SpA* [1976] ECR 1871.

7 The new and proposed EU law on financial consumer protection in the event of financial institution failure after the GFC

Depositors as investors?

Introductory note

In the context of the new EU financial architecture and law, the Deposit Guarantee Schemes Directive (DGSD) was amended and recast to be brought into line with the new EU resolution regime for financial institutions (FIs), while an initiative to review the Investor Compensation Schemes Directive (ICSD) was abandoned for the time being owing to political disagreement.

At the same time, a proposal to establish a European deposit insurance scheme has been advanced by the Commission.

These developments and the emerging new framework bring up again the central question of the status of financial consumers under EU law in the event of FI failure.[1]

7.1 The Revised Deposit Guarantee Schemes Directive (DGSD Recast)

As the global financial crisis (GFC) had already escalated to a critical point, in mid-2010 the Commission submitted, among an array of other proposed measures, a proposal for the amendment of the DGSD,[2] which led to a new DCSD DGSD.[3]

1 See, in general, MOLONEY, N. (2015) 'Regulating the Retail Markets' in FERRAN, E., MOLONEY, N. and PAYNE, J. (eds) The Oxford Handbook of Financial Regulation, Oxford: OUP, p. 736; KINGSFORD SMITH, D., DIXON, O. (2015) 'The Consumer Interest and the Financial Markets' in FERRAN, E., MOLONEY, N. and PAYNE, J. (eds) *The Oxford Handbook of Financial Regulation*, Oxford: OUP, p. 695; ATHANASSIOU, P. (2014) 'On the Legal and Economic Treatment of Bank Deposits as Investments: Some Reflections', *JIBLR*, 29(12), pp. 715–20.

2 COM(2010) 368 final, 12.07.2010. This proposal was supplemented by a Commission Report to the EP and the Council on the review of the DGSD examining issues raised in particular by the review of DGSD, Articles 7(1) and 12(1).

3 Reference to Directive 2014/49/EU as the DGSD (Recast) is made in this study in order to make a distinction for practical reasons from Directive 94/19/EC, to which we refer as the DGSD; however, according to EU terminology and general references on the matter, both Directives are referred to as the DGSD.

This proposal was introduced at the same time as the EU institutions were examining in general and *ab initio* the architecture of financial supervision in the EU, and whilst the discussion regarding the possible role of DGSs in the context of bank recovery and resolution (BRR) procedures was still under way.

The 2010 Commission proposal was based on the consideration that 'the existing, fragmented [DGSs] system has not delivered on the objectives set by [the DGSD], in terms of maintaining depositors' confidence and financial stability in times of economic stress'.[4]

Indeed, beyond certain urgent measures (decrease of time limit for payment of depositor claims and increase of coverage level) introduced by Directive 2009/14/EC, the broader review of the DGSD remained outstanding.

In the context of its proposal to review the DGSD, the Commission undertook an in-depth examination of the issue and conducted an extensive impact assessment,[5] taking into account the critical issues related to deposit guarantee schemes (DGSs) per se, and also in relation to investor compensation schemes. (ICSs)

Identifying the problems of the EU DGS regime to be addressed in the review, the Commission inter alia referred to the divergence in the level and scope of coverage by DGSs, noting that in times of stability depositors might base their choice of credit institution on the merits of the DGS that covers it, which might cause distortion to competition since credit institutions have no choice as to their DGS.[6]

In relation to the definition of deposits, it noted the lack of an EU law definition of deposits beyond that of the DGSD, which it characterised as not being very concise. However, it considered that 'it seems to be clear from the general meaning of the word deposit (i.e. to place for safekeeping or in trust) that deposited items usually have to be returned in full'.[7]

It further noted that the DGSD definition of 'deposit' might be interpreted as encompassing structured products which, however, incur market risk (which was not covered by any protection scheme);[8] considering the potential overlap between the DGSD and the ICSD, in certain cases of securities and money linked to transactions in investment, it observed the disparities in protection ensuing

4 COM(2010) 368 final, p. 2.

5 SEC(2010) 834 final, 12.07.2010. For the results of the public consultation held by the Commission with regard to the proposed amendment, see http://ec.europa.eu/internal_market/consultations/2009/deposit_guarantee_schemes_en.htm. For relevant reports and impact assessment results, see http://ec.europa.eu/internal_market/bank/guarantee/index_en.htm. See also the European Forum of Deposit Insurers (EFDI) at www.efdi.eu.

6 SEC(2010) 834 final, 12.07.2010, p. 11.

7 Ibid., p. 14. Importantly, it proposed that deposits be defined more clearly and narrowly, so that structured products, certificates or bonds would not be considered as deposits for its purposes, distancing the risk associated with investment services; COM(2010) 368 final, p. 6. According to the relevant definition as proposed by the Commission, 'deposit means any credit balance which results from funds left in an account or from temporary situations deriving from normal banking transactions and which a credit institution must repay under the legal and contractual conditions applicable'; ibid., proposed Article 1.

8 SEC(2010) 834 final, 12.07.2010, p. 11.

from the different level of coverage and mechanism between these Directives and from the discretion of Member States to choose which scheme relevant claims would fall under.[9]

It also commented on the exemption of mutual guarantee schemes and voluntary guarantee schemes from the DGSD, expressing its concern in case of a mutual system collapse for depositor claims, and noting that voluntary and mutual guarantee schemes have a contractual basis and do not provide rights to depositors to claim reimbursement in the event of a bank failure.[10]

In considering policy options in relation to the DGSD review, the Commission assessed the effectiveness, efficiency and coherence with other objectives of EU policies the options examined.[11]

Concerning the level of coverage, it opted for maximum harmonisation, which in its view would ensure proper functioning of the Internal Market, while it considered minimum harmonisation to be 'ineffective as regards protecting depositor wealth and … incoherent with the Treaty objective to ensure the proper functioning of the Internal Market'.[12]

It further examined policy options in relation to exemptions from the coverage level, taking into account the option of adopting a high coverage for temporary high deposit balances (THDBs) from specific life events (an option at the time reflecting policies of only a few Member States) as well as the option of gradually phasing out such Member States' regimes after a transitional period, but allowing a general protection of old-age provision products.[13]

The Commission noted that an introduction of a THDB protection regime would require the definition of covered events, a maximum coverage level and a maximum time limit at the EU level, since if left to the discretion of the Member States it might entail competitive distortions.[14]

The Commission also took into account that most stakeholders who participated in the relevant public consultation were against any exemptions, on the grounds that they run counter to harmonisation and are confusing to depositors, are complicated, distort competition, and delay payout process, and therefore opted for the gradual phasing-out of THDB protection regimes.

Overall, the 2010 Commission proposal focused mainly on the simplification and harmonisation of DGSs, in particular in relation to eligibility, coverage and pay-out mechanism, the further reduction of the time limit for payment of depositors, the financing of DGSs (proposing funding on the basis of a mixed system of *ex ante* and *ex post* bank contributions calculated according to both risk-based and non-risk-based elements in partial harmonisation of national provisions) and the introduction of a mutual borrowing facility between DGSs

9 Ibid., pp. 15–16.
10 Ibid, p. 24.
11 Ibid., p. 30.
12 Ibid., p. 33.
13 Ibid., p. 34.
14 Ibid., p. 35.

on certain conditions.[15] It proposed that the scope of the DGSD should be extended to encompass all credit institutions and all schemes, without distinction, and that mutual or voluntary guarantee schemes, referred to as Institutional Protection Schemes (IPSs), should be allowed to be recognised as DGSs (on certain conditions).[16]

The impact assessment examined also the issue of establishing a pan-EU DGS, for which three structural options were taken into account by the Commission: a single entity acting as a pan-EU DGS replacing existing schemes, or an EU DGS additional to Member State DGSs, on a network of existing DGSs including a mutual borrowing facility.[17] The Commission had expressed its positive view of a pan-EU DGS, but only as a long-term project owing to legal issues relating also to the new EU financial supervisory architecture and the emerging (at that time) bank recovery and resolution regime, opting for the time being for a network of DGSs.[18]

Overall, the 2010 Commission proposal was characterised, in our view, by the intention to clarify the field of application of the DGSD, as the mandate of deposit guarantee systems was understood at the time,[19] and enhance its effectiveness through maximum harmonisation where possible.

In its Opinion on the revision of the DGSD proposed by the Commission, the ECB expressed its general agreement, since the proposal encompassed certain of its earlier recommendations on the matter of DGSs.[20] In particular, it agreed with the requirement for all credit institutions to become members of harmonised DGSs funded by mainly *ex ante* contributions. It also noted that while it does not provide comments on the ICSD, 'it considers it important that the Union regulatory framework continues to be based on the assumption of different risk profiles of depositors and investors'.[21]

However, the EP, at the first reading of the Commission proposal in 2012,[22] proposed major modifications affecting the policy orientation of the initial Commission proposal.

In adopting its position, the EP took into account the fact that during the GFC, uncoordinated increases in the coverage levels in DGSs in the EU led to the

15 In relation to eligibility criteria, see proposed Article 2(1), point (a). Cf. proposed Article 4(1), point (k); regarding rules on the determination of the repayable amount, see proposed Articles 6 and 2(1), point (a).

16 At the time of the proposal, the applicable Directive was Directive 2006/48/EC; in its Article 80(8) it referred to IPSs as mutual guarantee schemes between credit institutions providing protection to each other in terms of liquidity and solvency. See now CRR, Article 113(7).

17 COM(2010) 369 final, p. 4.

18 Ibid., pp. 4–5.

19 In the historical context of the problematic on bank rescue without recourse to public funding, the Commission also considered the mandate of DGSs in the context of a recovery and resolution regime and mentioned the possible use of DGSs, on certain conditions, as facilities to avert credit institution failure, although it did not propose specific rules to this direction. See also the relevant Impact Assessment, (n. 17), pp. 64–66. Cf. COM(2010) 369 final, p. 5.

20 OJ C 99/1, 31.03.2011. Cf. Impact Assessment, (n. 17), pp. 67–70.

21 Ibid., p. 2, para. 2.

22 OJ C 249E/81, 30.08.2013.

shifting of deposits to Member States where deposit guarantees were higher (and thus causing liquidity problems to the credit institutions from which they were moved),[23] and to the fact that existing DGSs 'proved unable' to carry all losses in such a way as to protect depositors.[24] The EP's position was connected to the requirement, as stated, to create sufficient flexibility to enable DGSs to implement prevention and support measures.[25] In this direction, the EP position interconnected depositor protection to the possibility of preventing the failure of credit institutions by means of appropriate measures,[26] which is in line with the reasoning of the BRR regime, and which introduces a spectrum of powers of DGSs, ranging from providing reimbursement only ('pay box' function),[27] building early warning systems regarding the status of credit institutions,[28] deciding on support measures or using their resources for the purposes of the orderly winding-up of failing credit institutions.[29]

However, the EP noted that the establishment of a European mechanism to resolve banking crises should not affect the protection of depositors through a deposit guarantee system.[30]

In relation to the scope of the DGSD, the EP position attempted a new delineation of the ambit of deposit guarantee as it confirmed that certain financial 'products' with an investment character should not be covered,[31] while certain others should be protected,[32] and that in certain cases deposits may be fully protected (beyond coverage level).[33]

One of the important modifications brought to the DGSD by the EP related to the exemption regime, since the EP opted for the introduction of THDB clauses into the new DGSD.

Also, in relation to State and competent authorities' liability relating to the operation of DGSs, the EP added in the Preamble of the proposed DGSD that 'it is possible' that the DGSD does not result in such liability if Member States have ensured that 'one or more schemes guaranteeing deposits or credit institutions themselves' have been introduced and officially recognised, 'ensuring the compensation or protection of depositors under the conditions prescribed in [the DGSD]'.[34]

23 Ibid., Preamble, recital 11 as introduced by Amendment 13.
24 Ibid., recital 11a as introduced by Amendment 14.
25 Ibid., Preamble, recital 3 as introduced by Amendment 3; also recital 22 as introduced by Amendment 19.
26 Ibid., Preamble, recital 6 as introduced by Amendment 6.
27 Ibid., recital 9b as introduced by Amendment 9.
28 Ibid., recital 9c as introduced by Amendment 10.
29 Ibid.
30 Ibid., recital 34a as introduced by Amendment 28.
31 Ibid., recital 17 as introduced by Amendment 37.
32 Ibid., recital 18 as introduced by Amendment 18. Cf. ibid., Article 4(1) point (j) and Article 4(2a), as introduced by Amendments 59 and 60, respectively.
33 Article 5(1a) points (b) and (c), as introduced by Amendment 61. Cf. Article 2(1) point (a) as introduced by Amendment 36. See also Amendment 37.
34 Ibid., recital 30 (Amendment not enumerated in Position).

Political agreement was reached between the EP and the Council in December 2013, following a long period during which the Council (according to the EP) was 'unwilling to negotiate',[35] with the new measures introduced following the first reading by the Council being the alignment of the DGSD (Recast) with the political agreement on the proposal for the BRRD and the national option to use DGS funds in the context of national insolvency proceedings (on certain conditions).[36]

The political agreement, diverging importantly from the original Commission proposal, led to the adoption of the new DGSD (Recast) in April 2014,[37] which constitutes, in our view, a compromise on the aims of deposit guarantee, between the differing trends reflected in the relevant ongoing policy discussions.

The DGSD (Recast) appears to be attempting a balance between the wish to bring DG systems in line with the new developments in EU financial supervisory architecture and law, and the need to enhance depositor confidence.

In relation to the determination of the nature and mandate of DGSs, the DGSD (Recast) adopts a functional approach regarding its field of application (encompassing all forms of DGSs and IPSs so as to avert regulatory *arbitrage*).[38]

Concerning the interrelation of DGSs with the BRR regime, the DGSD (Recast) clearly subsumes the function of DGSs to the needs of the BRR, as determined by the resolution authority, under the general rule that the financial means of DGSs will primarily be used to repay depositors.[39]

The participation of DGSs in bank failure prevention as well as national insolvency procedures is also permitted on certain conditions by the DGSD (Recast), the main being that relevant costs for DGSs do not exceed the 'pay-box' function costs for DGSs.[40]

In this context, while legal certainty and predictability regarding DG systems are sought by the DGSD (Recast), it is not certain that they are achieved, at least with regard to the designation of insured deposits.

Delimitation of insured deposits under the DGSD (Recast)

In relation to the first, central issue of defining insured (eligible and covered) deposits – and thus delimiting the field of protection available – the new applicable provisions under the DGDS (Recast) examined together may be considered as ambiguous.

First, concerning the notion of deposit, the DGSD (Recast)I states that:

> 'deposit' means a credit balance which results from funds left in an account or from temporary situations deriving from normal banking transactions and

35 See EP Recommendation for Second Reading, A7-0216/2014, 21.03.2014.

36 See COM(2014) 140 final, 04.03.2014, p. 4.

37 Directive 2014/49/EU of the European Parliament and of the Council of 16 April 2014 on deposit guarantee schemes (recast), OJ L 173/149, 12.06.2014. The time limit for the transposition of the main provisions of the directive into national law was 03.07.2015; ibid., Article 20.

38 See BRRD, Article 1.

39 Ibid., Article 11(1) and (2).

40 Ibid., Article 11(3) and (6).

> which a credit institution is required to repay under the legal and contractual conditions applicable, including a fixed-term deposit and a savings deposit, but excluding a credit balance where: (a) its existence can only be proven by a financial instrument ... unless it is a savings product which is evidenced by a certificate of deposit made out to a named person and which exists in a [Member State] on 2 July 2014; (b) its principal is not repayable at par; (c) its principal is only repayable at par under a particular guarantee or agreement provided by the credit institution or a third party.[41]

While this definition of deposit, as finally adopted, is rather clear (despite the use of certain vague notions such as 'normal banking transactions'), it is applicable in conjunction with the provisions on eligibility of deposits[42] and coverage level.[43]

The latter provides that Member States are obliged to ensure that the coverage level for the aggregate deposits of each depositor is 100,000 euros;[44] but also that:

> [i]n addition [Member States] shall ensure that the following deposits are protected above EUR 100 000 for at least three months and no longer than 12 months after the amount has been credited or from the moment when such deposits become legally transferrable: (a) deposits resulting from real estate transactions relating to private residential properties; deposits that serve social purposes laid down in national law and are linked to particular life events of a depositor such as marriage, divorce, retirement, dismissal, redundancy, invalidity or death; (c) deposits that serve purposes laid down in national law and are based on the payment of insurance benefits or compensation for criminal injuries or wrongful conviction.[45]

In this way, while the minimum amount of deposit coverage per credit institution in the EU is clearly defined, at the same time the DGSD (Recast) introduces a new THDB protection rule, according to which maximum deposit coverage has to be provided for a limited period of time but according to vague criteria.

The compulsory coverage of eligible deposits beyond the minimum specified amount is thus influenced by two parameters, one relating to time and the other to the source or intended use of a deposit.

Further, while such temporary maximum coverage is provided as compulsory for Member States, the latter of the two parameters is left to Member States to specify, according to national law.[46]

In this way, and taking into account that the protection of retail depositors

41 DGSD (Recast), Article 2, para. 1(3).

42 Ibid., Article 5.

43 Ibid., Article 6.

44 Ibid., Article 6(1). The limit of moneys payable applies to aggregated deposit placed with the same credit institution (irrespective of number of deposits, currency and location in the EU); ibid., Article 7(1).

45 Ibid., Article 6(2).

46 See, however, how this decision may be transferred to EU organs, on the basis of the SRM framework; see Ch. 8.2.

and their confidence in the financial market is one of the proclaimed aims of EU financial law, it appears that deposit protection under the DGSD (Recast) is to an important extent connected not only to what is defined by it as a deposit eligible for protection, but also to what is the source or aim of a deposit and according to the personal life choices and events of each financial consumer and in application of national law.

The emerging legal uncertainty is apparent, in our view, since not only does the DGSD (Recast) result in harmonisation by reference to diverting national law regimes and provide for a legal obligation under EU law for Member States on the basis of national law, but most importantly it parameterises the notion of covered deposit on the basis of personal depositor choices and random events.

Beyond possible legal difficulties in specifying and rendering such provisions applicable in practice, they also appear, in our view, to be directly influencing the concept of depositing money with a bank and the status of (retail) depositors vis-à-vis (retail) investors.

Indeed, if it is accepted that financial consumer choices are formed on the basis of a wider understanding of the public as to the workings and operation of the financial market, and not always on the basis of accurate information and exact assessment of the risks associated with it,[47] then such a provision of conditional maximum coverage of deposits may affect the behaviour of financial consumers.

In this sense, while in order to avert moral hazard the bank resolution regime provides – at least according to its design – incentives for consumers to make informed choices and to assess the FIs they trust with their assets, at the same time the risk of trusting an FI may be relevant not to the type of transaction of financial consumer with the FI (e.g. depositing in a savings account): it may, instead, depend on the underlying transaction which led in the past to the accumulation of the monetary property (e.g. from real estate transactions), or to the envisaged future transactions reflecting personal financial consumer choices and random conditions.[48]

Thus, it could be argued that in the new EU deposit-protection regime under the DGSD (Recast) deposits are covered not only on the basis of eligibility criteria, but also on the basis of derivative and vague criteria according to factors external to the basic deposit contract of a retail depositor with a credit institution.

At the same time, upon the expiry of the relevant high-protection time limit, and the higher protection awarded to certain deposits according to the new THBD regime, and the amount of deposit above the minimum harmonised covered amount by the DGSD (Recast) will no longer be protected and will also be susceptible to resolution measures, such as bail-in.

Thus, this new system provides a possible explicit 'blanket' coverage of certain deposits according to such unharmonised criteria, and for a limited time, while

47 This is on the same premise that systemic risk in the banking sector is understood to operate in the case of 'bank runs' caused by lack of financial consumers' confidence.

48 The DGSD (Recast) Preamble offers little explanation regarding the *rationale* of the new rules; see recitals 19 and 26, in particular.

after the expiry of such time period of high protection the assets of the retail depositor above minimum coverage appear to be treated as a *quasi*-investment, which may be lost at any time in the context resolution procedures.

Beyond legal considerations as to the clarity and certainty of such rules, it also appears reasonable to assume that such provisions may be the basis for a new form of moral hazard, as pressure may be exercised to decision-makers at any level as to the operation of the THBD regime.

7.2 The proposal for a European Deposit Insurance Scheme (EDIS)

By its Communication of November 2015 to the EP, the Council, the ECB, the EESC and the CoR, *Towards the Completion of the Banking Union*,[49] the Commission noted that while single rulebook establishing the new EU regulatory framework for banks has been achieved (by the introduction of the CRDIV/CRR, the BRRD and the DGSD Recast), and while the SSM and the SRM have been established, as the two pillars of the Banking Union, the third pillar, i.e. a common deposit insurance scheme, was still missing.[50]

Reminding that '[a] key objective of the Banking Union is to reverse fragmentation of financial markets since the euro crisis, by weakening the link between banks and their national sovereigns (whereby bank failures can imperil public finances, and sovereign stress can destabilise banks)',[51] the Commission noted that its earlier proposal, in the context of the DGSD review, to establish mandatory mutual borrowing and lending between national DGSs, had not been accepted, and that despite improvements brought by the review of the DGSD, depositors remained vulnerable to large local shocks while a level playing field 'for depositors and banks' in the Banking Union was still missing.[52]

The Commission proposed to establish the EDIS on the same basic structure as other Banking Union institutions, i.e. with a single rulebook such as the DGSD (Recast) for all Member States, complemented by the EDIS; it also referred to an array of other measures necessary to be introduced together with establishing the EDIS in order to reduce risk in the Banking Union. According to the proposal, the EDIS would initially combine reinsurance and co-insurance elements gradually moving to full insurance.

49 COM(2015) 587 final, 24.11.2015.

50 In this context the Commission referred to the earlier June 2015 'Five Presidents' Report' of the Presidents of the EP, the European Council, the Commission, the Eurogroup, and the ECB, on completing the EMU, by which it was considered that a common EU deposit insurance scheme would increase resilience against future crises, '[a]s the current set-up with national deposit guarantee schemes remains vulnerable to large local shocks (in particular when the sovereign and the national banking sector are perceived to be in a fragile situation' (p. 11); available at http://ec.europa.eu/priorities/economic-monetary-union/docs/5-presidents-report_en.pdf. See also IMF (2013) *A Banking Union for the Euro Area*, SDN/13/01.

51 Ibid., p. 3.

52 Ibid., pp. 5–6.

The proposed regulation to establish the EDIS

In parallel to its Communication,[53] the Commission submitted in November 2015 its proposal for a Regulation of the EP and of the Council amending Regulation No. (EU) 806/2014 (the SRM Regulation), in order to establish the EDIS.[54]

According to the Commission proposal, the EDIS will address the misalignment between EU supervision and resolution of banks in participating Member States, and the effectiveness and credibility of national DGSs in case of bank failure pursuant to the DGSD. This will be achieved by attributing to a Single Resolution and Deposit Insurance Board (SRDI Board) the powers of decision-making, monitoring and enforcement powers over the DG framework.[55] In its view, 'in a system where the responsibilities for bank supervision and resolution are shared, the circumstances under which a national DGS may be used are already not any longer under national control'.[56]

Further, according to the Commission, '[s]upervision can only be effective and meaningful if an adequate deposit insurance system, corresponding to the developments in the field of supervision, is created'.[57]

However, if the EDIS is successful, then it might be argued that the recurrent problematic of moral hazard is reintroduced, this time at EU rather than at Member State level.

In this regard, the Commission proposes that safeguards should be introduced into the EDIS, and in particular that DGSs build up their funds in accordance with DGSD requirements, that they bear a fair share of loss themselves, that DGSs should repay the SRDI Board from insolvency proceeds and that the SRDI Board should have the powers to recover all or part of the funding in case of DGSs not complying with key obligations.[58]

According to the proposal, the EDIS will be governed centrally by the SRDI Board and will make use of the proposed Deposit Insurance Fund (DIF), to be funded directly by banks (which will continue, in parallel, to fund DGSs) mainly on an *ex ante*, risk-based basis.[59] However, according to the Commission, the EDIS would be cost-neutral for the banks and their DGSs.[60]

The provisions applicable to the SRM regarding privileges and immunities, actions before the court of justice, liability, and others, will also apply to the SRDI Board when exercising its functions within the EDIS.[61]

Whilst at the Member State level the proposal for the EDIS is debated, at the EU level it appears that it has been accepted that:

53 See n. 50.
54 COM(2015) 586 final, 24.11.2015.
55 Ibid., pp. 3–4.
56 Ibid., p. 6.
57 Ibid., p. 20.
58 Ibid., p. 22.
59 Ibid., p. 23.
60 Ibid.
61 Ibid., p. 17.

> [a] single banking system is the mirror image of a single money. As the vast majority of money is bank deposits, money can only be truly single if confidence in the safety of bank deposits is the same irrespective of the Member State in which a bank operates. This requires single bank supervision, single bank resolution and single deposit insurance.[62]

7.3 The withdrawn proposal for the revision of the Investor Compensation Schemes Directive

Together with its proposal for a revision of the DGSD, in mid-2010 the Commission submitted to the EP and the Council a proposal to amend the ICSD.[63]

The proposal referred to the need to review the ICSD, which was adopted, as the Commission noted, as a complement to the ISD, not only to take account of the developments relating to the introduction, at the time, of the MiFID and of the emerging EU legislation as a response to the GFC, but also to address *lacunae* in the regulatory and supervisory system, which had led to 'numerous investor complaints about the application of the ICSD in a number of important cases involving large investor losses'.[64]

According to the Commission, the proposal aimed 'at improving the practical functioning of the ICSD, at clarifying the scope of the ICSD … at reducing gaps in the regulatory system and disparities between the protection of clients of investment firms and of banking depositors'.[65]

The Commission stressed that the different underlying objectives of the DGSD and the ICSD had to be taken into account, stating that while the first 'has a prevailing bank stability objective because banks are susceptible to the risk of a run if depositors believe that their deposits are not safe and try to withdraw them at the same time', the latter 'protects investors against the risk of frauds or administrative malpractices or operational errors making the investment firm unable to return assets to clients',[66] noting that the proposal 'preserves the specificities of the sectoral legislation'.

In terms of alignment of the ICSD with the MiFID, the proposal noted that the scope of the MiFiD is broader than that of the ISD, and therefore adaptation of the scope of the ICSD to that of the MiFID is required.

In this direction, the Commission proposed a number of amendments to adapt

62 See 2015 'Five Presidents' Report' (n. 50), p. 11.

63 COM(2010) 371 final, 12.07.2010. For the results of the consultation of interested parties by the Commission, see http://ec.europa.eu/internal_market/consultations/2009/investor_compensation. The work of the ESME and the ESC was also taken into account by the Commission. The 2005 study by OXERA, 'Description and assessment of the national investor compensation schemes established in accordance with Directive 1997/9/EC', was also taken into account; available at http://ec.europa.eu/dgs/internal_market/docs/evaluation/national-investor-rep2005.pdf. For the impact assessment analysis conducted by the Commission on the proposal, see SEC(2010) 845.

64 Ibid., p. 2.

65 Ibid., p. 4.

66 Ibid., p. 5.

the scope of the ICSD to that of the MiFID, including inter alia a new definition of 'investment business' which shall mean 'investment business and activities as defined in Article 4(1)(2) of [the MiFID] and the ancillary service referred to in point 1 of Section B of the Annex I to [the MiFID]'.[67]

In relation to the classification of clients of an investment firm, it proposed that while the ICSD is potentially applicable to all categories of investors, national legislation may provide that 'professional investors' and 'institutional investors' (according to the definitions provided by the ISD) can be excluded from coverage of the ICSD.[68]

However, as the Commission further noted, this classification does not coincide with the one in the MiFID, so that problems in providing protection may arise, as 'clients classified as professionals for the provision of services may not correspond to the clients which may be excluded from coverage according to the ICSD'.[69]

In order to ensure legal certainty and more effective protection (especially for medium-sized enterprises that may be excluded from protection under the ICSD but are classified as retail investors under the ICSD), the Commission proposed the correlation of the ICSD with the definition of investors provided by the MiFID.

More importantly, the proposal noted that one of the issues that had arisen was the coverage of firms depending on the scope of their authorisation – relating to whether or not an investment firm is authorised to hold client assets.

In this respect, an important proposal was advanced by the Commission: that all investment services and activities covered under the MiFID should be subject to the ICSD and that 'if firms de facto hold client assets (irrespective of restrictions on their authorisation or the nature of their investment service), then clients should be entitled to compensation under the ICSD'.[70]

In the same direction, the proposal noted that the right of clients to compensation in such a case 'would be irrespective of whether the firm is doing so [i.e. holding clients' assets] in contravention of any limitation on its authorisation (e.g. preventing it from holding client assets or from dealing with retail clients) and irrespective of the nature of the investment service it provides'.[71]

Thus, in relation to coverage of investment services and compensation payable to investors, the new rules propose the introduction of a provision that '[Member States] shall ensure that the schemes provide coverage where financial instruments or monies are held, administered or managed for or on behalf of an investor, irrespective of the type of investment business being carried on by the firm and of whether or not the firm is acting in accordance with any restriction set out in its authorisation', thus covering also the case of *lato sensu* investors.[72]

It is interesting to note that the Commission proposed the introduction of

67 Ibid., Article 1(1)(a) of the proposed Directive.

68 See ICSD, Article 4(2) and Annex 1.

69 COM(2010) 371 final, pp. 5–7.

70 Ibid., p. 5.

71 Ibid.

72 Ibid., Article 1(2)(c) of the proposed Directive; cf. proposed recital 5.

these provisions regarding the coverage of clients' assets that are de facto held by investment firms not as a new rule, but as a clarification of the existing rule. This signifies, in our view, that the Commission considered such an interpretation of rules in force as valid in the context of applicable law.

Specifically, the Commission noted that 'the proposed amendment clarifies that ... if firms de facto hold client assets ... then clients should be entitled to compensation'.[73]

Another critical feature of the proposal, which signifies, in our view, the new approach of the Commission regarding the status of investors, is that the 'co-insurance principle'[74] as a measure to address moral hazard and to raise investor awareness regarding the selection of investment firms, is not fair since 'arguably it is unrealistic to expect retail investors to be able to identify which firms are more or less likely to be affected by fraud or systems failures'.[75]

In relation to payment of compensation, beyond a proposal to increase the level of compensation,[76] the Commission noted that when monies are deposited in a bank in the context of the provision of investment services, in cases of doubt 'the investor is to be compensated under the DGSD (which provides a higher level of coverage)'.[77]

Furthermore, the Commission took into consideration the particular characteristics of investment firm failure as a result of fraud, proposing the amendment of the ICSD mechanism on payment of compensation, in connection to claim verification.[78]

In relation to the critical issue of eligibility of claims and on the verification of claims, the proposal advanced two new rules, which confirm, in our view, that the current normative structure of EU law on investor compensation is problematic.

The first proposed rule stated that '[Member States] shall ensure that compensation schemes may participate in insolvency or judicial procedures that may be relevant in establishing the eligibility and the amount of a claim'.[79] Certainly, Member States are not prohibited, under the ICSD as currently in force, to provide that compensation schemes may participate in such procedures. What appeared as a clarification, in the Commission proposal, did not provide, in our view, useful directions as to how insolvency or judicial procedures would be correlated in the national legal order to verification of claims procedures under EU

73 Ibid., p. 5.

74 ICSD, Article 4(4); cf. ICSD, Preamble, recital 13. Cf. the co-insurance principle in the DGSD and the DGSD (Recast).

75 COM(2010) 371 final, p. 11.

76 To a fixed amount of EUR 50,000; ibid., p. 8; proposed Article 1(4). Further new rules are proposed with regard to the funding of ICSs and borrowing mechanisms between ICSs; ibid., pp. 9–10, proposed recitals 13–19, proposed Article 1(5).

77 Ibid., p. 9. Cf. Article 1(2)(f) and recital 8 of the proposed Directive.

78 Ibid., p. 12 and proposed Article 1(7). The proposal provides that the investor compensation scheme must be in a position to pay an investor's claim as soon as possible and at the latest within three months of the establishment of the eligibility and the amount of the claim (extension of delay and partial compensation payment provided on certain conditions).

79 Ibid., proposed Article 1(7) introducing new Article 9 to the ICSD; cf. new proposed recital 21.

and national law on investor compensation. While this may be attributable to considerations relevant to the institutional autonomy of Member States, including rules on the organisation of justice and on procedural law matters, it is not clear, in our view, how the investor compensation regime may be harmonised at the European level, if the law on verification of claims remains a secluded national domain.

The second proposed rule stated that the rule above 'shall be without prejudice to schemes being able to adopt other methods to determine the eligibility or amount of a claim'.[80] This proposed rule was no less ambiguous, since it confirmed that (at least) two sets of national rules on claim verification may be validly applicable for the purposes of investor protection (i.e. one set of rules regarding national judicial procedures in general and/or one set of rules regarding national insolvency proceedings, which may be governed by general insolvency law or by specific insolvency law for investment firms, plus one set of rules applicable specifically by ICSs).

The position of the EP that was adopted at first reading regarding the Commission proposal for the amendment of the ICSD[81] took inter alia into account the reasoned opinions of the Swedish Parliament and the UK House of Commons, according to which the proposal contravened the principle of subsidiarity.[82]

The amendments introduced by the EP at first reading of the draft legislation did not in general alter the essence of the proposed new rules.

Some of the more important amendments introduced by the EP include, in our view, the broadening of the definition of 'investor', encompassing any natural or legal person, including micro-entities, non-profit organisations and public local authorities,[83] and the broadening of the conditions for failure of investment firm to include beyond fraud, malpractice or operational error, as per the Commission proposal, also bad advice, regarding CoB obligations when providing investment services to clients.[84] In relation to the issues concerning claim eligibility and verification rules, the EP position did not include any amendments to the Commission proposal. Interestingly, however, the EP proposed that the level of compensation payable per retail investor should be 100,000 euros, i.e. equal to that payable to

80 Ibid.

81 OJ C 033E/328, 05.02.2013.

82 Ibid. The UK House of Commons issued a reasoned opinion, pursuant to Article 6 of Protocol (No. 2) on the Application of the Principles of Subsidiarity and Proportionality, according to which the Commission proposal to amend the ICSD was not compatible with said principle, as regards the borrowing last resort mechanism between national schemes in proposed new Article 4(b) of the ICSD. Available at www.parliament.uk/pagefiles/54364/Reasoned%20 Opinion%2025.10.10.pdf. The Commission replied that it has already taken into account the concerns expressed by the House of Commons in its proposal; see http://ec.europa.eu/dgs/ secretariat_general/relations/relations_other/npo/docs/united_kingdom/2010/com20100371/ com20100371_commons_reply_en.pdf.

83 OJ C 033E/328 (n. 81), proposed Article 1(1)(a)(4).

84 Ibid., proposed Article 1(2)(b) amendment 20.

depositors under the DGSD.[85] It also proposed the *ex ante* ICSs funding on the basis of risk-weighted criteria [86] and inter-ICS lending at the EU level.[87]

However, negotiations stalled. Although in the case of the DGSD lengthy negotiations took years and ended in a political compromise and the adoption of the DGSD (Recast), in the case of the ICSD the negotiations did not show any signs of progress. Finally, the Commission proposal to review the ICSD was withdrawn in 2015.[88]

The Commission has issued an Action Plan on Building a Capital Markets Union,[89] in the context of which EU aims and instruments in the area of investment services will be re-assessed.

Interim concluding remarks

While financial consumer protection has been announced by EU law as one of the aims of financial law, in the event of FI failure, the protection offered to retail depositors and retail investors by EU law has been limited to the payment of minimum *ex lege* compensation under national rules very little harmonised by EU law.

The DGSD and the ICSD were introduced in the EU legal order as instruments of minimum harmonisation aiming primarily at the avoidance of distortions in the competition among FIs and thus at the completion of the internal financial market, while also aiming in parallel at enhancing financial consumers' confidence in the financial market.

Examined per se and in conjunction with each other, they did not constitute a coherent system of law providing protection in a coherent way; recent case law of the ECJ appears to be aiming at redressing certain inconcistencies in the protective ambit of these Directives.

Despite progress in the area of financial consumer protection in the event of FI failure, the new THDB rules in the DGSD (Recast) introduce new strong elements of uncertainty with regard to the effectiveness of protection awarded, as the conditions and level of protection may depend on a number of fluctuating parameters: thus the protection available may reflect financial market conditions and overall systemic protection considerations.

In the same context, both the recent ECJ case law in this area as well as the normative content of the new DGSD (Recast) and the reasoning in the proposal for a revision of the ICSD reveal an approximation of the characteristics of the financials consumers that are perceived as retail depositors to those that are perceived as retail investors, in particular in the event of FI failure.

The more risk is directly or indirectly recognised to be associated with depositing money with a FI, the more difficult it is to justify a different legal

85 Ibid., proposed Article 4(1).
86 Ibid., proposed Article 4a.
87 Ibid., proposed Article 4b.
88 OJ C 80/17, 07.03.2015.
89 COM(2015) 468 final, 30.09.2015.

treatment of retail depositors and retail investors seeking protection after the collapse of a FI.

Beyond legal considerations, an approximation (or even unification) of the protective regimes for these two categories of financial consumers – at least in the area of FI failure – may enhance credibility of the financial market and raise public confidence in it, as the award of protection will not depend on an uncertain classification of financial consumers or financial instruments, which has proven incoherent and unable to follow market developments.

Furthermore, such a protective environment may promote financial activity and encourage participation of financial consumers in the financial markets, as well as discourage regulatory arbitrage based on the classification of financial consumers or financial instruments.

8 The new EU law on the recovery and resolution of financial institutions

A realignment of the status of financial consumers

Introductory note

One of the most important effects of the global financial crisis (GFC) on the EU legal order has been the introduction of the new resolution regime for financial institutions (FIs), and the rearrangement of the EU financial law that it has entailed.[1]

In order to address the concerns regarding systemic stability, the Commission submitted in mid-2010 a Communication to the EP, the Council, the ECSC and the ECB entitled *Bank Resolution Funds*.[2] This Communication followed the G-20 meeting of September 2009 in Pittsburgh,[3] which had been politically supported by the EU,[4] that bank losses should not be covered by the taxpayers (as in traditional 'bail-outs').

In this direction, the Commission proposed two complementary ways of treating credit institutions' failure: by the provision of better supervision, corporate governance, and regulation on the one hand, and by an appropriate mechanism for orderly and timely bank resolution should failure occur, endorsing relevant proposals by international *fora*.[5]

1 See, generally, ALEXANDER, K. (2015) 'European Banking Union: A Legal and Institutional Analysis of the Single Supervisory Mechanism and the Single Resolution Mechanism', *ELRev*, 40(2), pp. 154–87; WYMEERSCH, E., HOPT, K. J. and FERRANINI, G. (eds) (2012) *Financial Regulation and Supervision: A Post-crisis Analysis*, Oxford: OUP; GRUNEWALD, S. (2014) *The Resolution of Cross-border Banking Crises in the European Union*, The Hague: Kluwer Law International; CAPRIGLIONE, F. and SEMERATO, G. (2012) 'Financial Crisis and Sovereign Debt: The European Union between Risks and Opportunities', *Law and Economics Yearly Review*, vol. 1, pt. 1, p. 4.

2 COM(2010) 254 final, 26.05.2010. See also the Council (ECOFIN) conclusions (17006/1/10) calling for an EU framework for crisis prevention, management and resolution, aiming at 'preserving financial stability by protecting public and market confidence; putting prevention and preparation first; providing credible resolution tools; enabling fast and decisive action; reducing moral hazard and minimising to the fullest possible extent the overall costs to public funds, by ensuring fair burden sharing among the financial institutions' stakeholders; contributing to a smooth resolution of cross border groups; ensuring legal certainty; and, limiting distortions of competition'.

3 See Ch. 3 (n. 5).

4 See ECOFIN Council Conclusions of 18 May 2010.

5 For an overview, see generally BABIS, V. (2012) 'EU Recovery and Resolution Framework: Financial Assistance between Banking Group Members', University of Cambridge Faculty of

In the latter case, the Commission supported through its Communication, 'the establishment of ex ante resolution funds, funded by a levy on banks [including investment firms for the purposes of its Communication] to facilitate the resolution of failing banks in ways which avoid contagion, allow the bank to be wound down in an orderly manner and in a timeframe which avoids the "fire sale" of assets (*principe de prévoyance*)'.[6]

The Commission also recalled the 'polluter pays' principle, noting that political support for its application in the financial sector is also growing, in the sense that those responsible for causing a crisis will (have to) pay for the relevant costs (without, however, clarifying how responsibility is to be defined and attributed).[7]

The Commission further took into account moral hazard concerns, noting in particular that '[s]hareholders (up to the value of their investment) and creditors (excluding depositors which are guaranteed by deposit guarantee schemes) must be the first to face the consequences of a bank failure and … resolution funds must not be used as an insurance against failure or to bail out failing banks, but rather to facilitate an orderly failure'.[8]

In this way, the Commission proposed in this Communication: (a) that resolution funds should be used in connection to (all) FI failures, the aim of financial law being not to avert FI failures (at any cost) but to control FI failures; and (b) that creditors are responsible for bearing the consequences of a FI failure (depositors being protected up to the limit of applicable deposit guarantee).

Thus, already in mid-2010 the Commission had proposed a change in the policy of implicit total deposit guarantee (entailing FI rescues by the use of public funds), without entering into detailed analysis regarding the constant concern of financial law to protect trust in the financial system.

According to the Commission, the issue of resolution funds should be addressed at the EU level, in the context of establishing wider integrated crisis management and supervisory arrangements, forming part of a range of measures to address the GFC, focusing on the prevention of FI failure, but allowing for orderly FI failures irrespective of size.[9]

Law Research Papers, vol. 15, June, http://ssrn.com/abstract=2091194; SCHILLIG, M. (2012) 'Bank Resolution Regimes in Europe I – Recovery and Resolution Planning, Early Intervention', April http://ssrn.com/abstract=2136101; *idem* (2012) 'Bank Resolution Regimes in Europe II – Resolution Tools and Powers',. August, http://ssrn.com/abstract=236084.

6 COM(2010) 254 final, pp. 2–3.

7 Ibid. In our view, the issue of 'responsibility' for causing a financial crisis is very wide and may extend from a micro-analysis point of view of the responsibility of FIs (as in the case of unfit management of SIFIs) to creditor responsibility (e.g. as in the case of professional investors supporting high-risk portfolio management) to regulatory and supervisory authorities' responsibility (as in the case of not duly exercising their powers) to political responsibility (for not acting in an effective way either as legislature or as public administration to protect the market and participants). Each category of responsibility may be connected to a final negative result (a financial crisis) but the intensity of causality differs.

8 Ibid., p. 3.

9 This Commission initiative was followed by a Commission proposal in 2012 for a Bank Recovery and Resolution Directive (BRRD); COM(2012) 280. See n. 25.

Further, by its Communication of 20 October 2010, *An EU Framework for Crisis Management in the Financial Sector*,[10] the Commission addressed a number of pertinent issues and proposed a European framework for controlling the GFC.

Noting, at that time, that EU Member States had committed aid to rescuing FIs amounting to around 30per cent of EU GDP (while the aid used at that time amounted to 13per cent), and that such public interventions also had a significant impact on the level playing field within the internal market, it referred to its two earlier Communications on crisis management and resolution,[11] and to a relevant report by the EP,[12] and taking into account the work of the FSB and the G-20, the Commission stated that '[t]he overriding objective of a European resolution framework should be that ailing institutions of any type and size, and in particular systemically important institutions, can be allowed to fail without risk to financial stability whilst avoiding costs to taxpayers'.

In relation to the scope of such framework, the Commission explained that both credit institutions and systemically important investment firms should fall within it.

Interesting comments were made to this Commission Communication by the European Economic and Social Committee (EESC).

In its Opinion of 16 June 2011,[13] the EESC shared the view that the support of failing FIs at the cost of public finances and of the level playing field within the internal market is no longer acceptable in the future and supported in principle the proposed comprehensive EU framework, recommending that the Commission renders compulsory for all Member States the IMF/World Bank Financial Sector Assessment Programmes as also proposed by the *De Larosière* Report.

The EESC noted inter alia that the Commission's Communication proposes a crisis management framework for 'all cross-border and domestic credit institutions and some investment firms' without clear definition of proposed application as to investment firms, encouraging the Commission also to assess whether the resolution tools and powers suggested its Communication would be sufficient to address adequately all specific problems related to the failure of an investment firm.

In relation to 'bail-in', the EESC posed a series of questions as to the proportional allocation of losses and the criteria for including creditors among contributors, asking when, and to what extent, one specific creditor is to be called to bear the losses, and whether there should be a distinction between 'guilty' or 'imprudent' creditors and others; and, on what basis, and under what circumstances, the losses would be covered by the whole banking industry.[14]

Further, the EESC expressed the hope that the options proposed by the Commission for FI resolution 'would not be misused in political, economic and social emergencies'.

10 COM(2010) 579 final, 20.10.2010.

11 COM(2009) 561 and COM(2010) 254.

12 European Parliament, A7-0000/2010, Committee on Economic and Monetary Affairs (the *Ferreira Report*).

13 [2011] OJ C 248/101.

14 Ibid.

In relation to the enhanced supervision proposed by the Commission, the EESC, noting the enhanced responsibilities and powers of supervisors under the proposed regime, concluded that '[i]n practice, supervisors become super-managers of the institutions'.[15]

As the GFC progressed and deepened, the Commission issued its 2011 Communication, 'A roadmap to stability and growth',[16] in which it noted that '[t]he crisis threatens to become systemic', emphasising that '[a] solution to break the vicious circle between doubts over the sustainability of sovereign debt, the stability of the banking system and the EU's growth prospects is more necessary than ever', and proposed elements of such a solution. Among measures to this aim, the Commission proposed inter alia that '[b]anks should first use private sources of capital, including through restructuring and conversion of debt to equity instruments'. Also, a new system of regulation for the financial sector (including reinforced rules on credit rating agencies, transparency and market conduct, market abuse, and a European framework on bank resolution), as well as the proposed Financial Transaction Tax (FAT).[17]

The Liikanen Report

On 02 October 2012, shortly after the publication of the Commission Communication, *A Roadmap towards a Banking Union*,[18] the High Level Expert Group on reforming the structure of the EU banking sector, which was established by the Commission in February 2012, and chaired by E. Liikanen, issued its final report (known as the *Liikanen Report*).[19]

With a view to considering whether or not there is a need for structural reforms in the EU banking sector, and to make relevant proposals appropriate, in order to establish a stable and efficient banking system, the Report took into account aggregate EU banking sector developments, the diversity of banking business models in Europe,[20] existing and proposed regulatory reforms of the EU banking sector.[21]

15 Ibid.
16 COM(2011) 669 final, 12.10.2011.
17 Ibid.
18 COM/2012/0510 final.
19 Available at http://ec.europa.eu/internal_market/bank/docs/high-level_expert_group/report_en.pdf.
20 In relation to banking business models, risk profile, and performance during the first years of the GFC, see AYADI, R., ARBAK, E., De GROEN, W. P. and LLEWELLYN, D. T. (2012) *Regulation of European Banks and Business Models: Towards a New Paradigm*, Brussels: CEPS; AYADI, R., De GROEN, W. P. and LLEWELLYN, D. T. (2011) *Business Models in European banking: a pre- and post-crisis screening*, Brussels: CEPS; AYADI, R. and SCHMIDT, R. (eds) (2009) *Investigating Diversity in the Banking Sector in Europe: The Performance and Role of Saving Banks*, Brussels: CEPS.
21 Specifically in relation to recovery, resolution and 'bail-in' instruments, the *Liikanen Report* observed inter alia that during the period of October 2008 to the end of 2010, European governments used a total of 1.6 trillion euros of state aid to support the banking sector, in the form of guarantees and liquidity support, recapitalisation and asset relief measures, noting that the available evidence

The *Liikanen Report*, taking into account international initiatives regarding financial markets structural reforms, examined in particular two structural reform avenues that may be useful in order to further limit the likelihood of bank failures, to improve resolvability of banks, and to reduce use of public funds to rescue banks. These two avenues, reflecting relevant proposals at the international level,[22] are: (a) the introduction of non-risk weighted capital buffer for trading activities and contingent functional separation of significant trading activities; and (b) the introduction of immediate functional separation of significant trading activities.[23]

The Report concluded that reform is necessary, and proposed measures in that direction.[24]

8.1 The new Bank Recovery and Resolution Directive (BRRD)

Endorsing many of the proposals by international *fora*, EU institutions and think-tanks, the first EU law instruments for the recovery and resolution of FIs were adopted in 2014 by the Bank Recovery and Resolution Directive (BRRD), issued in parallel with the Single Resolution Mechanism (SRM) Regulation.

Despite the emergency presented by the GFC not only for MS financial markets and economies, but also for the Euro area and the single currency at large, this new resolution framework took years to develop and to agree at the EU level, which is indicative of the level of difficulties faced during the legislative procedure.

Owing to the importance of these new instruments of EU law regarding retail investor and retail depositor protection, it is useful to first examine the legislative

suggests that the transfer of resources from the government to the banking system through implicit subsidies has been significant, and that 90% of all implicit subsidies were channelled to the largest institutions. As the Report noted, such subsidisation causes distortions, in terms of competitiveness (banks benefiting from implicit subsidy vis-à-vis banks not benefiting from it), excessive risk-taking, and misallocation of resources. Further, that due to the lack of an adequate crisis management mechanism in the EU, only a few liquidations of small banks took place in the EU during the GFC; ibid., p. 25, wherein there are further references.

22 Ibid., pp. 97–99. For a critical analysis of different separation models, see BLUNDELL-WIGNALL, A., ATKINSON, P. and ROULET, C. (2014) 'Bank business models and the separation issue', *OECD Journal: Financial Market Trends*, vol. 2013/2, pp. 69–91.

23 Ibid., pp. 95–97.

24 Among such measures, it was proposed by the *Liikanen Report* that proprietary trading and other significant trading activities should be assigned to a separate legal entity if the activities to be separated amount to a significant share of a bank's business, or if the volume of such activities can be considered significant in terms of financial stability. As a consequence, the report stated, deposits and the explicit and implicit guarantees they carry, would no longer directly support risk trading activities. In particular, the report concluded that it is necessary to require legal separation of certain risky financial activities from deposit-taking banks within a banking group; the activities to be separated should include proprietary trading of securities and derivates, and activities closely linked with securities and derivatives markets. It further supported inter alia drawing-up and maintainance of effective and realistic recovery and resolution plans, and agreed that the use of designated bail-in instruments should be supported, and that banks should have a large quantity of debt to be used in case of bail-in. Ibid., pp. 99 *et seq.*

process that led to their adoption, as well as their normative structure and content, and then to focus on the new bail-in regime.

The 2012 Commission proposal for a BRRD and the legislative process for the adoption of BRRD

The Commission proposed in June 2012 a Directive of the EP and of the Council establishing a framework for the recovery and resolution of credit institutions and investment firms (the BRRD),[25] with a view to fundamentally changing the structure of EU financial law according to the new ideas on how to treat failing FIs; and thus affecting critically the regime of retail depositor and retail investor protection in the EU.

The BRRD proposal built on the 2010 Commission Communication, *An EU Framework for Crisis Management in the Financial Sector*,[26] the G-20 political decisions in the context of which the FSB *Key Attributes of Effective Resolution Regimes for Financial Institutions*[27] were also endorsed. It also took into account extensive consultations with the financial industry and other stakeholders and experts.[28]

By its 2012 BRRD proposal, the Commission appears to have altered its initial position in relation to the legal context of bank resolution, explaining that, while in case of failure banks should be wound down according to the usual insolvency proceedings, the systemic risk posed by banks (in case of a domino effect as a result of loss of confidence in the financial system) and the important economic function of the FIs would necessitate a special framework for the management of bank failures; and that where no public interest considerations are raised, an FI may be subject to the usual insolvency proceedings.[29]

In this regard, the Commission observed that 'by removing the implicit certainty of a publicly-funded bail out for institutions, the option of resolution should encourage uninsured creditors to better assess the risk associated with their investments'.[30]

Since uninsured creditors include depositors (for the amount of their deposit beyond deposit guarantee protection), it appears that the Commission in its proposal regards such depositors as making an investment decision (in a wide sense)

25 COM(2012) 280 final. On 12.12.2013, an agreement was reached between the EP and the Member States of the EU for the adoption of the proposed BRRD. See http://europa.eu/rapid/press-release_MEMO-13-1140_en.htm?locale=en.

26 See n. 10.

27 See Ch. 3.1.

28 See http://ec.europa.eu/internal_market/bank/index_en.htm. The Commission also prepared an impact assessment (available at the same site) according to which the proposed resolution framework 'will achieve the objectives of enhancing financial stability, reducing moral hazard, protecting depositors and critical banking services, saving public money and protecting the internal market for financial institutions' while '[t]he costs of the framework derive from a possible increase in funding costs for institutions due to the removal of the implicit certainty of state support, and from the costs related to resolution funds'; ibid.

29 Ibid.

30 Ibid., p. 5.

when depositing money with a bank – that is in practice when selecting a credit institution to entrust it with their money since no other material decision is taken by retail depositors in this context.

Moreover, according to the Commission BRRD proposal, while losses are to be allocated between the shareholders and the creditors of the FI according to national insolvency law, the following principles for the allocation of losses should apply irrespective of national insolvency law: (a) that the losses should first be allocated in full to the shareholders and then to the creditors; and (b) that creditors of the same class might be treated differently if this is justified by reasons of public interest and in particular in order to underpin financial stability.[31] These principles were to be complemented according to the proposal by the 'no creditor worse off than in liquidation' principle.[32]

The Commission BRRD proposal noted that national authorities will be able to retain specific national tools and powers to deal with failing FIs (on the condition of compatibility with EU law and if they do not impede effective group resolution), observing however that 'ring-fencing' would thus not be compatible with the proposed legislation.[33]

It further advanced proposals in relation inter alia to the 'bail-in' tool, the hierarchy of claims subject to the 'bail-in' power, the temporary stay of rights to enforce claims by counterparties and creditors,[34] as well as by restriction on judicial proceedings against the resolution authorities (that would be liable only for paying compensation for the damages suffered by affected persons) and against the FI under resolution.[35]

By its Opinion of November 2012 on the proposed BRRD,[36] the ECB noted its full support of the development of a recovery and resolution framework and the removal of obstacles to effective crisis management at FIs, applicable both to credit institutions and investment firms.[37] It observed that resolution requires a clear hierarchy, so that where there is no public interest concern (i.e. for the prevention of systemic risk), failing FIs should be liquidated under insolvency proceedings normally applicable under national law.[38]

Noting that resolution measures 'should be adopted in justified circumstances and accompanied by appropriate conditions to limit moral hazard',[39] the ECB considered that bail-in should be used for FIs that are unviable and only in exceptional and justified cases in order to maintain a failing FI as a going concern.[40]

In relation to the function of DGSs in the context of BRR procedures, as in the

31 Ibid., p. 11, para. 4.4.8.
32 Ibid.
33 Ibid., p. 12, n. 15.
34 Ibid., p. 14.
35 Ibid.
36 Opinion of the ECB of 29.11.2012 (OJ C 39/1, 12.2.2013).
37 Ibid., p. 1.
38 Ibid., p. 2.
39 Ibid.
40 Ibid., pp. 2–3.

proposed BRRD, the ECB considered of the utmost importance that it 'does not compromise in any way the core DGS function in protecting insured deposits',[41] and advocated that legal certainty is ensured 'by clearly defining the role of the DGS in resolution financing, regardless of which resolution tool is chosen and how the measures are applied'.[42]

Lastly, the ECB noted that the diversity in insolvency laws across Member States impacts considerably on the implementation of resolution and asked for efforts to minimally harmonise national insolvency legislation to be continued.[43]

The EESC provided its Opinion on the proposed BRRD in December 2012,[44] by which it generally supported the Commission proposal, but also noted the need for clarification of the bail-in tool,[45] stressing that the BRRD should introduce provisions 'guaranteeing that the DGS can perform its main function to protect retail depositors at all times'.[46] It further expressed its concern that the wide range of powers attributed to the resolution authorities according to the proposed BRRD would be incompatible with judicial control of insolvency procedures and of the actions of administrative authorities.[47]

As also recommended by the ECB, the EESC recommended that the proposed BRRD should guarantee that DGSs can perform their main function to protect retail depositors at all times.[48]

The EP, in its Position of 15 April 2014,[49] proposed a number of modifications to the Commission proposal, which were accepted by the latter.

The BRRD was finally adopted in 15 May 2014,[50] and entered into force in June 2014,[51] with a general transposition period until the end of 2014, and regarding the bail-in tool until one year later.[52]

The BRRD poses centrally the issue of financial consumer protection under EU law, as well as the particular question regarding the relation of the legal status of retail depositors vis-à-vis retail investors under EU law.

41 Ibid., p. 6.
42 Ibid.
43 Ibid., p. 7.
44 OJ C 44/68, 15.02.2013.
45 Ibid., pp. 69, 74.
46 Ibid., p. 69, para. 1.12. It also asked for a clear definition of the terms 'creditors' and 'depositors' to be used in the proposed BRRD, since depositors are also creditors and noting that the ranking of depositors as creditors is not harmonised in Member States; ibid., p. 73.
47 Ibid., pp. 69 and 74.
48 Ibid., p. 75.
49 Position of the European Parliament of 15.04.2014 adopted at first reading (EP-PE_TC1-COD(2012) 0150).
50 Directive 2014/59/EU of the European Parliament and the Council of 15 May 2014 (OJ L 173/190, 12.6.2014.
51 BRRD, Article 131.
52 Ibid., Article 130.

The BRRD general structure and normative content

The main structure of the BRRD consists inter alia of provisions on the preparation of recovery and resolution (title II), on early intervention measures (title III), on resolution (title IV), on cross-border resolution (title V), on relations with third countries (title VI), and on financing agreements (title VII).

The BRRD is based on the fundamental acceptance that the GFC showed the lack of an adequate mechanism at the EU level 'to deal effectively with unsound or failing credit institutions and investment firms'.[53]

The notion of access to funding in equivalent conditions for credit institutions, in order to avoid failure,[54] and the notion of interconnectedness of institutions across integrated markets raising systemic risk[55] are at the basis of the BRRD's aim to enhance mutual trust between Member States and credibility of the internal market in the area of financial services.

The BRRD recognises that there is no harmonisation at the EU level for the resolution of FIs; and that relevant national law is very diversified while corporate insolvency law is not only very different from one Member State to another, but also may not always ensure financial market stability.[56]

Thus, the BRRD is portrayed as a regime 'needed to provided authorities with a credible set of tools to intervene sufficiently early and quickly in an unsound or failing institution so as to ensure the institutions critical financial and economic functions, while minimising the impact of an institution's failure on the economy and financial system'.[57]

Further, a basic notion of the BRRD is that 'in order to avoid moral hazard, any failing institution should be able to exit the market, irrespective of its size and interconnectedness, without causing systemic disruption', and that such a failing FI should in principle be liquidated under normal insolvency proceedings save where public interest considerations would dictate applying the resolution tools under the BRRD rather than normal insolvency proceedings.[58]

Within the field of application of the BRRD fall credit institutions and investment firms established in the EU,[59] and its definitions follow the general definitions applicable as per relevant EU instruments.[60]

53 Ibid., Preamble, recital 1.
54 Ibid., recital 2.
55 Ibid., recital 3.
56 Ibid., recital 4.
57 Ibid., recital 5.
58 Ibid., recital 46.
59 Ibid., Articles 1(b) and 2(23). Credit institutions are defined as in point (2) of Article 4(1) of Regulation 575/2013 CRR, but not including the entities referred to in Article 2(5) of CRD IV, i.e. not including central banks and certain categories of public institutions. Investment firms are defined as in point (2) of Article 4(1) of CRR, which is subject to the initial capital requirements of Article 28(2) of CRD IV.
60 See e.g. the definitions of DGSs, covered deposits, eligible deposits, depositor and investors in BRRD, Article 2(73), (94), (95), (104) and (105), respectively.

Central to the structure and operation of the BRR system is the role of the Resolution Authorities (RAs).

According to the BRRD, the RAs shall be public administrative authorities or authorities entrusted with public administrative powers designated by Member States and responsible for resolution; they may be national central banks, ministries or other public administrative authorities, and must be operationally independent from any other supervision or other functions or authorities.[61]

Regarding the preparation of recovery and resolution, the BRRD provides for the obligation of Member States to ensure that competent authorities and RAs have in place adequate recovery and resolution plans relevant to each institution and on the basis of various scenarios of failure and the possible systemic repercussions thereof.[62]

Particularly important is the assessment of the 'resolvability' of an institution for the purposes of application of the BRRD.

An FI shall be deemed resolvable 'if it is feasible and credible for the [RA] to either liquidate it under normal insolvency proceedings or to resolve it by applying the different resolution tools and powers to the institutions while avoiding to the maximum extent possible any significant adverse consequences for financial systems … with a view to ensuring the continuity of critical functions carried out by the institution'.[63]

The ensuing vagueness of notions to be specified by RAs with a view to applying resolution is evident: neither the notion of what is considered to be 'feasible and credible' in order for an RA to proceed to either liquidation or resolution, nor the notion of the need to avoid 'to the maximum extent possible' adverse 'significant' consequences for financial systems, are elaborated by BRRD.

Despite certain minimum criteria provided in Section C of the Annex to the BRRD, and the provision for draft regulatory standards by the EBA,[64] wide discretion as to the resolvability of an FI is left by the BRRD to the RAs.[65]

Furthermore, important powers are attributed to the RAs in relation to addressing or removing impediments to the resolvability of FIs: the RAs may, after consulting the competent authority, and if the measures proposed by an FI are not effective in removing impediments to their resolvability, resolve to taking a series of important measures, including requiring the FI to divest specific assets,

61 Ibid., Article 3.

62 Ibid., title II.

63 Ibid., Article 15(1).

64 Ibid., Article 15(4). The EBA does not decide on the resolvability of institutions under the BRRD, which is left to the discretion of Member State RAs, the latter being under obligation to notify the EBA of their decision as to resolvability; ibid.

65 In relation to the assessment of the resolvability of groups, the relevant discretion rests with group-level RAs, which examine resolvability together with RAs of subsidiaries after consulting their consolidating supervisor and competent authorities as well as RAs of jurisdictions where significant branches are located; ibid, Article 16, and concerning the decision making procedure ibid., Article 13.

to limit or cease specific existing or proposed activities, or to change its legal or operational structure.[66]

Despite the obligation of RAs to issue reasoned decisions and the right of FIs to an appeal, the discretionary powers of RAs are wide and not dependent on the prior consent of any other public authority. RAs are only required to take into account 'the potential effect of those measures on the particular institution, on the internal market for financial services, on the financial stability in other [Member States] and Union as a whole'.[67] The potential effect of such measures on shareholders, creditors and other stakeholders is not mentioned as a parameter to be taken into account by RAs in determining relevant measures.

The BRRD further provides for a number of early-intervention measures,[68] which Member States must ensure that their competent authorities have at their disposal in order to treat the rapidly deteriorating condition of FIs. Such measures are connected to the activation of RAs,[69] as well as of intra-group financial support,[70] and may include the removal of senior management and the management body of an FI,[71] as well as the appointment of a temporary administrator.[72]

It is interesting to note in this regard the very wide discretion of RAs regarding the powers of such temporary administrator, as well as relevant disclosure obligations: the RAs are attributed the exclusive power to specify 'the role, duties and powers of the temporary administrator and any requirements for the management body of the institution to consult or to obtain the consent of the temporary administrator prior to taking specific decisions or actions'.[73]

Thus, the RAs are provided exclusive power to appoint (for a term of up to a year)[74] and remove temporary administrators, while there are no criteria provided for such attribution of powers, save that the competent authorities shall specify the powers of the temporary administrator 'based on what is proportionate in the circumstances' and that such powers must comply with applicable company law.[75]

Beyond the wide powers attributed to RAs in relation to the appointment and powers of the temporary administrators, the BRRD further provides that Member States may limit the liability of temporary administrators in accordance with national law, for acts or omissions in the discharge of their duties.[76]

While the BRRD provides a number of provisions relating to the recovery of an FI in distress, attributing important powers and leaving very wide discretion

66 Ibid., Article 17.
67 Ibid., Article 17(7).
68 Ibid., title III.
69 Ibid., Article 27(2).
70 Ibid., Articles 19–26.
71 Ibid., Article 28.
72 Ibid., Article 29.
73 Ibid., Article 29(4).
74 Ibid., Article 29(7).
75 Ibid., Article 29(2).
76 Ibid., Article 29(9).

in this regard to RAs, in cooperation with the EBA, the focus of the BRRD is on resolution, which occupies most of the normative content of the Directive.

Resolution and bail-in under the BRRD

As resolution objectives, the BRRD states the following:

> (a) to ensure continuity of critical functions; (b) to avoid significant adverse effects on financial stability, in particular by preventing contagion, including to market infrastructures, and by maintaining market discipline; (c) to protect public funds by minimising reliance on extraordinary public financial support; (d) to protect depositors covered by [DGSD] and investors covered by [ICSD]; (e) to protect client funds and assets.[77]

Through this definition of resolution objectives, the BRRD introduces the whole problematic of the new legislation relating to the failure of FIs and presents the diverse parameters of this problematic as concurrent and even compatible with each other: resolution aims – according to the BRRD definition – at achieving both market stability and financial consumers' and taxpayers' protection, while ensuring continuity of critical financial functions.

The BRRD further clarifies that '[s]ubject to different provisions of this Directive, the resolution objectives are of equal significance, and resolution authorities shall balance them as appropriate to the nature and circumstances of each case'.[78] This provision is, in our view, important, despite the obvious difficulty in practice to reconcile and equally uphold the differential aims of resolution as stated by the BRRD, because it clearly places – or at least announces – all such aims to be *a priori* of equal significance.

In this sense, it allows at first for a systematic interpretation of the relevant EU law, as formulated under the new regime following the GFC, in the direction that under EU law financial consumer protection is an equal aim to financial market stability protection, and that *a priori* such two aims are regarded as not competitive and mutually exclusive.

Moreover, it is important in placing the protection of retail depositors on an equal footing in relation to the protection of retail investors and to the protection of taxpayers.

Beyond this important *a priori* position, said BRRD fundamental rule is subjected by the Directive to two conditions: first, that no other provisions of the BRRD dictate otherwise, i.e. provide for a hierarchy in these aims of resolution; and, second, that the task of balancing such objectives belongs to RAs which are again provided with wide discretion to act as they consider appropriate on a case-by-case basis.

The wide discretion attributed to RAs raises issues not only of delegation of

77 Ibid., Article 31.
78 Ibid., Article 31(3).

power by EU law but also of legal certainty and predictability of the rules to be applied. The general rule of the BRRD, that all resolution objectives are of equal significance, may become relevant in a critical situation, since RAs have a discretion to prioritise certain objectives over others, as they deem appropriate on a case-by-case basis.

The conditions for RAs to proceed to resolution of an FI are, *grosso modo*, that competent authorities have determined that the FI is failing or likely to fail, that there are no viable alternatives to resolution and that resolution is 'necessary in the public interest',[79] i.e. 'if it is necessary for the achievement of and is proportionate to one or more of the resolution objectives ... and winding up of the institution under normal insolvency proceedings would not meet those resolution objectives to the same extent'.[80]

These criteria, for RAs to decide whether to proceed to resolution, in our view, further complicate the inter-relation between different resolution objectives as stated by the BRRD.

The reference to 'public interest' provided by the BRRD, as a condition justifying the option to proceed to resolution instead of normal insolvency proceedings, may not be considered as a definition or even a delimitation of the notion of public interest: for resolution to be in the public interest, according to the BRRD, on the one hand, it has to fulfil the vague criterion to be necessary and proportionate for the achievement of at least one resolution objective and, on the other hand, it has to fulfil the equally vague criterion that winding up under normal insolvency proceedings would be less effective in meeting the same objective(s).

As the BRRD provides no mechanism to resolve a possible conflict between *a priori* equal resolution aims, it appears to be in the discretion of RAs to decide whether to follow resolution proceedings, as being more effective than winding up proceedings, even where one or more resolution objectives may be better served by it, while others are not.

The exercise of such discretion also appears to be on the basis of a justification that seems difficult to refute in practice as only an estimation is requested as justification.

Furthermore, the BRRD sets a number of 'general principles' governing resolution, which are in broad terms that: (a) shareholders bear first losses; (b) creditors bear losses after shareholders in accordance *a priori* with the order of priority of their claims under normal insolvency proceedings; (c) the management body and senior management are in principle replaced; (d) the management body and senior management provide all necessary assistance; (e) national and legal persons are made liable, subject to Member State law, under civil or criminal law for their responsibility for the failure of the institution; (f) creditors of the same class are *a priori* treated in an equitable manner; (g) no creditor shall incur greater losses than if winding up under normal insolvency proceedings;[81] (h) covered deposits

79 Ibid., Article 32(1).
80 Ibid., Article 32(5).
81 The 'no creditor worse off than in liquidation' principle. The effect of the BRRD includes specific

are fully protected; and (i) resolution action is taken in accordance with BRRD safeguards.[82]

These general principles of resolution bind RAs in the exercise of their powers and the BRRD calls Member States to ensure their application.

In the context of resolution, RAs are empowered by the BRRD to appoint a 'special management' of the FI under resolution, operating under the control of the RA and aiming at the implementation of the resolution.[83]

The powers of this special management correspond to those of the temporary administration in the context of early-intervention measures, and are even greater; the BRRD even provides that '[t]he special manager shall have the statutory duty to take all the measures necessary to promote the resolution objectives ... and implement resolution actions ... Where necessary, that duty shall override any other duty of management in accordance with the statutes of the institution or national law, insofar as they are inconsistent'.[84]

The emerging problematic on whether a general provision of EU secondary law may entail overriding any inconsistent provision of national law is apparent; moreover, it is not clear who is to decide whether there is such an inconsistency.

The BRRD further provides certain rules relating to the valuation which has to be carried out before resolution action or bail-in takes place, by a person independent from any public authority, including the RA and the FI, and which has to value the assets and liabilities of the FI in a 'fair, prudent and realistic' way.[85]

The 'resolution tools' provided by the BRRD for RAs to deploy are the 'sale of business tool', the 'bridge institution tool', the 'bail-in tool', and the 'asset separation tool' (to be applied by RAs only together with another resolution tool);[86] writing down and conversion of capital instruments are also applicable by RAs when the application of a resolution tool would result in losses being borne by creditors or the claims being converted.[87]

Furthermore, the BRRD equips such resolution tools with the provision that Member States have to ensure that national insolvency law rules relating to voidability or unenforceability of legal acts detrimental to creditors do not apply to transfer of assets, rights or liabilities by virtue of resolution.[88]

In order for resolution tools to be applied in an effective way, the BRRD provides for a number of resolution powers, which it distinguishes into 'general powers' and other, specific powers.[89]

The general resolution powers that Member States are required by the BRRD

rules on the ranking of deposits in insolvency hierarchy, providing that Member States have to adapt their legislation accordingly. See BRRD, Article 108.

82 Ibid., Article 34(1).

83 Ibid., Article 35.

84 Ibid., Article 35(3).

85 Ibid., Article 36(1).

86 Ibid., Article 37(3) and (5).

87 Ibid., Article 37(2).

88 Ibid., Article 37(8).

89 Ibid., Chapter VI.

to ensure RAs may exercise, either individually or in combination, include powers: (a) to request information; (b) to take control of the institution under resolution; (c) to transfer shares and instruments of ownership; (d) to transfer rights, assets and liabilities of the institution under resolution; (e) to reduce eligible liabilities; (f) to convert eligible liabilities; (g) to cancel debt instruments; (h) to reduce the nominal amount of shares and instruments of ownership; (i) to request the issuance of new shares and other instruments of ownership or capital instruments; (k) to close out and terminate financial contracts or derivative contracts; (l) to remove or replace the management; and (m) to require the competent authority to assess buyer of qualifying holding.[90]

The BRRD further provides that Member States are obliged to ensure that when applying resolution tools or exercising resolution powers, RAs are not subject to national law statutory or contractual requirements, such as to obtain approvals or to follow procedural requirements (including to notify, publish notices or prospectuses or file or register documents) prior to the exercise of powers.[91]

Beyond general resolution powers, the BRRD provides for a series of ancillary powers necessary for the effective exercise of resolution powers,[92] as well as for an array of specific powers of RAs, such as the power to require the provision of services and facilities,[93] the power to enforce crisis-management measures or crisis-prevention measures by other Member States,[94] and powers in respect of assets, rights, liabilities, shares and other instruments of ownership in third countries.[95]

Moreover, Member States are required by the BRRD to ensure that RAs have the power to suspend certain obligations for a period of time, including payment obligations, with the exception inter alia of eligible deposits and eligible claims under the ICSD.[96] Other RA powers provided by the BRRD include the power to restrict enforcement of security interests,[97] and the power to temporarily suspend termination rights.[98]

To remove any possible doubt, the BRRD further clearly states that Member States shall ensure that RAs are able to exercise control over the FI under resolution, so as to: (a) operate and conduct its activities with all the powers of its shareholders and management body; and (b) manage and dispose of its assets and property.[99]

It also provides that control of the FI under resolution by the RA may be exercised either directly by the RA or by a person appointed by the RA, and

90 Ibid., Article 63(1).
91 Ibid., Article 63(2).
92 Ibid., Article 64.
93 Ibid., Article 65.
94 Ibid., Article 66.
95 Ibid., Article 67.
96 Ibid., Article 69.
97 Ibid., Article 70.
98 Ibid., Article 71.
99 Ibid., Article 71(1).

that Member States have to ensure that RAs may take resolution action through executive order in accordance with national administrative law.[100]

Thus, the new EU law on the BRR provides RAs with a panoply of mechanisms to enforce the resolution of an FI in distress; however, the relevant provisions of the BRRD are characterised by an important degree of vagueness.

This, in our view, may be due not only to the legal form of the BRRD as a directive, i.e. as an instrument of harmonisation of Member States' legislation, but also to the design of the new BRR regime as a wide, all-encompassing crisis management legislation which aims to provide RAs with very extended competences, to be applied virtually at their sole discretion, on a case-by-case basis.

In this way, it might be argued that the BRRD is creating a financial law of emergency – which may be set in action according to technical criteria following very rapid procedures, and while aiming at the prevention or control of systemic risk may entail important changes in the financial position of retail depositors or retail investors of distressed FIs or of local financial markets in danger of destabilisation.

In such an extreme factual situation, the new EU law opts for maximum concentration of competence by RAs and for maximum flexibility – without, however, providing a balancing mechanism providing legal certainty and predictability in the application of the overall new BRR regime; perhaps such a balance could be searched for not in the context of the BRRD (together with SRM), but in the wider context of the wider emerging new Banking Union, if the new measures under the DGSD (Recast) were to be effective, and in particular if the proposed EDIS were to be achieved and to operate on the basis of a well-regulated mechanism, running like clockwork.

It also appears possible that the application of the BRRD, through national implementation measures, may raise legal issues as to its interpretation and application, as it plainly entails extensive modification or disuse of relevant national legal rules if inconsistent.

In this direction, the BRRD provides for two levels of control: substantive and procedural safeguards in the application of resolution, and judicial control.

In relation to substantive safeguards, the basic rules provided by the BRRD are that in case of partial transfers of rights, assets and liabilities and the application of the bail-in tool, the 'no creditor worse off than in liquidation' principle applies.[101]

In relation to procedural safeguards, the BRRD provides for notification obligations (that an FI is failing or likely to fail, of the decision of the RA and of the relevant measures decided),[102] for RAs to issue reasoned decisions whether or not to take resolution action, the action intended and relevant measures, including the RA determination to apply for winding up, for the appointment of an administrator or any other measure under applicable normal insolvency proceedings or under national law.[103]

100 Ibid., Article 71(2).
101 Ibid., Articles 73–80.
102 Ibid., Articles 80–84.
103 Ibid., Article 82(2).

Among the procedural obligations relevant to the notification requirements regarding resolution, the BRRD includes provisions on notification obligations of RAs[104] and also on confidentiality.[105] RAs have to notify the FI under resolution of any order or instrument by which it exercises its powers and which indicate the date from which resolution is effective; they also have to notify the same documents to a number of authorities, including the competent authorities, the central bank, the DGS, the competent ministry, the Commission, the ECB, the ESMA, the EIOPA, and others.[106] Also, they have to publish such document on the internet, 'or a notice summarising the effects of the resolution action, and in particular on retail customers'.[107]

Thus, the information publishable by RAs as soon as they take a resolution action is set by the BRRD at a minimum level.

On the other hand, extensive confidentiality restrictions are imposed by the BRRD on the persons involved in the resolution procedure.

RAs, competent authorities, the EBA, competent ministries, special managers, temporary administrators, potential acquirers, auditors, accountants, legal and professional advisors, valuers and experts, administrators of DGSs and ICSs and others are placed under professional secrecy obligations relating to 'confidential information received during the course of their professional activities or from a competent authority or from a [RA] in connection with its function under [the BRRD]'.[108]

The nature or content of such confidential information is not provided by the BRRD, which adopts a very wide scope of the relevant definition, qualifying it only as necessary for the resolution action to be possible to be planned or carried out,[109] and enhancing it with the addition of provisions on civil liability for infringement.[110]

The BRRD does not specify the duration of the relevant obligation *ratione temporis*; it does not provide any time limit, before which relevant information or assessments may be accessible by the public.

On the contrary, the BRRD imposes an obligation on Member States to ensure that even disclosure to the public of actions preliminary to resolution is controlled: '[Member States] shall ensure that no confidential information is disclosed … and that the possible effects of disclosing information on the public interest as regards financial, monetary or economic policy, on the commercial interests of natural and legal persons, on the purpose of inspections, on investigations and on audits are assessed'.[111]

It also provides that the procedure for checking the effects of disclosing

104 Ibid., Article 83.
105 Ibid., Article 84.
106 Ibid., Article 83(1), (2) and (3).
107 Ibid., Article 83(4). Cf. ibid., Article 84(7).
108 Ibid., Article 84(3).
109 Ibid., Article 84(4) and (5).
110 Ibid., Article 84(3) and (6).
111 Ibid., Article 84(3).

information shall include a specific assessment regarding the contents and details of recovery and resolution planning and of resolvability assessment.[112]

This rule of the BRRD does not provide any standard against which such potential effects of disclosure on public interest, and the other categories of interest stated, are to be measured by Member States.

Thus, it could be argued that the potential of disclosure impinging on practically any, public or private, interest – which may prove not difficult to support – will provide grounds for denying any disclosure, not only of initiatives directly relevant to setting the resolution procedure in effect, but also any other initiatives including preliminary inspections, investigations and audits.

While these obscure provisions of the BRRD provide little explanation as to the *ratio* and content of such extensive secrecy requirements, the preamble to the directive appears more elaborate, explaining that 'as information obtained by [RAs] and their professional advisers during the resolution process is likely to be sensitive, before the resolution decision is made public, that information should be subject to an effective confidentiality regime'.[113]

Moreover, that '[a]ny information provided in respect of a decision before it is taken, be it on whether the conditions for resolution are satisfied, on the use of a specific tool or of any action during the proceedings, must be presumed to have effects on the public and private interests concerned by the action'.[114]

While the preamble to a legal instrument, as in this case the BRRD, does not set legal rules, it is relevant to the interpretation of the *ratio* of such instrument. The presumption of any disclosure prior to resolution action representing risk, on public and private interests concerned by such action, as stated in the preamble of the BRRD, appears to be extremely strict against the interests of third parties, particularly financial consumers, and disproportionate since it amounts to a requirement of negative proof.

Indeed, it is not clear how, when and by whom such a presumption, which amounts to an *argumentum ad ignorantiam*, may be challenged.

Moreover, such a construction would be difficult to reconcile with the basic concept of the BRRD, especially in relation to bail-in, that '[t]he bail-in tool will … give shareholders and creditors of institutions a stronger incentive to monitor the health of an institution during normal circumstances'.[115]

It is not clear how such an incentive may operate if all crucial information is presumed not disclosable, especially since indications of an unhealthy condition of an FI may be present a long time before the FI is in danger of failing, but may be identifiable only following an inspection, investigation or audit conducted by authorities or persons bound by the extensive BRRD confidentiality requirements.

In such a case, even if financial consumers carefully monitor the health of an FI during what will appear to be normal circumstances, in the wording of the

112 Ibid.

113 Ibid., Preamble, recital 86.

114 Ibid. This part of recital 86 was added by the EP during the co-decision procedure.

115 Ibid., Preamble, recital 67.

BRRD, they will not be allowed to have access to information, perhaps indicating that the FI is facing important problems and even the risk of failing, if such information is available but presumed confidential.

In other words, in such a case, and for the duration of the uncertain and financially dubious period preceding the failure of an FI, financial consumers will have to form their investment decisions on which FI and by which instrument and conditions to trust with their assets, only on the publicly available general corporate and capital markets information, while, however, competent authorities, RAs and in general Member State organs may possess crucial information in the opposite direction.

Such a result would appear difficult to reconcile with the position that market stability and financial consumer protection constitute equal aims of EU financial law.

In this regard, it is interesting to note the general rule of the BRRD, that resolution objectives, amongst which is the protection of the financial market, of retail depositors and of retail investors, are *a priori* of equal significance in the context of resolution – i.e. subject to different provisions in the BRRD.

While it could be argued that, in the case of confidentiality of information in relation to resolution, the protection of retail depositors and retail investors is subordinate to financial market protection, and so public interest considerations in this context justify the imposition of secrecy to the potential detriment of financial consumers connected to a particular FI or group of FIs, such a consideration may not be accurate.

According to the BRRD, the RAS shall have regard to resolution objectives 'when applying the resolution tools and exercising the resolution powers'.[116]

So, according to the BRRD, RAs may under certain conditions (if necessary, proportionate and suitable) subordinate financial consumer protection to the need to protect public funds when applying such tools and powers, in the context of resolution proceedings.[117]

However, if financial consumer protection and financial market protection are to be considered of equal importance, as dual aims of EU financial law, such an extraordinary discretion of the RAS not to fully protect retail investors and retail depositors has to be interpreted and applied in a strict sense, i.e. in the application of resolution tools and powers when resolution has already commenced (with the application of resolution tools and powers) and not in a general way or indefinitely.

In this context, an obligation of absolute secrecy indefinitely in time, regarding crucial information on the status of an FI, may not be considered to be in harmony with the dual aim of EU financial law or proportionate.

An interpretation of the relevant obligations in light of general EU financial law rules on financial consumer protection and according to a criterion of proportionality would entail disclosure of important information by public authorities – at

116 Ibid., Article 31(1).
117 Ibid., Article 31(1)(c) and (5).

least if financial consumers are to bear the consequences of trusting a FI with their money.

If competent authorities, even in cases where they are also RAs,[118] inform and protect financial consumers when there are indications that an FI is representing a danger to them (as in the case of suspicion of excessive risk taking, fraudulent behaviour, technical inefficiency, etc.), or at least do not disallow the dissemination of relevant information, then burden sharing by financial consumers is set on a different basis.

Thus, a critical parameter with regard to disclosure and financial consumer protection in conjunction with market stability considerations is timing.

However, the BRRD does not provide any rule distinguishing the crucial period in which an FI is in imminent danger of failing from a possibly long period during which an FI may be in distress (but not failing); aiming to protect financial market stability and to avoid bail-out by public funds it appears to be allowing for the imposition of an absolute secrecy regime to be partially lifted only when resolution measures are already taken and officially announced.

Keeping the balance between predictability and flexibility can prove difficult in crisis management, which is the BRR regime, for public authorities.

As a result, it appears that the heavier the obligation of secrecy authorities impose on the financial condition of an FI before the BRR, the more difficult it will be for authorities to claim immunity for their acts and omissions in relation to the BRR, especially in relation to financial consumers' claims bearing the cost of their inaccurate assessment of an unviable FI.

This issue is relevant in particular to the application of bail-in measures, which appear to form the first line of defence of the new EU financial law to control FI failures.

The 'bail-in' resolution tool

The BRRD provides that the bail-in resolution tool may be applied by RAs in order: (a) to recapitalise an FI that meets the conditions for resolution to restore its ability to comply with conditions for authorisation, and to sustain sufficient market confidence in it,[119] and only if there is a reasonable prospect that such action will restore its financial soundness and long-term viability;[120] and (b) to convert to equity or reduce the principal amount of claims or debt instruments that are transferred to a bridge institution or under the sales of business tool or the asset separation tool.[121]

The basic rule of the BRRD regarding bail-in is that it is *a priori* applicable to all liabilities of an FI.[122]

118 Ibid., Article 3(3).
119 Ibid., Article 43(2)(a).
120 Ibid., Article 43(3).
121 Ibid., Article 43(2)(b).
122 Ibid., Article 44(1). See, in general, Communication from the Commission on the application, from 1 August 2013, of State aid rules to support measures in favour of banks in the

This rule is qualified by the prohibition imposed by the BRRD to RAs to exercise the write-down or conversion powers in relation to a number of liabilities such as: covered deposits (for the covered amount), certain secured liabilities, liabilities arising out of holding of client assets or money if protected under applicable insolvency law, liabilities arising by virtue of fiduciary relationship if the beneficiary is protected under applicable insolvency law, liabilities to FI with original maturity of less than seven days owed to systems or system operators, liabilities to employees for certain payments, liabilities to commercial or trade creditors of the FI arising out of the provisions of goods or services critical to the daily functioning of its operations, liabilities to tax and social security authorities where preferred under applicable law, and liabilities to DGSs.[123]

This list of categories of liabilities, which the RAs are prohibited to include in the bail-in, was included in the majority of liabilities it includes, in the original proposal of the Commission for the BRRD and perhaps reflects a consideration to achieve equilibrium between the perceived need to treat creditors as debtors so as to protect public funds, but also in the context of the 'no creditor worse off than in liquidation' principle and of protecting certain sensitive interests which could be regarded as reflecting general good considerations.

However, the BRRD includes a list of further categories of liabilities which RAs may exclude 'in exceptional circumstances' from the application of the write-down or conversion powers.[124]

This list includes rather a general description of instances where RAs may

context of the financial crisis ('Banking Communication'), OJ C 216/1, 30.07.2013. In this Communication the Commission refers in particular to EU state aid law in conjunction with the new BRR regime. The Commission inter alia refers to 'burden sharing', noting that 'State support should be granted on terms which represent an adequate burden-sharing by those who invested in the bank' and that 'some Member States had to go beyond minimum requirements under State aid rules and by introducing new legal frameworks enforce stricter *ex ante* burden-sharing requirements. That development led to diverging approaches to burden sharing across Member States, namely those that have limited themselves to the minimum requirements under State aid rules and those which have gone beyond those requirements, requiring bail-in of investors or creditors. Such differences in the approach to burden sharing between Member States have led to divergent funding costs between banks depending on the perceived likelihood of a bail-in as a function of a Member State's fiscal strength. They pose a threat to the integrity of the single market and risk undermining the level playing field which State aid control aims to protect' (ibid., paras 15, 18). Taking these considerations into account, the Commission urged by its Communications for the minimum requirements for 'burden sharing' to be raised, so that '[b]efore granting any kind of restructuring aid, be it a recapitalisation or impaired asset measure, to a bank all capital generating measures including the conversion of junior debt should be exhausted, provided that fundamental rights are respected and financial stability is not put at risk', and that 'before granting restructuring aid to a bank Member States will need to ensure that the bank's shareholders and junior capital holders arrange for the required contribution or establish the necessary legal framework for obtaining such contributions' (ibid., para. 19). With regard to the Banking Communication, a reference for a preliminary ruling is pending before the ECJ, in Case C-526/14, *Tadej Kotnik and others v Državni zbor Republike Slovenije*, OJ C 81/3, 09.03.2015.

123 Ibid., Article 44(2).

124 Ibid., Article 44(3).

decide to exclude liabilities from bail-in rather than specific types of liabilities or sources thereof.

Such are the cases where 'it is not possible to bail-in that liability within a reasonable time notwithstanding the good faith efforts of the resolution authority', where 'the exclusion is strictly necessary and proportionate to achieve the continuity of critical functions and core business lines in a manner that maintains the ability of the institution under resolution to continue key operations, services and transactions', where 'the exclusion is strictly necessary and proportionate to avoid giving rise to widespread contagion, in particular as regards eligible deposits held by natural persons and micro, small and medium enterprises, which would severely disrupt the functioning of financial markets … in a manner that could cause a serious disturbance to the economy of a [Member State] or of the Union', or where non-exclusion from bail-in would cause a destruction in value of the relevant liabilities.[125]

The relevant provisions, which were added by the EP in the co-decision procedure, include very ample criteria for exclusion of any liabilities from bail-in on the basis of presumption by RAs.

Although they probably reflect a protective policy by the EP, to extend the exclusion from bail-in to practically any type of liability and for any sensible reason, in the opinion of RAs, the emerging legal uncertainty is apparent.

The BRRD sets certain rules for the application of such exclusions, relating in particular to relevant contributions (MREL rules)[126] and to notification requirements,[127] but in essence the decision to exclude wide categories of liabilities from bail-in (beyond liabilities already excluded *ex lege*) rests at the discretion of RAs, according to a case-by-case assessment.

Also taking into account the wide discretion allowed in the context of the new THDB protection regime under the DGSD (Recast), the new EU law creates a protection regime for retail depositors that is not only flexible and changeable, but even adaptable according to Member State policies on a case-by-case basis.

Retail depositors may see, for any of the reasons stated in the DGSD (Recast) or the BRRD, their assets totally protected for a limited time, even beyond covered deposit levels; or only partly protected, up to the level of covered amount; or fully or partly protected above the covered amount, owing to a partial or total exclusion from bail-in.

This protean form of retail depositor protection, emerging from the new EU financial law, is connected to a treatment of retail depositors – according to a functional if not legal analysis – as making an investment decision when trusting an FI with their money, in the absence of a state guarantee of banks.

The legal situation may become even more complicated, where relevant decisions regarding the treatment of financial consumers in case of FI failure are to be taken at the EU level, on the basis of the SRM rules, so that the problematic of conferral of powers to agencies is also added to the equation.

125 Ibid.
126 Ibid., Article 44(4)–(8); cf. Article 45.
127 Ibid., Article 44(12).

8.2 The new SRM Regulation

Following its Communication of 12 September 2012, *A Roadmap towards a Banking Union*,[128] and as discussions on the proposed new DGSD and BRR regimes were continuing, the Commission proposed in July 2013 the adoption of a SRM Regulation to establish uniform rules and a uniform procedure for the resolution of FIs, as well as to establish a Single Resolution Mechanism (SRM) and a Single Bank Resolution Fund (SRF).[129]

The Commission proposed the introduction of the SRM as the framework in which the SRB, a new EU agency overseeing resolution procedures and managing the SRF, would facilitate resolving the interdependence of banks and sovereigns, arguing that such a structure would provide key benefits for Member States, taxpayers and banks, and financial and economic stability for the EU; and also, that the introduction of the SRM within the EU legal and institutional framework would protect the democratic and institutional order of the EU, avoiding the deployment of *ad hoc* intergovernmental instruments.

The initial Commission proposal envisaged an enhanced role of the Commission in the initiation of the resolution procedure, providing that the Commission would indicate to the SRB the resolution framework to apply. The ability of the SRF to pool resources would render it a Euro-area insurance mechanism in banking crises, to absorb shocks, but not to be used as a bail-out fund, with Member State DGSs contributing up to the amount of covered deposits in application of the 'no creditor worse off than in liquidation' principle.

In its opinion of November 2013,[130] the ECB expressed its full support to the establishment of the SRM,[131] stressing that a strong and independent single RA should be at the centre of the SRM, agreeing with the Commission that such a single mechanism is better placed to guarantee optimal resolution action than a network of national RAs.[132] It further welcomed the centralised structure proposed, and 'in particular the fact that no party, specifically national resolution authorities, will have a power of veto in the decision-making of the [SRB]'.[133] It was, however, concerned about the issue of compatibility of SRB extended competences with the *Meroni* doctrine,[134] as well as in relation to the supervisory competency of the ECB.[135] It also noted inter alia the lack of provisions on judicial review.[136]

The EESC in its Opinion[137] also expressed its agreement to the proposal,

128 COM(2012) 510 final.
129 COM(2013) 520 final.
130 OJ C 109/2, 11.4.2014.
131 Ibid.
132 Ibid., p. 3.
133 Ibid., p. 4.
134 Ibid.
135 Ibid. pp. 5–6.
136 Ibid., p. 9.
137 OJ C 67/58, 06.03.2014.

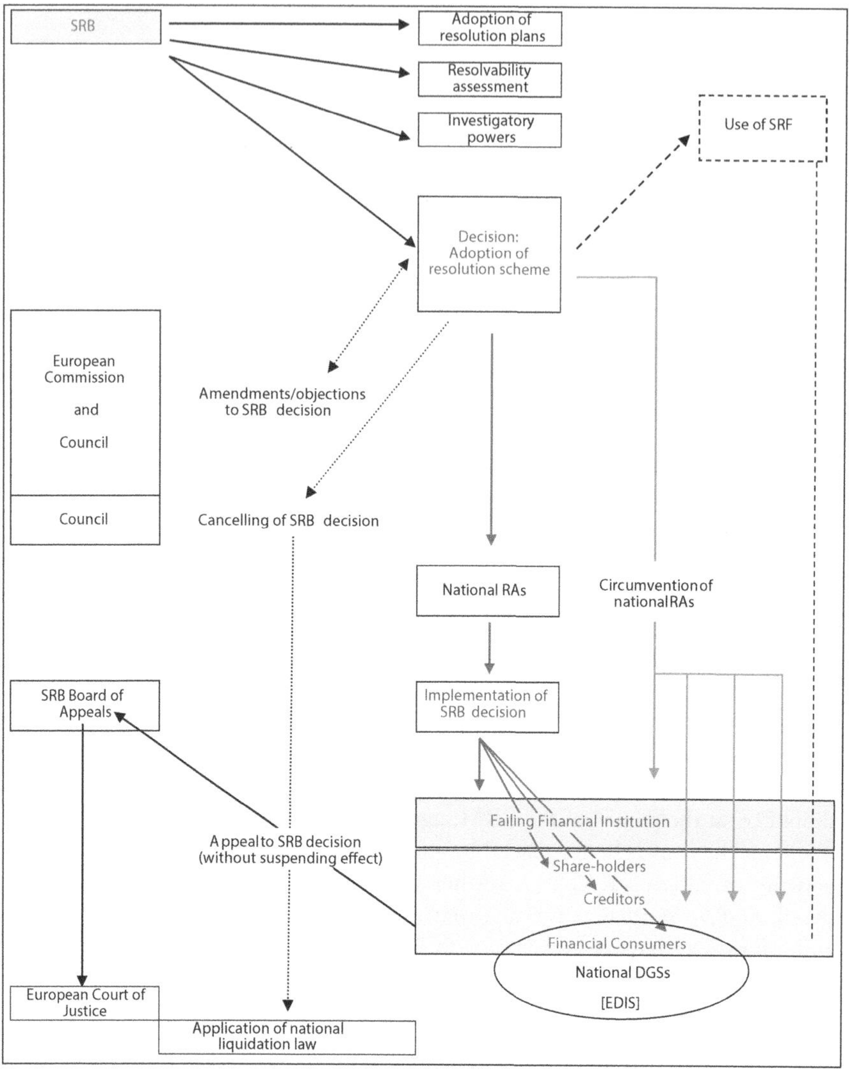

Figure 3 The operation of resolution under the SRM.

stressing inter alia the need for independence and democratic scrutiny in the operation of the SRB and for a clear division of powers with the supervisory authorities.[138]

138 Ibid., pp. 61–62.

The SRM Regulation: general structure and normative content

The SRM Regulation was adopted in July 2014,[139] and builds on the BRRD structure, reflecting the new EU financial supervisory architecture according to which national competent authorities are supervised, directed and even replaced in the exercise of their competence by a central EU agency with extended competence – the SRB.[140]

The uniform rules and procedure for the resolution of FIs falling within the ambit of SRM Regulation shall be applied by the SRB, together with the Council and the Commission according to the rules provided by it, and by the support of the SRF set up by the SRM Regulation. The use of the SRF is clearly stated by the SRM Regulation to be contingent upon the entry into force of agreement among participating Member States on transferring funds to the SRF.[141]

The scope of the SRM Regulation is wide: it encompasses the resolution of all SIFIs established in participating Member States (Euro-area Member States and others wishing to participate, according to the relevant rules of the SSM Regulation), i.e. to all credit institutions established in participating Member States, to parent undertakings established in one of the participating Member States when subject to consolidated supervision, and to investment firms and FIs as defined therein,[142] established in participating Member States when covered by consolidated supervision according to the SSM Regulation.[143]

The SRM Regulation provides a number of general principles for the exercise of competence by the SRB, the Council and the Commission in the context of the SRM.[144] Such general principles inter alia include the prohibition of discrimination on grounds of nationality or place of business,[145] a duty of care for the unity and integrity of the internal market,[146] and an obligation when measures concern groups established in more than one Member State to take into consideration resolution objectives and the impact of measures for the Member State where the group operates, balancing the interests of involved Member States.[147] In addition, decisions or actions of the SRB, the Council or the Commission shall not require Member States to provide extraordinary

139 Regulation (EU) No, 806/2014, OJ L 225/1, 30.07.2014.

140 The normative structure of the SRM Regulation generally reflects its foundation on the BRRD: it is divided in three parts, where Part I includes the general provisions (Articles 1–7), Part II the specific provision of the SRM (Articles 8–41), and Part III the institutional framework (Articles 42–99), wherein are the titles for the SRB and the SRF.

141 Ibid., Article 1.

142 Reference to CRR, Article 4(1). While the SRM Regulation is also applicable under conditions to investment firms, and although its aim is to protect also retail investors, rules on the interconnection between the SRM regime with ICSs appear to be missing, except for certain general references such as this.

143 Ibid., Articles 3 and 4.

144 Ibid., Article 6.

145 Ibid., Article 6(1).

146 Ibid., Article 6(2).

147 Ibid., Article 6(3).

public financial support nor impinge on budgetary sovereignty and fiscal responsibilities of Member States.[148]

The main rule under the SRM Regulation is that the SRB is 'responsible for the effective and consistent functioning of the SRM'.[149]

Subject to a general provision for cooperation with Member State RAs,[150] the SRB is competent for the drawing up of resolution plans and adopting all decisions relating to resolutions for FIs that are not part of a group and for groups which are significant according to the SSM Regulation or in relation to which the ECB has decided to exercise directly its powers under the SSM Regulation, as well as cross-border groups.[151]

In relation to other FIs, Member State RAs may exercise a number of tasks which relate to preparatory actions (resolution planning, resolution assessment, adopting early-intervention measures and others) and exercising writing down and converting capital instruments to restore viability of an FI; however, they may adopt resolution decisions and apply resolution tools only where such action does not require the use of the SRF – if so, the SRB is competent to adopt the resolution scheme.[152]

In the exercise of tasks under the SRM Regulation, Member State RAs are to apply the relevant SRM Regulation provisions, and all references in such applicable provisions to the SRB are to be considered as references to Member State RAs, which for that purpose shall exercise the powers conferred on them under national law transposing the BRRD.[153]

Most important, the SRB may at any time and on its own initiative exercise directly all relevant powers under the SRM Regulation in relation to any FI[154] – thus revoking the exercise of any tasks from Member State RAs *a priori* falling within their competence under the SRM Regulation. Moreover, when performing tasks and exercising such powers *a priori* falling within Member State RAs' competence, the SRB is to be considered to be the Member State RA for the application of both the SRM Regulation and the BRRD.[155]

And furthermore, Member States may assign even the exercise of tasks falling *a priori* within Member State RAs competence to the SRB.[156]

Thus, the SRB is attributed very extensive competence by the SRM Regulation, covering in total the issue of FI resolution, in what appears to have been an effort by EU institutions to render the SRB autonomous and powerful in the application of the SRM, with a view to render the latter effective in managing the crisis

148 Ibid., Article 6(7).
149 Ibid., Article 7(1).
150 Ibid., Article 31.
151 Ibid., Article 7(2).
152 Ibid., Article 7(3).
153 Ibid.
154 Ibid., Article 7(4)b.
155 Ibid., Article 5.
156 Ibid., Article 7(5).

connected to FIs' failure – in our view, beyond and despite any considerations regarding the conferral of powers principle.[157]

Before examining the SRB more closely, it would be useful to broadly review the SRM structure and functions, in the context of FI resolution at the EU level.

The SRM Regulation provides for the competence of the SRB to draw up and adopt resolution plans for SIFIs,[158] after consulting the ECB or national competent authorities and Member State RAs, as relevant, and to conduct assessment of their resolvability, also following relevant consultation.[159]

While the SRM Regulation provisions on resolution planning, including determining the MREL,[160] and assessment of resolvability reflect the relevant provisions of the BRRD *mutatis mutandis*, it also provides for the power of the SRB to take a reasoned decision on resolvability and instruct Member State RAs to require an FI to take measures in order to remove impediments to resolvability, which Member State RAs are bound to implement.[161]

The SRM rules on early intervention,[162] resolution and its objectives and general principles,[163] valuation,[164] general principles of resolution tools,[165] and the various resolution tools,[166] also generally reflect the relevant provisions of the BRRD, *mutatis mutandis* and with the implication of the SRB central position and extensive competence in the normative structure.

In the context of writing-down and conversion of capital instruments under the SRM Regulation, the relevant competence is also exercised by the SRB, but following an assessment by the ECB on the viability of the FI; the SRB will also determine whether writing-down and conversion is to be exercised in combination with a resolution action.[167]

The SRM Regulation further provides in relation to the order of priority of claims, that the SRB, the Commission, or where applicable Member State RAs, shall decide on the exercise of bail-in,[168] and Member State RAs shall exercise such powers in accordance with the reverse order of priority of claims as per national law.[169]

In relation to the resolution procedure, the SRM Regulation provides for the

157 For a critical review of the SSM and the wide discretion attributed to the SRB, in relation in particular to the *Meroni* doctrine, see ALEXANDER, K. (2015) 'European Banking Union: A Legal and Institutional Analysis of the Single Supervisory Mechanism and the Single Resolution Mechanism', (n. 1), pp. 176–87.

158 Ibid., Articles 8 and 7(2).

159 Ibid., Article 10.

160 Ibid., Article 12.

161 Ibid., Article 10(10)–(13).

162 Ibid., Article 13.

163 Ibid., Articles 14–16.

164 Ibid., Article 20.

165 Ibid., Article 22.

166 Ibid., Articles 24–27.

167 SRM Regulation, Article 21.

168 In accordance with SRM Regulation, Article 27.

169 In accordance with BRRD, Articles 47, 48 and 108.

extensive competence of the SRB to adopt a resolution scheme for SIFIs,[170] when it assesses that the FI is failing or likely to fail, having regard to the timing and other circumstances of the situation at hand, and that a resolution action is necessary 'in the public interest', as defined by the SRM Regulation. [171]

In such a case, the SRB shall adopt a resolution scheme placing the FI under resolution and determining the application of resolution tools and the use of the SRF.[172] The resolution scheme adopted by the SRB establishes the details of the resolution tools to be applied to the FI under resolution, to be implemented by Member State RAs in accordance with the BRRD.[173] Member State RAs are then required, under the SRM Regulation, to implement the resolution scheme as per the SRB resolution scheme.[174] The resolution scheme may be updated and amended by the SRB as necessary in the course of the resolution process.[175]

Once such a decision of the SRB to adopt a resolution scheme has been taken, a procedure for its application commences, revealing the orientation of the new EU financial law: the SRM Regulation provides that immediately after the adoption of the resolution scheme, the SRB transmits it to the Commission, which may, within 12 hours from transmission from the SRB, propose to the Council to object to the resolution scheme on the grounds that it does not comply with the public-interest criterion, or to approve or object to a material modification of the amount of funding by the SRF as provided for in the resolution scheme;[176] the Commission has in total 24 hours from the transmission from the SRB either to endorse the resolution scheme or to object to it in relation to discretionary aspects other than those relating to public interest and funding considerations.[177] Upon objection of the Council in relation to funding, the SRB has to modify the resolution scheme accordingly within eight hours.[178] Also, the Commission may prohibit or require amendments to the exclusion of liabilities in the resolution scheme, where it involves contribution by the SRF or alternative sources.[179]

Thus, both the Commission and the Council are competent to raise reasoned objections to the resolution scheme as proposed by the SRB and to influence its final form;[180] however, only the Council has the power to block the decision of the SRB to place an FI in resolution, on the grounds of public interest, in which case the FI shall be wound up according to applicable national law.[181]

170 According to SRM Regulation, Article 2.
171 SRM Regulation, Article 18(1) and (5).
172 Ibid., Article 18(4).
173 Ibid., Article 23.
174 Ibid., Article 18(9). Regarding implementation by Member State RAs of SRB decisions, see ibid., Article 29. Regarding the monitoring by the SRB of the execution of the resolution scheme by Member State RAs, see ibid., Article 28.
175 Ibid., Article 23.
176 Ibid., Article 18(7), first and second subparagraphs.
177 Ibid., Article 18(7), third subparagraph.
178 Ibid., Article 18(7), seventh subparagraph.
179 Ibid. Article 18(7), eighth subparagraph, and Article 27.
180 Ibid., Article 18(7), sixth subparagraph.
181 Ibid., Article 18(8).

Thus, neither the Commission (which would according to its initial SRM Regulation proposal be competent for the placing of FIs under resolution) nor the ESAs, the ECB or Member States may, under the SRM Regulation, cancel a decision by the SRB to place an FI under resolution, while the Council may do so but only for reasons connected to public interest considerations, as these are understood in the context of the SRM Regulation.

Taking into account the very short time limits for the Commission and the Council to respond to the transmission of a resolution scheme by the SRB, the irreversibility of the factual situation emerging from placing an FI under resolution, and the procedural requirements and the duration of proceedings for the judicial review of the decisions of EU institutions and agencies, it emerges that in practice the critical decision of placing an FI under the EU resolution regime or under a national winding-up regime rests ultimately with the Council.

Although it is reasonable that the decision whether or not to place an FI under resolution is both of an urgent and of a sensitive nature, in particular in terms of public interest, it is difficult, in our view, to see how an individual decision, such as placing an FI under resolution or not, may fall under the exclusive competence of the Council, taking into account its status under the Treaties, relating mainly to legislative, budgetary, policy-making and coordinating functions.[182]

In terms of state aid and SRF aid, the SRM Regulation provides rules for the application of EU competition law in the context of the SRM, with relevant decision-making and investigatory powers of the Commission.[183] The adoption of resolution schemes involving the granting of state or SRF aid depends on the issuing of a decision on the compatibility of such with the internal market by the Commission.[184]

The Commission may inter alia decide that the SRB's proposed use of the SRF would be incompatible with the internal market, in which case the SRB has to revise the resolution scheme accordingly,[185] and also request the recovery of SRF aid, if it considers that its decision has been violated and the aid has been misused.[186]

However, even when the Commission considers SRF aid to be incompatible with the internal market, the Council upon application by an Member State, acting unanimously, may decide within seven days of the application that such aid shall be considered compatible, due to exceptional circumstances.[187] This rule reflects the preoccupation of the new EU financial law with the avoidance of any systemic risk connected to an uncontrolled failure of an FI, in which case EU competition law rules may be bent for SRF funding to be available.

The extraordinary powers of the SRB are complemented by its competence to circumvent Member State RAs (not applying its decisions or not complying with

182 See TEU, Article 16.
183 SRM Regulation, Article 19.
184 Ibid., Article 19(1).
185 Ibid., Article 19(3), fifth subparagraph.
186 Ibid., Article 19(5).
187 Ibid., Article 19(10).

them or applying them in a way which poses a threat to resolution objectives or implementation of the resolution scheme) and to directly order a FI under resolution to adopt any necessary action to comply with its decision,[188] the FI being under obligation to comply, and the SRB orders prevailing over any previous Member State RAs decisions.[189]

The SRB is further equipped with an array of investigatory powers under the SRM Regulation, which it may exercise directly or through Member State RAs.[190] Such powers include requests for information from the failing FI, its employees, and third parties to whom the failing FI has outsourced functions or activities, general investigations of any such person established or located in a participating Member State, and on-site inspections at the business premises of such persons. In relation to authorisation for on-site inspections by the SRB, the SRM Regulation provides that the examination of the relevant application by the national judicial authority will be limited to the control of the authenticity of the decision of the SRB and to the control that the coercive measures envisaged are neither arbitrary nor excessive having regard to the subject matter of the inspection; however, the national judicial authority 'shall not review the necessity for the inspection or demand to be provided with the information on the [SRB] file', the ECJ being the only competent forum to review the lawfulness of the SRB decision.[191] In our view, such a prohibition is difficult to reconcile with the procedural autonomy of Member States and national constitutional rules on the independence of national judicatures.

The SRB may impose severe financial penalties to non-complying FIs, which have the rights to a hearing and a defence, and a right of access to the SRB file, but not extending to confidential or internal preparatory documents of the SRB.[192]

It is useful to discuss first the Single Resolution Fund before examining the SRB structure and powers more closely.

The Single Resolution Fund (SRF)

The SRF is established by the SRM Regulation as a fund, without legal personality, belonging to the SRB.[193]

The financing of the SRF is based upon contributions by FIs,[194] i.e. indirectly by financial consumers, and neither the EU budget nor national budgets may be held liable for expenses or losses of the SRF.[195]

188 Ibid., Article 29(2).
189 Ibid., Article 29(3).
190 Ibid., Articles 34–37.
191 Ibid., Article 37(2).
192 Ibid., Articles 38–41.
193 Ibid., Articles 67–79.
194 Ibid., Article 67.
195 Ibid., Article 67(2). The addition of national budgets in this provision was effected during the co-decision procedure by the EP.

In case the funding raised by risk-adjusted *ex ante* contributions[196] by FIs falling within the field of application of the SRM is not adequate to cover SRF needs, then *ex post* contributions may also be raised.[197]

Voluntary borrowing between resolution financing arrangements[198] and alternative funding means are also provided,[199] while access to public financial arrangements is subject to contracting by the SRB.[200]

The target level of SRF funds at the end of a transitional period is at least one per cent of the amount of covered deposits of all credit institutions authorised in all of the participating Member States,[201] so that when fully financed, the SRF will be holding an immense amount of liquidity in the EU.

The mission of the SRF as stated by the SRM Regulation is to ensure the effective application of resolution tools for the purposes of the SRM, including 'to pay compensation to shareholders or creditors if ... they have incurred greater losses [than] they would have incurred ... in a winding up under normal insolvency proceedings';[202] however, the SRF may not be used directly to absorb losses of an FI or to recapitalise it.[203]

Moreover, as stated in the general provisions regarding the SRM, the use of the SRM shall be contingent upon the agreement of participating Member States to transfer to the SRF contributions raised at the national level according to the BRRD; until that time, the SRB shall use the SRF 'in accordance with principles founded on a division of the [SRF] into national compartments corresponding to each participating [Member State]'.[204]

Rules are also provided in relation to the participation of DGSs in the context of resolution; DGSs shall be liable for the amounts payable by them as per the BRRD,[205] to be decided by the SRB following consultation of the competent authority of the DGSD (Recast),[206] and with the limit that the participation of a DGS under the SRM may not exceed the losses it would have incurred in a winding up under normal insolvency proceedings.[207]

While the SRF may not burden the EU or national budgets, the SRB is to invest

196 Ibid., Article 70. The calculation of individual contributions is effected by the SRB following consultation with the ECB or national competent authorities and in cooperation with Member State RAs, and the application of the methodology for the calculation of individual contributions and for allocation of risk factors is effected by the Council by the adoption of delegated acts following a proposal of the Commission; ibid., Article 70(2) and (7).

197 Ibid., Article 71.

198 Ibid., Article 72.

199 Ibid., Article 73.

200 Ibid., Article 74.

201 Ibid., Article 69.

202 Ibid., Article 76(1)(e).

203 Ibid., Article 76(3).

204 Ibid. Article 77. Reference to this contingent use of the SRF is also made in Article (3).

205 Ibid., Article 79(1).

206 Ibid., Article 79(3).

207 Ibid., Article 79(5).

the amounts held by the SRF 'in obligations of the [Member States][208] or intergovernmental organisations, or in highly liquid assets of high credit worthiness',[209] the Commission being empowered to adopt acts on the rules for the administration of the SRF and the general principles and criteria for its investment strategy.[210]

The establishment of the Single Resolution Board (SRB) as a new powerful EU agency

The SRB is established by the SRM Regulation as a new EU agency 'with a specific structure corresponding to its tasks',[211] having legal personality and enjoying the most extensive legal capacity of legal persons under national law,[212] the privileges and immunities of the EU,[213] and being the owner of the SRF.[214]

The SRB is composed of a Chair, four full-time members, and a member appointed by each Member State representing Member State RAs.[215] The Chair and the four full-time members are selected by the Council, acting on qualified majority, on the basis of a shortlist of candidates proposed by the Commission following an open selection procedure and approval by the EP.[216]

The SRB is required to act in compliance with EU law, and 'in particular with the Council and the Commission decisions pursuant to [SRM] Regulation'; [217] moreover, the SRM Regulation specifies that '[t]he Chair, Vice-Chair and the members [selected by the EU institutions] shall perform their tasks in conformity with the decisions of the [SRB], the Council and the Commission'.[218]

At the same time, it is provided that the SRB and the Member State RAs shall act independently and in the general interest,[219] as well as that the SRB members selected by the EU institutions shall act independently and objectively in the interest of the EU as a whole.[220]

208 The initial version of the provision, as proposed by the Commission, referred to 'obligations of participating' Member States. The deletion of the word 'participating' may reflect a decision to invest SRF money in participating and non-participating Member States, as per the SSM Regulation.

209 Ibid., Article 75(3). While the administration of the property of the SRF relates rather to policy and financial considerations than legal, it is not evident how the amounts deposited with the SRF will be readily available or sufficient in case of abrupt distress in the EU financial markets, especially in connection to sovereign debt issues, if such amounts are invested by the SRB in Member States' sovereign debt. In our view, a new form of negative interconnectedness between sovereign debt SRF creditworthiness might emerge in this way.

210 Ibid., Article 75(4).

211 Ibid., Article 42(1).

212 Ibid., Article 42(2).

213 Ibid., Article 80; Protocol No. 7 to the TEU and TFEU.

214 SRM Regulation, Article 67(3).

215 Ibid., Article 43(1).

216 Ibid., Article 56.

217 Ibid., Article 44.

218 Ibid., Article 47(2).

219 Ibid., Article 47(1).

220 Ibid., Article 47(2).

The plenary session of the SRB is competent for decision taking on a closed number of issues provided by the SRM Regulation, such as adopting its annual work programme and its budget, using the SRF (for support required above a threshold of five billion euros), raising *ex post* contributions, and deciding on SRF investments;[221] as a general rule, the SRB in its plenary session decides on a simple majority of its members.[222]

Issues not belonging to the decision taking competence of the plenary session, including those on resolution, fall within the competence of the executive session, which is composed only of the Chair and the four members selected by the EU institutions, and in certain cases also by the member appointed by the Member State affected by a deliberation of the SRB on an FI.[223] As concerns the decision-making rules of the SRB in executive session, when the SRB is deliberating on an individual FI or group, if consensus cannot be reached within the time limit set by the Chair of the SRB, then the relevant decision is taken by simple majority only by the SRB members appointed by EU institutions.[224]

It emerges that in many cases, where resolution action is to be taken by the SRB, the SRB will be deciding in executive session and if members appointed by involved Member States disagree with the members appointed by the EU institutions, the crucial decision will be taken by the latter.

Overall, the concentration of powers by the SRB with direct implications for an individual FI, FI groups, Member States and financial consumers is remarkable, and probably unprecedented in the institutional history of the EU with regard to powers of EU agencies.

With an intention to dynamically intervene in emergent financial situations and avert dangers of bank runs and risk contagion in the EU financial market, the EU and its Member States have opted for granting the SRB a very high degree of power – and responsibility.

This brings into the fore accountability and liability issues.

Accountability, liability and judicial review

The attribution of enhanced competence and powers by EU law to an agency such as the SRB is understood to be aiming at effectiveness in crisis management and protection of financial market stability.

A first emerging issue, at the institutional and political level, is relevant to the political accountability for the operation of the SRM, and in particular for the

221 Ibid., Article 50.

222 Ibid., Article 52; for certain decisions relating to the use of SRF, mutualisation of national financial arrangements, raising of *ex post* contributions, and other relevant matters, an extra criterion of simple or qualified majority representing a specified percentage of contributions is provided; ibid.

223 Ibid., Articles 52 and 53.

224 Ibid., Article 55. The provision does not specify whether it is applicable only in the context of executive session decision-making of the SRB; as it falls under SRM Regulation, Part III, Title III, which refers to the executive session of the SRB, it appears correct according to systematic interpretation.

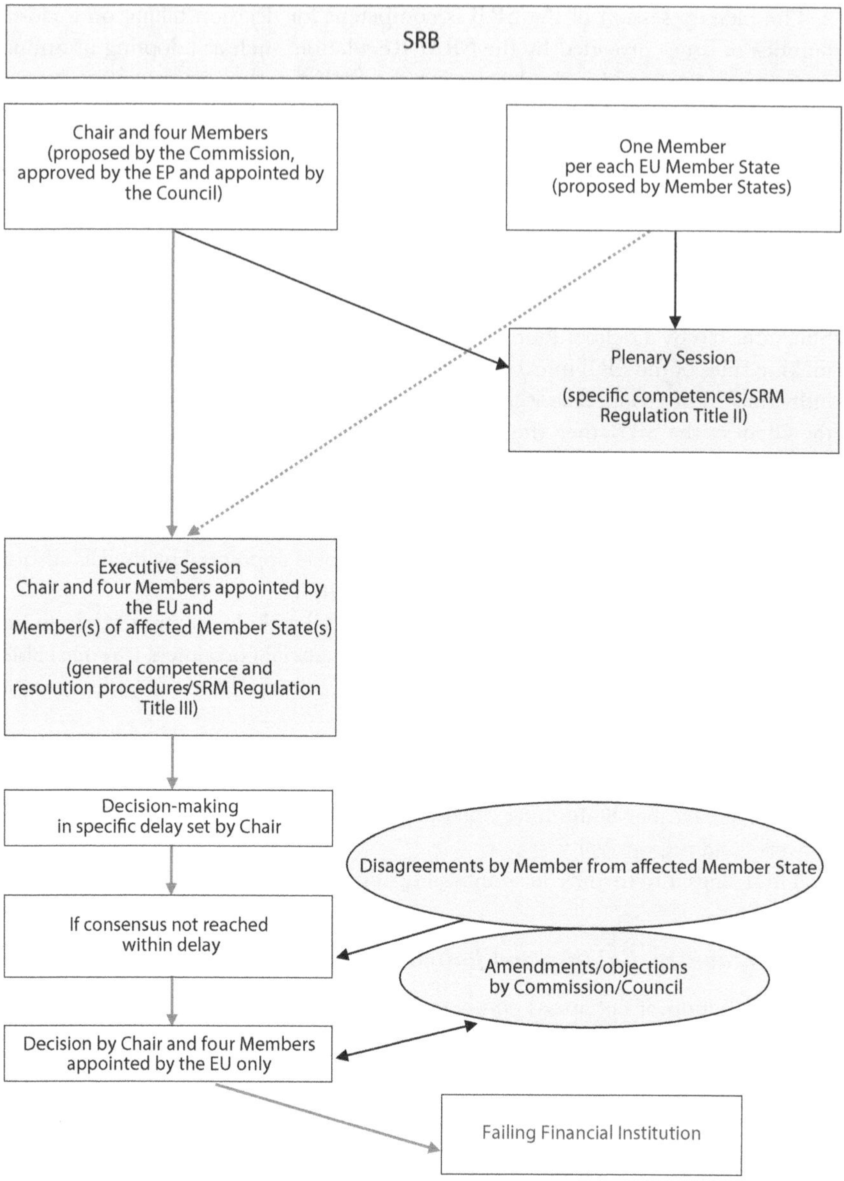

Figure 4 Structure and decision-making of the SRB.

SRB. The extent of powers attributed to the SRB and the degree of discretion allowed to it are difficult to conciliate with the principle of conferral of powers and ultimately with democratic accountability, institutional balance and transparency considerations.

In relation to institutional accountability, the SRB is accountable to the EP, the Council and the Commission for the implementation of the SRM Regulation,[225] while a mechanism of direct parliamentary questions by national parliaments of participating Member States to the SRB is also provided, to which the SRB has to reply directly.[226]

The SRB has to provide an annual report to the EP, national parliaments of participating Member States, the Council, the Commission and the European Court of Auditors; national parliaments may address to the SRB their reasoned opinion on the report.[227]

The introduction of provisions on the direct account given by the SRB to national parliaments, even in the form of information, acknowledges the strong interference and impact of the operation of the SRM in national affairs, in particular, in relation to Member State financial markets and hence to the national economic and social conditions.

However, despite the power of the SRB to autonomously and directly manage the resolution of individual FIs in Member States, which may have an important impact on financial consumers, the relationship of the SRB with financial consumers as established by the SRM Regulation is not bidirectional: at the political level, financial consumers may refer questions to the RSB only through their parliamentary representatives.

Beyond the political level, more options are available to individuals and entities wishing to contest the acts or omissions of the SRB: the SRM Regulation provides for a closed number of SRB decisions against which interested persons, including RAs, having direct and individual concern may appeal before an Appeal Panel established by the SRB.[228]

Such decisions are those relating to the direct instructions by the SRB to FIs for the removal of impediments to resolvability, to the simplified resolution planning, to determining the MREL, to the imposition of fines and relevant procedural safeguards, to the raising of *ex ante* and *ex post* contributions, and to access to SRB documents.[229]

However, filing such an appeal does not have suspensive effects on the SRB decision contested, although the Appeal Board may suspend the application of the decision.[230] If the Appeal Board accepts the appeal, it remits the case to the RSB, which is bound by the decision of the Appeal Board and has to adopt an amended decision.[231]

If the Appeal Board does not accept the appeal, confirming the decision of

225 Ibid., Article 45.
226 Ibid., Article 46(1).
227 Ibid., Articles 45(2) and 46(2).
228 Ibid., Article 85. The provision of a right to appeal before the SRB Appeal Panel was added by the EP during the co-decision procedure.
229 Ibid., Article 85(3) referring to Articles 10(10), 11, 12(1), 38–41, 65(3), 71 and 90(3).
230 Ibid., Article 85(6).
231 Ibid., Article 85(8).

the SRB, interested parties may bring proceedings before the ECJ.[232] The same applies for decisions of the SRB, where no right of appeal before the Appeal Board is provided.[233]

Furthermore, the SRM Regulation expressly provides not only for the SRB's contractual liability,[234] but also for its non-contractual liability.[235] The conditions for such non-contractual liability to attach will be provided by the general principles common to the laws concerning the liability of public authorities of the Member States,[236] and if found liable the SRB will have to make good any damage caused by it (or by its staff) in the performance of its duties.

The SRM Regulation provides specifically that the SRB will compensate Member State RAs for the damages which the latter have been ordered to pay by a national court, as a consequence of an act or omission committed by the Member State RA in the course of resolution under the SRM Regulation.[237]

Indeed, the exercise of very extensive powers on the basis of very wide discretion by the SRB, beyond considerations of a constitutional and institutional order, is certainly connected to non-contractual liability issues for damage caused by the acts and omissions of the SRB in the discharge of its competence. The extent of the powers attributed to the SRB by the SRM Regulation, in particular with regard to its very wide discretion as concerns resolvability assessments, resolution and use of resolution tools (such as the bail-in) and the use of the SRF, are in our view incompatible with the principle of conferral of powers, which may give rise to judicial proceedings.

In this way, a quasi-guarantor function seems to be attributed to the SRB, to cover damages payable by national RAs resulting from the application of its resolution decisions. The competence for the abjudication of such cases, of non-contractual liability of the SRB and of its responsibility to compensate Member State RAs, is attributed by the SRM Regulation directly to the ECJ.[238]

While the lack of immunity from extra-contractual liability of a European agency such as the SRB is in line with European *acquis* on EU institutions liability in tort,[239] it brings to the fore the wider problematic regarding the *locus standi* of individuals and the justicialibity of relevant rights, the conditions for such liability to attach, and the competent forum to abjudicate such actions.

The SRM Regulation provides a clear rule in relation only to the last issue; in relation to conditions for liability to attach, the SRM Regulation provides only for a five-year prescription period.

In the absence of EU law thereto, the ECJ is referred to apply the general principles common to the laws concerning the liability of public authorities of Member

232 Ibid., Article 86.
233 Ibid.
234 Ibid., Article 87(1).
235 Ibid., Article 87(3).
236 Ibid.
237 Ibid., Article 87(4).
238 Ibid., Article 87(5).
239 See Ch. 9.1.

States. The emerging uncertainty is enhanced by the intrinsic complexity of crises in financial markets.

The application of the relevant rules in practice may prove problematic, not least for reasons connected to causality.

However, actions for damages on grounds of non-contractual liability of the SRB may be one of the few remedies available to individuals, including FIs and financial consumers, under the new SRM regime.

Interim concluding remarks

The EU law on financial consumer protection in the event of FI failure has emerged from the GFC bearing an all-new mechanism of centralised EU power, exercised by the DGSD (Recast) and SRM/BRRD system with decision-making authority concentrated at the SRB agency.

Despite the intricate design of the SRM apparatus from a technical point of view, it is difficult to see how the competences attributed to it by the SRM Regulation having as their legal basis TFEU Article 114 may be in conformity with EU constitutional law – and probably with many Member State constitutional orders too.

It is additionally difficult to see how it can be in conformity with the principle of conferral of powers under EU law. Even if relevant grievances were not endorsed by the ECJ in its ruling in the *Short Selling* Regulation case, the case of the SRM Regulation is arguably different, as the range of discretion of the SRB is far wider and the criteria to exercise such discretion pursuant to the SRM Regulation far more vague.

And while the basic form of financial consumer protection in the event of FI failure –the payment of compensation – has not been fundamentally altered by the DGSD (Recast), DGSs have been rendered accessories to the SRM apparatus under the new legislation.

A number of factors, to be decided mainly by Member State or EU authorities on a case-by-case basis, and with wide discretion, has been added as variable parameters of the framework protecting financial consumers in the event of FI failure.

In this context, and while the status of retail depositors approaches that of retail investors at least in functional terms, the old differentiation of the philosophy concerning sensitive information in the banking and investment services sectors appears to be replicated in the new EU law instruments: while financial consumers are to be responsible for their choice to trust an FI, at the same time, information as to its financial status may be considered sensitive for market stability reasons and kept secret by public authorities for an undefined period of time.

In this legal framework, the *ratio* in differentiating the legal status and the protection awarded to retail depositors vis-à-vis retail investors is not evident – and appears all the more difficult to justify and to consider effective; an EU policy to incentivise financial consumers to behave as investors, either in the selection of an FI to trust their assets with, or in the selection of a financial product, necessitates a single coherent legal system of protection based on legal certainty and predictability.

And while the new BRR regime, and in particular the new bail-in mechanism, may at the technical financial level lead to a prevention of a disordered failure of FIs, thus *a priori* alleviating the risk of contagion and systemic risk, yet loss of confindence by the public to the market which is also a source of systemic risk may emerge by a very complicated regulatory structure which operates in unpredictable ways and which is not visible to financial consumers.

Indeed, beyond legal and institutional considerations, there are other parameters of this problematic which transcend such considerations, and which also have to be taken into account in a wider review of the SRM construction.

While the failure of a large FI in one or more Member States may have serious socio-economic, financial and legal consequences, to the extent that these are addressed by national institutions and authorities – or also by national institutions and authorities – public pressure may to an extent be alleviated, if financial consumers affected can identify possible causes and effects, perceive the dimensions of the problem affecting them, and possible ways to address it and to communicate with decision-makers affecting possible outcomes.

The transfer of all critical decision-making powers to an EU agency such as the SRB in the event of FI failure probably constitutes an unprecedented direct connection of decision-making at the EU level with large groups of individuals potentially affected by its decisions. In other words, the application of SRM may bring financial consumers face to face with EU organs, in the event of FI failure – if not literally, at least at the political level.

As individual decisions taken at EU level will have a direct effect on failing FIs and financial consumers, the latter not being able to turn to national authorities – whether administrative or even parliamentary – and with available administrative and judicial remedies of very limited preventive ability, the conditions appear to have been set for public discontent focusing on EU organs – and the EU edifice at large.

9 An EU right of financial consumer protection?

Following the examination of the development and *ratio* of EU financial law, and the mechanism created to provide minimum protection to financial consumers in the event of financial institution (FI) failure, it is necessary to examine in turn whether it is valid to consider that a right of financial consumers to be protected, and to what extent, may be recognised to exist under EU law.

In exploring this issue, we need to take into account the EU law *acquis* in the area of individual protection, as well as the relevant case law of the ECJ which, in addition, will be analysed in relation to the problematic of retail depositor vis-à-vis retail investor protection.

9.1 The *acquis* on individual protection in EU law and competent authorities' liability in tort

The recognition of justiciable individual rights is a precondition for the effective protection of the individual.[1]

In the EU, legal order is closely linked with the impetus provided to European integration by the ECJ, and the central position of individuals in the European legal foundations.[2]

1 For the notion of justiciability and the connection of remedies to rights, see generally FALLON, R. H. (2006) 'The Linkage between Justiciability and Remedies – And their Connection to Substantive Rights', *Virginia Law Review*, vol. 92, p. 633; HARRIS, B. V. (2003) 'Judicial review, Justiciability, and the Prerogative of Mercy', *CLJ*, vol. 62, no. 3, p. 631.

2 For a general account of the role of the ECJ in the evolution of EU law and European integration, see STONE SWEET, A. (2011) 'The European Court of Justice' in CRAIG, P., de BÚRCA, G., *The Evolution of EU Law*, Oxford: OUP, pp. 121–55; ARNULL, A. (2011) 'The Principle of Effective Judicial Protection in EU Law: An Unruly Horse?', *ELRev*, vol. 36, p. 51; WARD, A. (2007) *Judicial Review and the Rights of Private Parties in EU Law*, 2nd edition, Oxford: OUP; ARNULL, A. (1999) *The European Union and its Court of Justice*, Oxford: OUP; DEJOUSSE, R. (1998) *The European Court of Justice*, Macmillan; HARTLEY, T. C. (1998) *The Foundations of European Community Law*, 4th edition, Oxford: OUP; JACOBS, F. (2004) 'The evolution of the European legal order', *CMLRev*, vol. 41, pp. 303–16; LASOK, K. P. E. (1984) *The European Court of Justice: Practice and Procedure*, London: Butterworths; POIARES MADURO, M. (1998) *We the Court*, Oxford: Hart Publishing; TRIDIMAS, T. (1996) *The European Court of Justice and the EU Constitutional Order: Essays in Judicial Protection*, Oxford: Hart Publishing.

The EU legal order has gradually evolved from the initial recognition by the ECJ of the legal status of individuals in this particular legal order, to the recognition of the conditions for rights considered to be conferred by EU law to individuals, and further to the recognition of liability in tort of both Member States and EU institutions for breach of EU law causing damage to individuals, on certain conditions.[3]

According to the well-established case law of the ECJ, state liability for damage caused to individuals because of breach of EU law, and for which public authorities are responsible, is a principle of EU law intrinsic to the system created by the Treaty, which creates obligations of Member States. Therefore, state liability to compensate individuals in case of tort committed in breach of EU rights is based directly upon EU law. According to the case law of the ECJ, there are three conditions for state liability in tort for breach of EU law to attach: (a) that the rule breached confers rights upon individuals, (b) that the breach of the rule is sufficiently serious, (c) that there is direct causation (causal link) between the breach of the rule by the state and the damage suffered by the individual.[4]

Member States may not deny their responsibility for redress in such cases by invoking their internal distribution of competences and responsibilities between authorities existing in the national legal order or by claiming that the national

3 See among many, BEUTLER, B. (2009) 'State liability for breaches of Community law by national courts: is the requirement of a manifest infringement of the applicable law an insurmountable obstacle?', *CMLRev*, vol. 46, pp. 773–804; BECKER, F. (2007) 'Application of Community law by Member States' public authorities: between autonomy and effectiveness', *CMLRev*, vol. 44, pp. 1035–56; DAVIS, R. (2006) 'Liability on damages for a breach of Community law: some reflections on the question of who to sue and the concept of "the State"', *ELR*, vol. 31, no. 1, pp. 69–80; BENTLEM, G. (2005) 'Torts, a European ius commune and the private enforcement of Community law', *CLJ*, vol. 64, no. 1, March, pp. 126–48; BOUVERESSE, A. (2004) 'Responsabilité des Etats membres', *Europe*, vol. 12, p. 393; EILMANSBERGER, T. (2004) 'The relationship between rights and remedies in EC law: in search of the missing link', *CMLRev*, vol. 41, pp. 1199–246; ANAGNOSTARAS, G. (2001) 'The allocation of responsibility in state liability actions for breach of Community law: a modern Gordian knot?', *ELR*, vol. 26, no. 2, pp. 139–58; BAILEY, S. H. and BOWMAN, M. J. (2000) 'Public authority negligence revisited', *CLJ*, vol. 59, no. 1, March, pp. 85–132; CRAIG, P. (1997) 'Once more unto the breach: the Community, the State and damages liability', *LQR*, vol. 113, January, pp. 67–94; TRIDIMAS, T. (2001) 'Liability for breach of Community law: growing up and mellowing down?', *CMLRev*, vol. 38, no. 2, pp. 301–32; TALBERG, J. (2000) 'Supranational influence in EU enforcement: the ECJ and the principle of state liability', *Journal of European Public Policy*, vol. 7, no. 1, March, pp. 104–21; WOODS, L. and SMITH, F. (1997) 'Causation in Francovich: The Neglected Problem', *ICLQ*, vol. 46, no. 4, pp. 925–41; Van GERVEN, W. (2000) 'Of rights, remedies, and procedures', *CMLRev*, vol. 37, p. 501; *idem* (1996) 'Bridging the Unbridgeable: Community and National Tort Laws after Francovich and Brasserie', *ICLQ*, vol. 45, no. 3, pp. 507–44.

4 See, generally, ECJ decision of 19.11.1991 in joined cases C-6/90 and 9/90 *Andrea Francovich and Danila Bonifaci and Others v Italian Republic* [1991] ECR I-5357, para. 35; ECJ decision of 05.03.1996 in Joined Cases C-46/93 and C-48/93, *Brasserie du pêcheur and Factortame*, [1996] ECR I-1029, para. 31; ECJ decision of 26.03.1996 in Case C-392/93, *British Telecommunications* [1996] ECR I-1631, para. 38; ECJ decision of 23.05.1996 in Case C-5/94, *Hedley Lomas* [1996] ECR I-2553, para. 24; ECJ decision of 08.10.1996 in Joined Cases C-178/94 and C-188/94–C-190/94, *Dillenkofer etc.* [1996] ECR I-4845, para. 20; ECJ decision of 02.04.1998 in case C-127/95, *Norbrook Laboratories* [1998] ECR I-1531, para. 106.

authority, which committed the breach of EU law, did not possess the necessary competence, knowledge or means. It is for the Member State to ensure that individuals can achieve redress of the damage caused to them by breach of EU law, irrespective of the public authority that committed the breach and independently of which national authority is *a priori* responsible for redress according to applicable national law.[5]

Furthermore, non-contractual liability of the EU to compensate individuals for damage caused to them in breach of EU law is provided in the TFEU,[6] and has also been the subject of the jurisprudence of the ECJ: the action for damages under the TFEU is autonomous (and not dependent on any prior annulment or other action);[7] moreover, the damaging act (or omission) must be attributable to the EU,[8] and the action for damages has a five-year prescription period.[9]

The substantive criteria for an action in damages are, in line with Member State non-contractual liability for breach of EU law, that: 'the rule of law infringed must be intended to confer rights on individuals; the breach must be sufficiently serious; and there must be a direct causal link between the breach of the obligation resting on the State and the damage sustained by the injured'.[10]

As the ECJ has noted, 'The protection of the rights which individuals derive from Community law cannot vary depending on whether a national authority or a Community authority is responsible for the damage.[11]

Thus, two important factors for the extra-contractual liability of the EU, or EU institutions or agencies with autonomous legal personality are: (a) the conferral of (justiciable) rights by EU law to the individuals incurring damage, and (b) the breach of a legal obligation where there is no discretion or where the limits of discretion have been 'manifestly and gravely disregarded'.[12]

With regard to the new EU financial law that has emerged from the global financial crisis (GFC), very wide discretion and important powers have been attributed to both EU institutions and new agencies, in the context of the new EU financial supervisory architecture and the new BRR regime; however, the issue of conferral by EU law of (justiciable) rights to financial consumers continues to be complicated, and has to be addressed for the purposes of this study.

5 See, e.g. ECJ decision of 09.02.1994 in Case C-319/92, *Salomone Haim v Kassenzahnärztliche Vereinigung Nordrhein* [1994] ECR I-00425, para. 27 *et seq.*; ECJ decision of 01.06.1999 in case C-302/97, *Klaus Könle v Republik Österreich* [1999] ECR I-3099, para. 62.

6 TFEU, Articles 340 and 268. See generally BIONDI, A. and FARLEY, M. (2009) *The Right to Damages in European Law*, The Hague: Kluwer International.

7 See, generally, ECJ decision of 14.12.1962 in Joined Cases 31/61 and 33/62, *Lütticke et al v Commission* [1962] ECR 501.

8 See, generally, ECJ decision of 10.07.1985 in Case 118/83, *CMC Cooperativa muratori e cementisti and Others v Commission* [1985] ECR 2325.

9 See Protocol (No. 3) on the Statute of the Court of Justice of the European Union, annexed to the Treaties, Article 46.

10 See ECJ decision of 04.07.2000 in Case C-352/98P, *Bergaderm et al v Commission* [2000] ECR I-5291, para. 42.

11 Ibid., para. 41.

12 See ibid., paras 43–44.

9.2 Individual protection considerations in the area of financial markets in ECJ case law

Of the abundant case law of the ECJ connected to individual protection, only a few cases relate directly to individual protection in the area of financial markets, in the context examined by this study: the ruling of the ECJ in Case C-233/94, *Germany v European Parliament and Council,*[13] and Case C-222/02, *Peter Paul,*[14] merit particular analysis.[15]

The ECJ decision in case C-233/94, Federal Republic of Germany v European Parliament and Council

The critical issue of European financial law objectives was examined by the ECJ in Case C-233/94, which related to (retail) depositor protection under the DGSD, and is one of the few cases in which the ECJ had the opportunity to rule on some of the fundamental features of EU financial law.[16]

The case concerned an action by Germany against the European legislators for the annulment of the DGSD, on the ground that its legal basis (Article 57(2) of the EC Treaty) was inadequate and also on the ground that the DGSD did not state the reasons on which it was based (as required by Article 190 of the EC Treaty). In the alternative, the application asked for the annulment of the DGSD provisions: (a) on the 'export prohibition' rule (Article 4(1) of the DGSD), and (b) on the obligation of Member States whose DGS exceeded the level or scope of cover provided in another Member State to establish a DGS which branches of banks authorised in such other Member State may join in order to supplement their guarantee (Article 4(2) of the DGSD), and (c) on the obligation of banks to join a DGS (Article 3(1) second sentence of first subparagraph of the DGSD).

The German DGS provided a high level of protection to depositors, having the following essential characteristics at the time of the facts of the case: although banks having their head office in Germany were not obliged by law to be members of a DGS, most banks participated in such a scheme (except for 5 out of 300, while the *ratio* of unprotected to protected deposits amounted to approximately 1 in 1000).[17] The Federal Association of German Banks operated such a scheme, as a self-regulated and voluntary insurance body not under state control. However,

13 ECJ decision of 13.05.1997, Case C-233/94, *Federal Republic of Germany v European Parliament and Council of the European Union* [1997] ECR I-02405, ECLI:EU:C:1997:231.

14 ECJ decision of 12.10.2004 in Case C-222/02, *Peter Paul and Others v Bundesrepublic Deutschland* [2004] ECR I-9425.

15 See also recent judgments of the ECJ in Cases C-127/14 (Ch. 6.1) and C-671/13 (Ch. 6.2), which however are not directly relevant to the issue at hand.

16 See DASSESSE, M. (1998) 'Protection du consommateur: les arrêts Allemagne (garantie des dépôts) et Parodi', *Journal des tribunaux/droit européen*, pp. 9–10; LANDSEER, A. and Van EMPEL, M. (1998) 'The Directive on deposit-guarantee schemes and the directive on investor compensation schemes in view of Case C-233/94', *European Financial Services Law*, pp. 143–48.

17 See Opinion of AG Léger of 10.12.1996 in Case 233/94 (n. 13), points 18–23 and 155.

any bank not belonging to a DGS was under obligation to inform its customers thereof before an account was opened; further, the German supervisory authorities could prohibit a bank from receiving payments if it did not belong to a DGS and if there was danger of insolvency.

Furthermore, the deposit guarantee fund of the Federal Association of German Banks had been authorised by its members to obtain all necessary information from the Federal Supervisory Agency for Credit Institutions and from the Federal Bank of Germany, as well as to have access and examine member bank documents. Moreover, banks had to provide the national supervisory authorities with the verification reports drawn up by the DGSs they belonged to.[18] This system, while voluntary, was characterised as 'particularly effective', since it covered the majority of deposits, providing the highest level of depositor protection in the EC.[19]

As AG Léger noted, the DGSD was the first result of the conciliation process provided by the co-decision procedure of Article 189B of the EC Treaty.[20] Examining the principal claim of the action for annulment, the Advocate General first considered the position of Germany, that Article 57(2) of the EC Treaty could not constitute the sole basis for the DGSD, because the aim of the latter was 'rather to strengthen protection for depositors than to allow the completion of the single banking market',[21] and therefore that the adoption of the Directive could only be achieved on the basis of the unanimity required by Article 235 of the EC Treaty.[22] The European institutions, on the other hand, supported that the main purpose of the DGSD was to strengthen the stability of the banking system and to establish equal competition, 'whereas consumer protection is only an incidental effect, inherent in that purpose'.[23] In this regard, it is interesting to note that not only the Commission and the Council, but also the EP, considered depositor (consumer) protection to be only incidental in the DGSD.

However, as ensues from the long political process that preceded the adoption of the DGSD and from the positions advanced by the EP during this process,[24] the latter considered the introduction of the DGSD as important for depositor protection and acted in this direction.[25]

18 Ibid., points 18–23.
19 Ibid., point 24.
20 Ibid., points 7 and 9.
21 Ibid., point 27.
22 Ibid., point 28.
23 Ibid., point 29.
24 See Ch. 6.1.
25 In this direction, the EP had asked during the co-decision procedure for the limit of compensation to be raised from 15,000 ECU to 20,000 ECU (Decision of the Common Position [1993] OJ C115/91, Amendments Nos 1, 13 and 15), and for modifying initial Article 4(3), which read '[t]his Article shall not preclude the retention or adoption of provisions which offer a high guarantee ceiling' so as to provide that '[t]his Article shall not preclude the retention or adoption of provisions which offer more comprehensive cover for depositors, in particular by extending the categories of investors protected by the guarantee or raising the maximum level of compensation' (ibid., Amendment No. 14). While it appears that the reference to 'investor'

Taking the above into account, it might be argued that while the EP participated in the DGSD process with a view to achieve depositor protection as an aim of greater or equal importance to harmonisation, when the issue of the correct legal basis arose before the ECJ the EP concurred with the Council and the Commission in characterising the DGSD as a banking sector integration and stability measure.

AG Léger, in order to opine on the correct legal basis for the adoption of the DGSD, referred to the constant case law of the ECJ according to which the choice of legal basis for a measure must be based on objective factors which are amenable to judicial review, such as the aim and content of the measure.[26]

Recapping the case law of the ECJ on the correct legal base of a harmonisation measure having a dual objective, the Advocate General distinguished between European measures in which the two aims pursued are 'indissociable', and measures in which one aim must be considered incidental to the other.[27] Considering that the two objectives of the DGSD are, on the one hand, freedom of establishment and freedom to provide services in the banking sector, and, on the other hand, 'the stability of the banking system and protection for savers',[28] AG Léger proceeded in examining whether these aims are equally pursued by the DGSD or whether one is incidental to the other.[29]

AG Léger based this categorisation of the DGSD aims on the wording of the first recital in its Preamble,[30] and moved on to examine which of the two aims prevails[31] – thus treating as resolved the dilemma of whether the two aims are equal or whether one is incidental only to the other. However, the first recital stated that 'the harmonious development of the activities of credit institutions throughout the Community should be promoted through the elimination of all restrictions on the right of establishment and the freedom to provide services, while increasing the stability of the banking system and protection for savers': nothing in this wording appears to be subjecting one aim to the other. AG Léger,

instead of 'depositors' may be a mistake, the extension of the available protection by the national legal order not only in relation to the level of compensation payable but also to the categories of persons covered by it probably demonstrates the effort of the EP to achieve the widest protection possible.

26 Opinion of AG Léger in Case 233/94 (n. 13), point 31, and further references therein.

27 Ibid., points 33–34.

28 Ibid., point 35.

29 However, it is not perhaps indisputable that the two concurrent (equal or not) aims of the DGSD are to be classified in this way, i.e. freedom of establishment and freedom to provide services, on the one hand, and protection of market stability and depositors, on the other. It could perhaps also be argued that the two aims of the DGSD were protection of market stability and creation of a level playing field between banks achievable through harmonisation, on the one hand, and depositor protection, on the other hand (in relation to which, the effectiveness of the DGSD was seriously contested by the German Government in the same case). By grouping together market stability and depositor protection, as a single aim, the Advocate General appears to consider these to be necessarily interconnected; however, that depositor protection may constitute an autonomous aim of legislation, having as a parallel effect the protection of market stability through the creation of confidence in the public.

30 Opinion of AG Léger in Case 233/94 (n. 13), point 36.

31 Ibid., point 37.

noting correctly that both aims are referred to in numerous recitals, considered that a joint legal basis should be necessary.[32]

Proceeding further to examine the content of the DGSD, AG Léger noted the difficulty in establishing a hierarchy between the two aims, as 'the very purpose of a large number of the principles laid down by rules aimed at harmonizing bank deposit-guarantee schemes is to protect depositors'.[33]

Again, it is not clear why a hierarchy between the two aims had to be established, since there appears to be no evident reason not to consider them 'indissociable' or of equal importance.

Recognising that 'at first glance' the two aims of the DGSD may be considered as equal,[34] AG Léger explained why in his opinion the aim of harmonisation should be considered as prevailing.[35] The arguments forwarded by the Advocate General in this direction are interesting.

First, the general objective of establishing an internal market was noted; then, however, AG Léger presented a series of provisions of the DGSD which 'were dictated by considerations extraneous to or even, in fact, in conflict with any concern for consumer protection'.[36] Such provisions are, according to the Advocate General, for example those on the level of guarantee provided by Article 7(1) of the DGSD,[37] on the 'export prohibition' of Article 4(1) second subparagraph of the DGSD,[38] on the rule of Article 4(2) of the DGSD providing for the exclusive competence of the host Member State to organise a guarantee scheme which a branch of a bank may join to supplement the level of protection available to depositors in the home state,[39] and on the rule of Article 8 restricting the level of guarantee available by providing for guarantee per depositor per bank (whatever the number of deposits) and not per depositor per deposit per bank.[40] All of these provisions, according to AG Léger, were relevant to considerations extraneous, if not contrary, to depositor (consumer) protection – in other words, depositor protection was an externality to achieving harmonisation of national establishment and provision of services rules for banks to freely operate on a European level.[41]

However, AG Léger considered that while certain provisions of the DGSD were dictated by considerations extraneous to, or even in conflict with, any concern for consumer protection, yet on the contrary 'every provision in the Directive favourable to depositors can be related to the initial objective of harmonization with a view to completing the internal market',[42] moving on to provide certain examples

32 Ibid., point 37.
33 Ibid., point 38.
34 Ibid., point 38.
35 Ibid., point 39.
36 Ibid., point 41.
37 Ibid., point 42.
38 Ibid., point 43.
39 Ibid., point 44.
40 Ibid., point 45.
41 This position, although supported by important arguments and examples, does not explain the position held by the EP in the process of adopting the DGSD.
42 Opinion of AG Léger in Case 233/94 (n. 13), point 46.

of that.[43] In the opinion of the Advocate General, all articles which were invoked by the applicant to show that the main objective of the DGSD was protection provided rules 'without which no measure of harmonization aiming to establish the internal market could be complete'.[44] In this respect, the provisions of the DGSD referred to as examples of this were those on compulsory introduction of at least one DGS in each Member State (Article 3), on minimum guarantee provided (Article 7, on the obligations of banks to inform (Article 9), and on the setting of a common time-limit for payment of depositors' claims (Article 10. However, in our view, in this selective reference to certain provisions of the DGSD several other, important, provisions appear to have been omitted – such as those on the ability of Member States to retain or adopt provisions offering a higher or more comprehensive cover for deposits (Article 7(3) of the DGSD) or those providing for the right of depositors to take legal action against the national DGS, which do not seem to be indispensable to harmonisation.

Having concluded that the aim of the DGSD was the harmonisation of national rules on bank DGSs, the Advocate General considered that should a second legal basis be necessary for the DGSD to be lawful, it would have to be Article 129a(1)(b) of the EC Treaty and that since the Article 189b of the EC Treaty procedure used to adopt the DGSD was the same as that of Article 129a, the omission of any reference to the latter was a formal defect (since consultation of the EESC required by Article 129a had taken place) so that the DGSD was not null and void.[45] Therefore, AG Léger proposed that the plea of lack of legal basis should be rejected by the ECJ.

Following the proposal to dismiss the claim of lack of correct legal basis, the Opinion of AG Léger examined in turn the other grounds for annulment,[46] which he also proposed to be dismissed.

43 Ibid., points 47–51.
44 Ibid.
45 Ibid., points 52–65.
46 In relation to the plea of not stating the reasons to enact the DGSD, and the relevant issues of exercising competence with respect to the principle of subsidiarity, the Opinion considered that in the area to which the DGSD relates there is clearly exclusive competence of the Community, so there was no need to demonstrate that the principle of subsidiarity was respected; ibid., points 69–90. The pleas relating to the alternative claim of the applicant were equally proposed to be dismissed; ibid., points 91 *et seq.* Especially in relation to the plea of the German Government that the 'export prohibition' rule of the DGSD is incompatible with the objective of a high level of consumer protection laid down by Articles 3(s) and 129a of the EC Treaty, AG Léger referred to the correct, in his view, legal basis of the Directive, considering that since consumer protection was not the main objective of the DGSD and since the new rules of harmonisation introduced by the DGSD 'justify and counterbalance the "export" prohibition … by the lasting improvement in the general level of deposit-guarantee schemes', therefore the 'export prohibition' rule was not incompatible with the objective of a high level of consumer protection as provided by the EC Treaty; ibid., points 108–9. It is submitted, however, that this reasoning appears elliptic: even if depositor protection is not an aim equally pursued by the DGSD with the aim of harmonising national rules on DGSs, it is not clear why the relevant claim regarding depositor protection is to be dismissed without further examination in substance. Cf. the decision of the ECJ in Case 205/84 *Commission v Federal Republic of Germany* [1986] ECR 3755, published at the time the case under examination was brought before the ECJ.

The ECJ followed in general the reasoning of AG Léger, and dismissed the application. Regarding the plea of illegality of the DGSD on the ground that it was adopted on the wrong legal basis, following a presentation of certain relevant arguments of the German Government and of relevant provisions of primary EU law and case law,[47] the ECJ forthwith concluded that '[t]he effect of the machinery established by [the DGSD] is to prevent the [Member States] from invoking depositor protection in order to impede activities of credit institutions authorized in other [Member States]. Accordingly, it is clear that the Directive abolishes obstacles to the right of establishment and the freedom to provide services'.[48]

In relation to the plea of incompatibility with the objective of a high level of consumer protection (Articles 3(s) and 129a of the EC Treaty), the ECJ ruled that the DGSD 'aims to promote the right of establishment and the freedom to provide services in the banking sector … The reduction in the level of protection which may … result in certain cases through the application of the second subparagraph of Article 4(1) of [the DGSD] does not call into question the general result which the Directive seeks to achieve, namely a considerable improvement in the protection of depositors within the Community'.[49] In this wording, the ECJ appears to have supported the assertion that the aim of the DGSD was depositor protection – by means of harmonising national rules on DGSs which may in some cases entail lessening of the level of protection for an interim period, in order for harmonisation to be achieved smoothly (as in the case of the temporary 'export prohibition' of Article 4(1) of the DGSD).

Then, however, it is difficult to see how depositor protection was not an aim of the DGSD or is not an aim equal to achievement of market integration through freedom of establishment and freedom to provide services.

Case C-233/94 is important, in relation to the reasoning both of the ECJ and of the Advocate General, as it led to an examination by the ECJ of the *ratio* and objective of the DGSD.

The political disagreement of Germany to the DGSD was transformed in legal terms into an argument that since the DGSD was a depositor (financial consumer) protection measure, its adoption required unanimity (on the basis of Article 235 of the EC Treaty), in which case the DGSD could not have been adopted given the disagreement of Germany.

The decision of the ECJ may be considered, in our view, as unsatisfactory in terms of reasoning and legal certainty. By dismissing the plea of wrong legal basis, ruling that it is 'clear' that the DGSD abolished obstacles to market integration, the ECJ appears to have avoided entering into an in-depth discussion of the objective of the DGSD in relation to depositor protection, which might have led to a judicial examination of the wider issue of individual protection in the context of European financial law.

47 Case C-233/94 (n. 13), paras 10–18.
48 Ibid., para. 19.
49 Ibid., para. 48.

The ECJ decision in Case C-222/02, Peter Paul

The decision of the ECJ in *Peter Paul* is fundamental in relation to the issue of whether EU law, and in particular the DGSD/DGSD (Recast), confers justiciable rights on individual depositors.[50]

It is then necessary to proceed to a critical analysis of *Peter Paul*,[51] with a view to determine inter alia whether it may also be applicable in the field of investment services, and so to financial consumers in general; and if it may be applicable in the context of the EU financial law as it has been restructured following the GFC.

In *Peter Paul* the ECJ considered a preliminary reference by the German Federal Supreme Court of Justice on questions relevant to the interpretation of EU law on DGSs as well as on credit institutions, insurance undertakings and investment firms, and ruled that if the compensation of depositors prescribed by the DGSD is ensured, the DGSD (as well as the First Banking Directive, the Own Funds Directive and the Second Banking Directive) cannot be interpreted as precluding a national rule to the effect that the functions of the national authority responsible for supervising credit institutions are to be fulfilled only in the public interest, which under national law precludes individuals from claiming compensation for damage resulting from defective supervision on the part of that authority.

Specifically, the questions referred by the German Federal Court of Justice to the ECJ were relevant to the interpretation of Articles 3 and 7 of the DGSD, as well as to a number of provisions of Directives on credit institutions, insurance undertakings and investment firms.[52] The case in the main proceedings before the referring national court concerned three individuals who had opened term deposits accounts and had deposited money with a credit institution in Germany. The deposits took place while the transposition delay for DGSD had not yet lapsed (i.e. before 1 July 1995).[53] The credit institution had been licensed by the national competent authorities but was not a member of a DGS, having unsuccessfully applied for admission to such a scheme. When the licence (authorisation) of the credit institution was revoked, the claimants were not covered by any DGS (owing to the non-participation of the particular credit institution to any such scheme, as

50 See, among others, PISANI, P. (2006), 'Concorso di obligazioni indennitarie, risarcitorie e gestorie nella disciplina del rapporto tra autorità di vigilanza bancaria e risparmiatore depositante', Europa e diritto privato, pp. 865-91; TISON, M. (2005) 'Do not attack the watchdog! Banking supervisor's liability after Peter Paul', *CMLRev*, vol. 42, pp. 639–75; PROCTOR, C. (2005) 'Regulatory liability for bank failures: The Peter Paul case', *Euredia*, p. 73; CARRA, M. (2005) 'La (ir)responsibilità dello Stato per omessa vigilanza bancarisa', *Giornale di diritto amministrativo*, p. 1175; BINDER, J.-H. (2004) 'The Advocate-General's Opinion in Paul and Others v. Germany – Cutting back state liability for regulatory negligence?', *EBLR*, p. 463; BOUVERESSE, A. (2004) 'Responsabilité des Etats membres', *Europe*, vol. 12, p. 393.

51 See n. 14.

52 The Directives that the preliminary reference referred to were the First Banking Directive, the Own Funds Directive, the Second Banking Directive, the Second Consolidated Supervision Directive, CAD, ISD, and Directive 95/26/EC (the Post-BCCI Directive). See also Ch. 4.1.

53 *Peter Paul* (n. 14), para. 13; DGSD, Article 14(1).

well as the non-transposition of the DGSD into the German legal order at the time of the events, the DGSD being transferred in 1998).[54] Thus, they did not receive any compensation for the loss of their deposits. The depositors brought proceedings before the competent German Court of first instance against the German state asking for compensation in respect of the losses of their deposits, arguing that if the DGSD had been transposed in time then '*Bundesaufsichtsamt* [the competent national supervisory authority] would have taken supervisory measures vis-à-vis the ... Bank before the applicants made payments to that bank'.[55]

Thus, the claimants did not seek compensation on the basis of supervisory authorities' liability for breach of a duty to effectively exercise their competence, but on the ground of breach of EC law by reason of non-transposition of the DGSD in time.[56]

Summoned upon an appeal on a point of law, the German Federal Supreme Court of Justice considered that the decisive legal issue in case before it was whether a national rule, such as the German rule which limits liability for breach of official duty by the competent national authorities by imposing on them obligations only in the public interest, is compatible with applicable EC law.[57] It appears that it considered that for such a rule to be incompatible with EC law, the ECJ would have to rule that EC law imposed an obligation on national supervisory authorities to act not only in favour of the public interest, but also in favour of the individuals falling within the ambit of the Directive, i.e. of depositors, linking such an obligation to a right of the depositors 'to have the competent authorities take supervisory measures in their interest ...'[58]

The ECJ reaction to this preliminary reference was to rearticulate the relevant questions posed by the national court.[59]

Having rearticulated the questions, the ECJ ruled that the DGSD does not confer rights on individuals.

It is important for the purposes of this study to discuss this ruling in more detail.

The first preliminary question, as submitted, asked: (a) Whether the provisions of Articles 3 and 7 of the DGSD confer on the individuals the 'right to require that

54 Ibid., paras 11 and 14–15.

55 Ibid., para. 14. It seems that the claimants maintained that in this way they had been denied the opportunity not to deposit their money in the credit institution in the first place and thus not to have to suffer damage as a result of the failure of the institution. This point is not elucidated in the Court decision and, in general, there is some difficulty in understanding how the failure of the German state to transfer the Directive in time relates to the financial damage suffered by the claimants as a result of competent national authorities' misconduct, i.e. as a result of the latters' failure to perform their supervisory duties effectively. The causal link between the breach of law (by the German state and by the competent supervisory authority) and the incurring of damage by the claimants is not evident; however, probably neither the German Courts nor the Court insisted on this point. The latter considered that the questions referred to were not hypothetical but real and necessary for the referring national Court, and proceeded to answer them; see ibid., para. 24.

56 Ibid., paras 14–15 and 18.

57 Ibid., para. 20.

58 Ibid., paras 21 and 22, at 2 and 3.

59 Ibid., para. 24 *et seq.*

the competent authorities avail themselves of the measures mentioned' in Article 3(2)–(5, in addition to the right to be compensated by a DGS,[60] and (b) whether, if such a right is conferred on the individual, it also includes the right to claim compensation for damage resulting from the misconduct of the competent authorities, beyond the amount specified in Article 7(1) of the DGSD.[61]

The ECJ rearticulated the question, considering that 'the Bundesgerichtshof seeks essentially to ascertain whether [the DGSD] ... precludes a national rule to the effect that the functions of the national authority responsible for supervising credit institutions are to be fulfilled only in the public interest, which under national law precludes individuals from claiming compensation for damage resulting from defective supervision on the part of that authority'.[62]

This alteration of the question does not lead to a safe conclusion, in our view, as to whether the Court wished, in this way, to distinguish the notion of exercising supervisory competence not only in the public interest from the notion of the individuals having a right to require the competent supervisory authorities to act in their interest, but also whether the ECJ intended to provide an interpretation of applicable EC law specifically in relation to the issue of exercising supervisory competence only in the public interest.

In order to answer the first question as rearticulated, the ECJ proceeded to examine Articles 6 and 7 of the DGSD, then Article 3(2)–(5), and then Preamble, recital 24. The ECJ found that as long as payment of compensation is ensured by the national DGS(s), Article 3 of the DGSD does not confer on depositors a right to have the competent authorities take supervisory measures in their interest.[63] From this consideration, the ECJ reached the general conclusion that the DGSD does not preclude a national rule to the effect that the functions of the national authority responsible for supervising credit institutions are to be fulfilled only in the public interest.

It may be argued, however, in our opinion, that several long steps appear to have been taken in this line of reasoning by the ECJ; indeed, one statement does not seem to lead necessarily to the next. The ECJ does not explain which is the legal situation in case the compensation of depositors by a DGS is not ensured; furthermore, it does not explain why a depositor who suffered damage while the compensation system provided by the DGSD was not ensured (as e.g. in the case of breach of the obligation to transpose the DGSD in due course, within the applicable time limit) does not have a right under EU law to claim compensation – not from national supervisory authorities but from the Member State, as in the case at hand.

In order to support its reasoning, the ECJ referred specifically to Preamble, recital 24 of the DGSD;[64] however, the ECJ does not seem to have taken into

60 *Peter Paul* (n. 14), para. 23.
61 Ibid., para. 22, at 1.
62 Ibid., para. 25.
63 Ibid., paras 29 and 30.
64 Ibid., para. 31.

account all other recitals, of the DGSD and the other Directives mentioned in the questions of the referring national court, and did not make particular references to its case law on individual protection in case of breach of EU law.

The second question referred to the ECJ by the German Federal Supreme Court related to the issue of the *ratio*, scope and aim of EC law in relation to individual protection in the fields of banking, finance and insurance law. More specifically, question 2 sub-question (a) referred to the relevant Directives with a view to discover whether they 'confer on the saver and investor rights to the effect that the competent authorities of the [Member States] must take prudential supervisory measures, with which they are charged by those directives, in the interests of that category of persons and must incur liability for any misconduct' or whether '[the DGSD] contain[s] an exhaustive set of special provisions for all cases of unavailability of deposits'.[65]

Thus, it seems that there is a difference between the scope and content of this question and of the first question referred by the national court: the first question asked whether applicable EC law confers on depositors a 'right to require that the competent authorities avail themselves of the measures mentioned' in the law, whereas part (a) of the second question asked whether EC law confers on depositors and investors 'rights' which the competent national authorities are liable to protect. This sub-question was evidently wider in scope than the first, as it considered not only the case of depositors, but also the case of investors as individuals falling within the general ambit of EC law in the field of banking and finance. Moreover, in part (b) of its second question, the *Bundesgerichtshof* sought to find whether certain recitals of the second Consolidated Supervision Directive, CAD and ISD 'provide assistance with interpretation for the purpose of answering the [question], regardless of whether they otherwise contain law applicable in the present case'.[66]

In this sense, it appears that the national court was implying the existence of a common *ratio*, at least to some extent, in the EU law in relation to (retail) investor protection; indeed, the referring court appears to have argued that although the various Directives to which it referred in its second question 'do not contain any express reference to the protection of depositors',[67] yet they form part of an overall scheme of banking supervision rules which 'would be denied practical effectiveness if the national supervisory authority were to exercise its functions only in the public interest …'[68]

Despite the importance of the *effet utile* criterion as underlined by the national court, its position that banking Directives do not contain any express reference to the protection of depositors was not accurate in our view; in fact, taking into account only the provisions to which it explicitly referred in its question 2(a), several references are made to depositor protection *expressis verbis*.[69] Furthermore,

65 Ibid., para. 23, at 2.

66 *Peter Paul* (n.14), para. 23, at 2(b).

67 Ibid., para. 22.

68 Ibid.

69 Specifically, in the First Banking Directive: Preamble, recitals 4 and 12; Article 6(1); in the Second Banking Directive: Preamble, recital 11; Article 3. In Own Funds Directive no explicit reference

express reference to the protection of depositors and/or investors is made several times in the recitals to which the *Bundesgerichtshof* referred in part (b) of its second question.[70]

The ECJ did not provide any answer to this general second question of the national court, in relation to issues or provisions not directly related to banking Directives; nor did the ECJ explain the reasons for its silence on this matter. In fact, the only reference the ECJ made in general to part (b) of the second question, which referred to depositors' and investors' protection, was that '[i]n a number of the recitals in the preambles to the directives referred to in the second question, parts (a) and (b), it is stated in a general manner that one of the objectives of the planned harmonisation is to protect depositors'.[71] It is not clear, in our view, what is signified by the reference of the ECJ to the 'general manner' of the statement of the objective to protect depositors in the recitals it referred to.[72] It is possible that the ECJ indirectly referred to the case law, according to which the interpretation of a Directive may not be conducted only by reference to its recitals.[73] The position of AG Stix-Hackl on the issue seems to be in the same direction.[74]

Thus, although the recitals in these Directives refer not only to the objective of protecting depositors, but also to that of protecting investors, the ECJ narrowed the focus of its reasoning to the issue of depositor protection, tacitly excluding all analysis on investor protection and its interrelation to depositor protection.

In responding thus only to second question, part (a), and by referring to the 'general manner' of the statement of the objective of depositor protection in the Preamble of cited Directives and to the various supervisory obligations imposed by the same Directives upon the national competent authorities in relation to credit institutions,[75] the ECJ ruled that:

> [i]t does not necessarily follow either from the existence of such obligations or from the fact that the objectives pursued by those directives also include

to depositor protection is made in Articles 2–7 to which the German court referred; however, reference is made in Preamble, recital 1, which was omitted in the question referred. In Post-BCCI Directive: Preamble, recitals 11 and 15.

70 Specifically: in the Second Consolidated Supervision Directive, Preamble, recital 11. It is not clear why the German Federal Court did not place this reference in the context of part (a) of its second question. In CAD: Preamble, recital 8. In ISD: Preamble, recitals 2, 5, 29, 32, 41 and 42. It is not clear, however, why the national court referred only to recitals in the Preamble of ISD and not also to articles of the same Directive, which explicitly refer to investor protection, or which are closely connected to it. Indeed, numerous provisions of ISD explicitly referred to investor protection: Article 1(2); Article 10; Article 11(3); Article 12; Article 14(4); Article 17(3); Article 19(8), (9); Article 21(1)–(3).

71 *Peter Paul* (n. 14), para. 38.

72 Ibid.

73 See ECJ decision of 13.11.1990 in Case C-106/89, *Marleasing SA v La Comercial Internacional de Alimentación SA* [1990] ECR I-4135.

74 See Opinion of AG Stix-Hackl in *Peter Paul* (n. 14), points 135 and 136.

75 *Peter Paul* (n. 14), para. 39.

> the protection of depositors that those directives seek to confer rights on depositors in the event that their deposits are unavailable as a result of defective supervision on the part of the competent national authorities.[76]

Explaining this conclusion, the ECJ noted that 'it should first be observed that Directives 77/780, 89/299 and 89/646 do not contain any express rule granting such rights to depositors'.[77] The ECJ further referred to essential harmonisation and mutual recognition considerations,[78] also referring to Preamble, recitals 1 and 4 of the Second Banking Directive, and considering the conclusion to be drawn from these as 'clear'.[79] It also considered the necessity to coordinate national rules on liability in the event of defective supervision,[80] noting that 'it is not possible in a number of [Member States] for the national authorities responsible for supervising credit institutions to be liable in respect of individuals in the event of defective supervision'.[81]

Thus, it might be argued that instead of considering whether a national rule precluding claims of individuals for compensation by competent authorities is compatible with EU law, the ECJ stated the existing legal situation in certain Member States, which exactly precluded such claims.[82]

The above reasoning of the ECJ led to the negative answering of the third question of the preliminary reference, which was relevant to state liability issues for breach of EU law in the context of the case at hand, and particularly in the event of defective supervision on the part of the competent national authorities.[83]

Thus, the ECJ, in providing its ruling and in explaining its *ratio decidendi*, appears to have meticulously avoided making any reference to the field of investment services, despite the relevant direct and precise questions asked by the referring national court.

The issue that inevitably arises is whether this omission is an implicit way for the ECJ to state that the two relevant fields of law, i.e. EU banking and EU investment services law, have to be treated as distinct in relation to their *ratio*, scope and aim, at least in relation to the existence and nature of rights of (retail) depositors and (retail) investors, as *a priori* protected by EU law.

In this regard, it appears in our view that the examination of *Peter Paul* in its own merit, as well as taking into account the problematic of the interrelation of depositor and investor protection regime as provided by the relevant Directives, does not lead to any safe conclusions as to whether the *ratio decidendi* of the ECJ in *Peter Paul* may be extended to investment services in the context of EU law until

76 Ibid., para. 40.
77 Ibid., para. 41.
78 Ibid., para. 42; cf. ibid., paras 35 and 45.
79 Ibid., paras 36 and 37, respectively.
80 Ibid., para. 43.
81 Ibid., para. 44.
82 Regarding the banking supervisory liability regimes in the EC, see TISON (n. 50), pp. 646 *et seq.*
83 *Peter Paul* (n. 14), paras 23, 48 *et seq.*

the GFC;[84] indeed, arguments may be presented both in favour and against such an approach.

If it is considered that the *ratio* and aim of EU banking law and EU investment services law, in relation to individual (depositor or retail investor) protection, is the same or similar, then *Peter Paul* may be applicable in investment services.

If, on the other hand, it is considered that the *ratio* and aim of EU banking law in relation to individual (depositor) protection differs significantly from the respective *ratio* and aim of EU investment services law in relation to individual (retail investor) protection, according to the intrinsic characteristics of each sector especially in connection to risk, then *Peter Paul* should not be extended to apply in investment services.

While this dilemma may be more difficult to resolve in the context of EU law as in force pre-crisis, the evolution of EU finance law since the GFC may offer a solution to this ambiguity (at least *de lege ferenda*).

As discussed, the fundamental changes in EU financial law, both at the level of financial supervisory architecture and normative content, the creation of new central EU financial market authorities with important powers to regulate directly the market and FIs and to take individual decisions, with very wide discretionary powers, as in particular in the case of the SRB, cannot easily be reconciled with a regime of total immunity of EU authorities from non-contractual liability.[85]

The same would appear reasonable – and necessary – to apply, in our view, to the issue of non-contractual liability of Member State institutions and agencies applying the new EU financial law, as in particular the RAs.

Thus, the effectiveness of the new EU financial law, which is closely connected to the protection of confidence in the financial market system, has to be examined, in our view, in conjunction with effective protection of individuals: beyond the problematic on the differentiation of depositors vis-à-vis retail investors, it would be very difficult, in our opinion, to support the application of *Peter Paul* in the context of the new EU financial law.

While the ECJ ruling in *Peter Paul* did not take such considerations into account, it suffices, in our view, to consider that this ruling referred only to the EU financial law regime before the GFC, so that it may be considered as applicable to the new and emerging EU financial law regime. Certainly, a preliminary reference on such issues by a national court of law would prove useful.

Such an opportunity arose before the GFC in the UK *Three Rivers* case, and after the GFC in the EFTA Case E-16/11 which should also be briefly examined, as indicative cases in other jurisdictions applying EU law, and since *ad hoc* ECJ case law on the subject matter under examination is scarce.

84 For some considerations on the applicability of *Paul* in the context of public offering of securities as regulated by EU law, see TISON (n. 50), p. 674.

85 In this new context, even if competence is to be exercised in the public interest (but not 'only' in the public interest), this does not appear adequate to *a priori* preclude tortuous liability where the competent authorities have the authority and powers to regulate and supervise financial markets and FIs.

9.3 Individual protection considerations in the area of financial markets in the case law of other jurisdictions applying EU law

The Three Rivers *case in the UK*

In the *Three Rivers* case,[86] the House of Lords (UK) considered the question of whether EU law may be interpreted as conferring rights on individual depositors.

The Bank of Commerce and Credit International (BCCI) had been established in 1972. The activities of the BCCI group of companies raised the suspicions of supervisors. A report produced in 1991 by the auditors appointed by the Bank of England, in order to protect depositors' interests, revealed that BCCI was connected to international financial crime, including money laundering, and was involved in fraudulent activities.

Following evaluation of the report, the competent authorities terminated the operation of BCCI in 1991, affecting a large number of depositors. In the UK, an 'Inquiry into the Supervision of the Bank of Credit and Commerce International' was issued on 22 October 1992 chaired by Bingham LJ,[87] giving rise to claims on

86 *Three Rivers District Council v Governor and Company of the Bank of England* [2000] 2 WLR 1220 (HL), and [2000] 3 All ER 1; *Three Rivers District Council v Governor and Company of the Bank of England* [2001] UKHL 16 (HL) and [2001] 2 All ER 513; see also GRAY, J. (2008) 'Lessons from BCCI Saga for the Current Accountability Debate Surrounding Northern Rock', *JIBLR*, p.37; *idem* (2006) 'Court Castigates BCCI Liquidators' Claim against Bank of England, Legal and Regulatory Commentary', *JFRC*, vol. 4, p. 411; WALKER, G. A. (2006) *European Banking Law – Policy and Programme Construction: 6 (Sir Joseph Gold Memorial)* (see Ch. 1 n. 1), pp. 205 *et seq.*, and further references therein; FAIRGRIEVE, D. (2003) *State Liability in Tort – A Comparative Law Study*, Oxford: OUP; ANDENAS, M. (2000) 'Liability for Supervisors and Depositors' Rights – the BCCI and the Bank of England in the House of Lords', *Euredia*, p. 407. Although relevant English law issues arising fall out of the scope of this study, this case is significant as the House of Lords proceeded to carry out an extensive analysis and interpretation of applicable European law, and in particular of the First Banking Directive, with a view to determine whether breach of rights conferred to depositors by European legislation had occurred by the alleged omission of the Bank of England to effectively supervise and withdraw in time the authorisation of the BCCI bank.

87 Available at www.official-documents.gov.uk/document/hc9293/hc01/0198/0198.pdf. Bingham LJ noted inter alia that '[t]he problem of fraud is one to which explicit reference has not been made in the Basle Concordats of 1975 and 1983, or in the Community Directives, or in the Banking Act 1979'; ibid., para. 1.45, p. 17. Having investigated the facts of the case, LJ Bingham concluded in relation to the supervision as conducted by the Bank of England (at the time of the facts competent for the supervision of banks) inter alia that '[p]rime responsibility of course rests with those who devised, directed and implemented the frauds which were practiced. Whether the frauds could and should have been discovered by the auditors earlier is an issue I have not been asked to investigate. The history, however, makes clear that fraudulent management were able to exploit the structure of the group to facilitate and disguise the frauds. This might have been in part prevented, or brought to a head, much earlier, had strong and resolute action been taken to insist on structural change as a condition of continued authorisation and to impose on the group the supervisory regime it was known to require … The Bank did not pursue the truth about BCCI with the rigour which BCCI's market reputation justified. In later stages the Bank came to rely to an excessive extent, in my opinion, on the auditors: under the British system of supervision the auditors have a crucial role to play but the duty to supervise is placed on the Bank and it is a

the ground of liability in tort of the Bank of England[88] to compensate the claimant depositors who incurred financial damage due to the illegal activities of BCCI which led to its forced closure.[89]

In order to decide on the case, the House of Lords took into account the relevant European law, and specifically the issue of whether EC banking law Directives conferred rights on individual depositors, concluding that no such rights were conferred on individuals (so that the first condition of the *Francovich* case law was not met according to the House of Lords).

Lord Hope considered, taking into account the legislative background and the terms of the First Banking Directive, as well as the case law of the ECJ, that the First Banking Directive was an instrument of harmonisation (having to achieve both objectives, of protecting deposits and of creating conditions of equal competition between banks operating in more than one states) which did not necessitate the conferral of rights by the Directive to individual depositors; no provisions of the Directive conferring rights to individuals were thus identified by Lord Hope.

It is interesting to note, that while the House of Lords as supreme national court of justice at the time of the case was under the obligation to refer preliminary questions on the interpretation of European law to the ECJ (under the terms provided by Article 234 of the TFEU, then Article 177 of the EC Treaty), it was considered that no such reference was necessary since the issue was clear and as unanimity was reached by the House of Lords.[90]

Relevant to the problematic under examination is also the EFTA Court decision of 2013 in Case E-16/11, *EFTA Supervisory Authority v Iceland*, which distinguished *Peter Paul* from relevant cases on financial consumer protection and state liability issues and which also has to be taken into account.

The EFTA Court decision in Case E-16/11, EFTA Supervisory Authority v Iceland

While *Peter Paul* referred to the EU financial law regime as developed before the GFC, the reasoning of the ECJ in *Peter Paul* was taken into account in a recent case brought before the EFTA Court, relating to the interpretation of the DGSD in the

duty which cannot be delegated. It is the Bank, not the auditor, which is the supervisor. In these respects, the Bank's supervisory approach to BCCI was in my opinion deficient. How different the course of events would have been had these deficiencies not existed, one can only speculate'; ibid., para. 2.484, pp. 149–50). The Inquiry included a number of important recommendations; ibid., Chapter 3, pp. 181 *et seq.*

88 For the Bank of England as a competent authority, see HADJIEMANNUIL, C. (1996) *Banking Regulation and the Bank of England*, London/New York/Hong Kong: LLP.

89 The action against the Bank of England was based on the tort of misfeasance in public office, under English law. Cf. applicable at the time Banking Act 1987 (UK), section 1. See also ANDENAS, M. and FAIRGRIEVE, D. (2002) 'Misfeasance in Public Office, Government Liability and European Influences', *ICLQ*, vol. 51, p. 757.

90 The competent Court of Appeals had not considered the issue as *acte claire* but had also refrained from proceeding to a preliminary reference to the ECJ.

context of the European Economic Area (EEA) Agreement, following the collapse of the Icelandic banking sector during the GFC.

In Case E-16/11, *EFTA Surveillance Authority v Iceland*,[91] the EFTA Court was asked to declare that by failure to ensure payment of the minimum amount of compensation to *Icesave* (a branch of *Landsbanki Íslands hf*, a credit institution established in Iceland) in the Netherlands and the UK, within the relevant time limits, Iceland had failed to comply with its obligations resulting from the Agreement on the EEA relating to the transposition of the DGSD.[92]

Taking into account the Preamble to the DGSD,[93] as well as the provisions of the DGSD,[94] as well as the relevant national Icelandic legislation,[95] the EFTA Court considered three pleas of the applicant EFTA Surveillance Authority, the first being that Iceland was under an 'obligation of result' to ensure that a DGS is set up capable of guaranteeing that in the event of deposits being unavailable the aggregate deposits of each depositors are covered in all circumstances to the amount provided by Article 7(1) of the DGSD, and to ensure that duly verified claims by depositors are paid within the time limit laid down by Article 10 of the DGSD.[96]

In particular, the applicant contented that Iceland had not fulfilled its obligations simply by transposing the DGSD into national law, and setting up and recognising a DGS without any regard as to whether the compensation of depositors was in fact ensured on the conditions prescribed by the DGSD.[97]

In this regard, the EFTA Surveillance Authority argued that it follows from *Peter Paul* 'that the ECJ considers Articles 7 and 10 of [the DGSD] to require a clear and precise result to be achieved'.[98]

The Commission, intervening in support of the ESA, concurred that the DGSD imposed said obligation of result[99] to ensure capability of the DGS to repay covered deposits, noting that any other interpretation would render the provision ineffective to ensure the objective of the DGSD,[100] and agreed on the interpretation of *Peter Paul* by the EFTA Surveillance Authority.[101]

Moreover, the Commission noted that state liability vis-à-vis individual depositors would have to be established by national courts.[102]

91 EFTA Court decision of 28.01.2013 in Case E-16/11, *EFTA Surveillance Authority v Iceland* [2013]. EFTA Court Reports 7. See also BABIS, V. (2013) 'Bank Failures, State Liability, and Protection of Depositors in Foreign Branches: EFTA Surveillance Authority v. Iceland', *University of Cambridge Faculty of Law Research Paper*, vol. 5, http://ssrn.com/abstract=2216847.
92 EEA Agreement, Annex IX, point 19a.
93 And in particular recitals 1, 2, 3, 4, 7, 16, 23, 24 and 25 thereof.
94 And in particular Articles 1, 3, 4, 7, 8, 9 and 10 thereof.
95 I.e. Act No. 98/1999 (of the Republic of Iceland) on a Deposit Guarantee and Investor Compensation Scheme.
96 EFTA Court decision, Case E-16/11, paras 75–76.
97 Ibid., para. 77.
98 Ibid., para. 78. The ESA referred specifically to *Peter Paul* (n. 14), paras 26, 27 and 30.
99 Ibid., paras 86–87.
100 Ibid., para. 88.
101 Ibid., para. 89.
102 Ibid., para. 95.

On the contrary, Iceland submitted that the DGSD imposed no obligation of result on an (EEA) state to use its own resources in order to guarantee the pay-out of a DGS,[103] and that the DGSD placed an obligation upon the state 'to set up and supervise a deposit-guarantee scheme, but there is no suggestion whatsoever that it must pay compensation'.[104]

In particular, Iceland emphasised that '[t]he sole purpose of recital 24 in the preamble to [the DGSD] is to exclude State liability if the compensation of depositors is ensured'.[105]

Among other intervening parties, Lichtenstein argued that the DGSD was not intended to deal with the collapse of an entire banking system (as in the case of Iceland),[106] while the UK argued that the DGSD imposed an obligation on EEA states to ensure payment of prescribed compensation to eligible investors within the applicable time limit.[107]

The EFTA Court noted that 'there is a general obligation on the EEA States to ensure that the provisions of a directive are fully effective',[108] further referring to the various degrees of detail in the rules provided by various directives.[109]

Considering the question that state liability is not within the scope of the proceedings before it,[110] the EFTA Court proceeded to interpret the DGSD. In this context, noting the duality of the aims pursued by the DGSD,[111] the EFTA Court considered that the obligation of an EFTA state under the EEA is to ensure that within its territory one or more DGSs are introduced and officially recognised,[112] and that the depositor's right to compensation may be subject of an action by the depositor against the DGS,[113] and therefore that the DGSD does not lay down an obligation on an EFTA state and its authorities to ensure compensation if a DGS is unable to cope with its obligations in the event of a systemic crisis.[114]

Furthermore, the EFTA Court considered that the alleged obligation of result cannot be derived from *Peter Paul*[115] without providing, in our view, any reasoning as to this conclusion (except that the case it examined should be distinguished from *Peter Paul* on the facts, which is not satisfactory reasoning in our opinion).[116]

Thus, the first plea of the EFTA Surveillance Authority was dismissed by the EFTA Court.

103 Ibid., para. 96.
104 Ibid., para. 97.
105 Ibid., para. 100.
106 Ibid., para. 110.
107 Ibid., para. 114.
108 Ibid., para. 120.
109 Ibid., para. 121.
110 Ibid., para. 123.
111 Ibid., para. 125, referring also to the Opinion of AG Léger in Case C-233/94 (n. 13), para. 19.
112 Ibid., paras 126–130.
113 Ibid., paras 131–143.
114 Ibid., paras 144 and 178.
115 Ibid., para. 145.
116 Ibid.

The other pleas were also dismissed.[117]

While the ruling of the EFTA Court does not constitute a binding interpretation of the DGSD for EU Member States, Case E-16/11 is important in relation to the issues that were treated by the Court and the parties, including the European Commission, which took a clear position that the ECJ in *Peter Paul* acknowledged an obligation of result to be imposed on the Member States.

While in our opinion the EFTA Court provided a very narrow interpretation of the DGSD for the purposes of the EEA, its judgment took into account various aspects of the relevant problematic, especially when examined in the context of a systemic banking crisis, in which, as it noted, a severe financial crisis may turn into sovereign default if DGSs are underwritten by states.

In this regard, stating that '[h]ow to proceed in a case where the guarantee scheme is unable to cope with its payment obligations remains largely unanswered by [the DGSD]',[118] the EFTA Court unavoidably applied EU law as in force before the GFC.

In that respect, as with the ECJ ruling in *Peter Paul*, the reasoning of the EFTA Court in Case E-16/11 is in our view ultimately not relevant and not applicable in the context of the new EU financial law which has emerged from the GFC.

Interim concluding remarks

Beyond the payment of minimum *ex lege* compensation to financial consumers in the event of FI failure, EU law has proven to be – at least until the GFC – tacit if not hesitant to recognise the application of the *acquis* of EU law on individual protection in this area of the European legal order.

While an interpretative approach that EU law does not confer rights upon individual financial consumers may be relevant to EU law until the GFC, the same would not appear valid with regard to the new EU financial law that emerged from the GFC; the fundamental reform of EU financial law rather leads to the opposite conclusion.

Thus, and despite the uncertainties caused by the BRRD/SRM and DGSD (Recast)/ICSD regime regarding the legal status of retail depositors vis-à-vis retail investors, in our opinion the new EU financial law has to be interpreted as conferring rights upon individual financial consumers and allowing for non-contractual liability of EU and Member State authorities, in distinguishing the new EU law from EU law as in force and as interpreted at the time of the *Peter Paul* ruling.

However, this would solve only one of the two main problems in this area, the issue of causality remaining to a large extent unresolved.

While it will be for upcoming EU case law to address these issues, perhaps re-examining the corpus of EU case law in the area of financial consumer protection under the light of new legal developments, a possible solution might be reached through the recognition of some kind of strict liability in the area of financial consumer law, as in the past in other sensitive areas of the EU edifice.

117 The other two pleas related to discrimination contrary to the DGSD and to EEA, Article 4; ibid., paras 186–227.

118 Ibid., para. 160.

10 Conclusions

This study attempted to examine how effective is the protection awarded by EU law to retail depositors and retail investors, in the event of financial institution (FI) failure.

In approaching the complicated legal issues which form the parameters of this question, the *ratio* of EU financial law was first examined.

In this context, the work of international financial organisations and *fora* has gained important influence in the development of EU policies and law.

While prior to the global financial crisis (GFC) a sector-based regulation of financial markets and FIs was perceived as reflecting the enhanced systemic risk intrinsic to the banking sector in particular, the development of highly interconnected global financial markets and financial conglomerates proved in the context of the GFC that any sector of the market may be a source of systemic risk; at the same time, it proved that a financial market crisis may lead to a sovereign debt crisis, and vice versa, so that mechanisms to disconnect banks from sovereigns were sought in the wake of the GFC.

Thus, a reassessment of the *ratio* and *modus operandi* of financial law has emerged from the GFC.

At the same time, regarding the question of the double aim of financial law, it appears that under the new EU law resulting from the GFC, a hierarchy has been established, according to which financial consumer protection in case of FI failure is placed below financial market stability considerations.

The new EU financial law is characterised by the centralisation of authority and the concentration of power at the EU level, with the attribution of extensive powers and discretion to newly established EU agencies, together with EU institutions, to both regulate and supervise financial markets and FIs – if need be, even by circumventing MS authorities and issuing individual decisions which directly control distressed FIs and affect financial markets and financial consumers.

In this new context, financial consumers may be deprived of critical information by competent EU and national authorities as to the financial condition of a distressed FI, so as to avoid further worsening of its condition, and then may be called upon to contribute to its rescue, according to a burden-sharing approach rendering them responsible for their choice of the FI to trust their money with.

This central contradiction in the new bail-in regime may be addressed if it is accepted that the status of retail depositors approaches that of retail investors in the event of FI failure, in the context of the new EU financial law, and the two categories of financial consumers are treated in the same way, in case of FI failure.

Indeed, in the context of FI failure, the disparities of EU law in the protection of retail depositors *vis-à-vis* retail investors appear difficult to justify and reduce both the effectiveness of financial consumer protection and the stability of financial markets, as they cause new sources of legal uncertainty and unpredictability and allow for regulatory arbitrage.

A unified approach to effective protection of retail depositors and retail investors in the event of FI failure would comprise simple, specific and predictable rules as to the payment of a predetermined amount of compensation by the relevant fund to affected financial consumers, irrespective of their classification as retail depositors or retail investors and irrespective of the classification of their financial contracts as deposits, financial instruments, hybrid financial instruments or something else.

Furthermore, it would involve clear rules allowing individual financial consumers to claim damages against responsible EU or MS competent authorities, in case of non-contractual liability.

Thus, the new EU financial law, and in particular the new resolution regime and the bail-in mechanisms, may at the technical financial level achieve protection of public funds and avoidance or control of systemic risk, by the prevention of disordered failures of FIs.

The new EU financial law must also avert the emergence of systemic risk which may be caused by a wavering of the public confidence in the financial markets, if individual financial consumers are not effectively protected – because trust in the financial market is always built at the individual level: financial consumer trust in the EU financial market system necessitates a EU system of clear and predictable legal rules, effectively protecting their individual rights and the property they entrust to the financial market.

Bibliography

Reports

BCBS (2012) *Core Principles for Effective Banking Supervision*, www.bis.org/publ/bcbs230.pdf.

BCBS (2006) *Core Principles for Effective Banking Supervision*, www.bis.org/publ/bcbs129.htm.

BCBS (2004) 'Bank Failures in Mature Economies', *BCBS Working Paper No. 13*, www.bis.org/publ/bcbs_wp13.pdf.

BCBS (1999) 'Core Principles Methodology', www.bis.org/publ/bcbs130.htm.

BCBS (1997) *Core Principles for Effective Banking Supervision*, Basel: Bank for International Settlements.

BCBS (1975) *Report to the Governors on the Supervision of Banks' Foreign Establishments* (the 'Basel Concordat'), www.bis.org/publ/bcbs00a.htm.

BCBS and IADI (2010) *Core Principles for Effective Deposit Insurance Systems – Methodology and Compliance Assessment*, Basel: BIS.

BCBS and IADI (2009) 'Core Principles for Effective Deposit Insurance Systems', www.iadi.org/cms/secure/docs/JWGDI%20CBRG%20core%20principles_18_June.pdf.

CESR (2007) 'The Passport under MiFID', CESR/07-335b, Paris: CESR.

De Larosière Group of Experts (2009) 'Report', http://ec.europa.eu/internal_market/finances/docs/de_larosiere_report_en.pdf.

European Commission (2007) 'Supervision of Branches under MiFID', http://ec.europa.eu/internal_market/securities/docs/isd/mifid-branches_en.pdf.

European Forum of Deposit Insurers (EFDI) (2008) *Report on the Scope of Cover under National Deposit Guarantee Schemes (DGS): 'Deposits' and 'Depositors'.*

European Securities Markets Expert Group (ESME) (2008) *Role of Credit Rating Agencies.*

European Securities Markets Expert Group (ESME) (2008) 'Differences between the Definitions of "Qualified Investor" in the Prospectus Directive and "Professional Client" and "Eligible Counterparty" in MiFID: Is Alignment Needed?', http://ec.europa.eu/finance/securities/docs/esme/report-qualified-investor_en.pdf.

FDIC (2011) 'The orderly liquidation of Lehman Brothers Holding Inc. under the Dodd-Frank Act ', *FDIC Quarterly*, vol. 5, no. 2, p. 31.

FITCH (2011) *Global Trading and Universal Bank Review*, www.fitchratings.com.

FSA (2009) 'The Turner Review. A Regulatory Response to the Global Banking Crisis', www.fsa.gov.uk/pubs/other/turner_review.pdf.

FSA; Treasury; Bank of England (2005) 'A Framework for Guarantee Schemes in the EU', *Discussion Paper.*

FSB (2014) Key Attributes of Effective Resolution Regimes for Financial Institutions, www.fsb.org/wp-content/uploads/r_141015.pdf.

FSB (2012) 'Thematic Review on Deposit Insurance Systems', www.financialstability board.org/publications/r_120208.pdf.

FSB (2011) Key Attributes of Effective Resolution Regimes for Financial Institutions, www.fsb.org/wp-content/uploads/r_111104cc.pdf?page_moved=1.

FSB (2011) 'Shadow Banking: Strengthening Oversight and Regulation', www.financial stabilityboard.org/publications/r_111027a.pdf.

FSB (2010) 'Reducing the moral hazard posed by systemically important financial institutions', www.financialstabilityboard.org/publications/r_101111a.pdf.

FSB (2009) 'Improving Financial Regulation', www.financialstabilityboard.org/publica tions/r_090925.pdf.

FSF (2001) 'Final Report of the Working Group on Deposit Insurance', www.iadi.org/docs/FSF_Final_Report.pdf.

FSF (2001) *Guidance for Developing Effective Deposit Insurance Systems*, www.fdic.gov/deposit/deposits/international/guidance/guidance/finalreport.pdf.

FSF (2000) '*International Guidance on Deposit Insurance – A Consultative Process*', www.fsb.org/wp-content/uploads/r_0006.pdf.

G-20/OECD (2011) 'High Level Principles on Financial Consumer Protection', www.oecd.org/daf/fin/financial-markets/48892010.pdf.

House of Commons (2010) 'Reasoned Opinion on the Application of the Principles of Subsidiarity and Proportionality Draft Directive amending Directive 97/9/EC on investor-compensation schemes (12346/10)', www.parliament.uk/pagefiles/54364/Rea soned%20Opinion%2025.10.10.pdf.

House of Commons Select Committee on Treasury (1998) 'Accountability of the Bank of England', London: The Stationery Office Limited, www.publications.parliament.uk/pa/cm201012/cmselect/cmtreasy/874/874.pdf.

House of Lords European Union Committee (2009) 'The Future of EU Regulation and Supervision', London: The Stationery Office Limited, www.publications.parliament.uk/pa/ld200809/ldselect/ldeucom/106/106i.pdf.

IADI (2015) 'Integrated Protection Schemes', www.iadi.org/en/assets/File/Papers/Approved%20Research%20-%20Discussion%20Papers/IPS_Research_Paper_March_2015_FINAL_Version.pdf.

IADI (2007) *General Guidance for an Effective Deposit Insurance Mandate*, (draft) Guidance Paper, www.iadi.org/docs/IADI%20Draft%20Discussion%20Paper%20on%20Effective%20 Deposit%20Insurance%20Mandate_Basel_2007a.pdf.

IADI (2005) 'Key Conclusions of the APEC Policy Dialogue on Deposit Insurance and IADI Guidance Points', www.iadi.org/docs/IADI_APEC_Guidance.pdf.

IMF (2013) *A Banking Union for the Euro Area*, SDN/13/01, www.imf.org/external/pubs/ft/sdn/2013/sdn1301.pdf.

IMF (2011) 'Making banks safer: Can Volcker and Vickers do it?', *IMF Working Paper*, November.

IMF (2010) *United States: Publication of Financial Sector Assessment Program Documentation – Detailed Assessment of Implementation of IOSCO Objectives and Principles of Securities Regulation*, IMF.

Independent Commission on Banking (2011) *Final Report* ('The Vickers Report'), http://webarchive.nationalarchives.gov.uk.

IOSCO (2011) 'Survey Regimes for the Protection, Distribution and/or Transfer of Client Assets', www.iosco.org/publications/?subsection=public_reports.

IOSCO (2010) 'Objectives and Principles of Securities Regulation', www.iosco.org/library/pubdocs/pdf/IOSCOPD323.pdf.

IOSCO (2009) *Annual Report 2009*, www.iosco.org/annual_reports/annual_report_2009/.

IOSCO (2008) *Annual Report 2008*, at www.iosco.org/annual_reports/annual_report_2008/.
IOSCO (2003) 'Methodology for Assessing Implementation of the IOSCO Objectives and Principles of Securities Regulation', www.ebrd.com/downloads/legal/securities/IOSCOPD155.pdf.
IOSCO (1998) 'Objectives and Principles of Securities Regulation', www.iosco.org/library/pubdocs/pdf/IOSCOPD82.pdf.
IOSCO (1996) 'Client Asset Protection', www.iosco.org/library/pubdocs/pdf/IOSCOPD57.pdf.
IOSCO (1996) 'Measures Available on a Cross-Border Basis to Protect Interests and Assets of Defrauded Investor', www.iosco.org/library/pubdocs/pdf/IOSCOPD55.pdf.
IOSCO (1993) 'Protecting the Small Investor: Combating Transnational Retail Securities and Futures Fraud', www.iosco.org/library/pubdocs/pdf/IOSCOPD30.pdf.
Joint Forum (BCBS, IOSCO, IAIS) (2010) 'Review on the Differentiated Nature and Scope of Financial Regulation – Key Issues and Recommendations', www.bis.org/publ/joint24.pdf.
Joint Forum (BCBS, IOSCO, IAIS) (2008) 'Customer Suitability in the Retail Sale of Financial Products and Services', www.bis.org/publ/joint20.pdf.
Joint Forum (BCBS, IOSCO, IAIS) (2006) *Regulatory and Market Differences: Issues and Observations*, Basel: Bank for International Settlements, www.bis.org/publ/joint15.pdf.
Joint Forum (BCSC, IOSCO, IAIS) (2004) 'Financial Disclosure in the Banking, Insurance and Securities Sectors: Issues and Analysis', www.bis.org/publ/joint08.pdf.
Joint Forum (BCBS, IOSCO, IAIS) (2001) 'Core Principles – Cross-sectoral Comparison', www.bis.org/publ/joint03.pdf.
Joint Forum (BCBS, IOSCO, IAIS) (2001) *Risk Management Practices and Regulatory Capital – Cross-Sectoral Comparison*, Basel: Bank for International Settlements, www.bis.org/publ/joint04.pdf.
Joint Forum (BCBS, IOSCO, IAIS) (1999) *Fit and Proper Principles*, Basel: Bank For International Settlements.
Lamfalussy Committee (2001) 'Final Report of the Committee of Wise Men on the Regulation of the European Securities Markets, http://ec.europa.eu/internal_market/securities/docs/lamfalussy/wisemen/final-report-wise-men_en.pdf.
Liikanen High Level Group of Experts (2012) 'The Liikanen Report', http://ec.europa.eu/internal_market/bank/docs/high-level_expert_group/report_en.pdf.
Multidisciplinary Working Group on Enhanced Disclosure (2001) 'Final Report to BCSC, Committee on the Global Financial System of the G-10 Central Banks, IAIS, IOSCO'.
OXERA Consulting Ltd (2005) *Description and assessment of the national investor compensation schemes established in accordance with Directive 1997/9/EC.*
US Department of the Treasury (2009) 'Financial Regulatory Reform. A New Foundation: Rebuilding Financial Supervision and Regulation', www.treasury.gov/initiatives/Documents/FinalReport_web.pdf.
US Department of the Treasury (2008) 'Blueprint for a Modernized Financial Regulatory Structure', www.treasury.gov/press-center/press-releases/Documents/Blueprint.pdf.
US Department of the Treasury (2008) 'Blueprint for a Modernized Financial Regulatory Structure', www.treasury.gov/press-center/press-releases/Documents/Blueprint.pdf.
US Government Accountability Office (2004) 'Financial Regulation – Industry Changes Prompt Need to Reconsider U.S. Regulatory Structure', www.gao.gov/assets/160/157565.pdf.
VIRGOS M. and SCHMIT, E. (1996) *Report on the Convention on Insolvency Proceedings*, EU Council Document 6500/96.

World Bank (2012) *Good Practices for Financial Consumer Protection*, http://siteresources.worldbank.org/EXTFINANCIALSECTOR/Resources/Good_Practices_for_Financial_CP.pdf.

Books in English

ALEXANDER, K. and MOLONEY, N. (eds) (2011) *Law Reform and Financial Markets*, Cheltenham: Edward Elgar Publishing.

ALEXANDER, K., DHUMALE, R. and EATWELL, J. (2006) *Global Governance of Financial Systems: The International Regulation of Systemic Risk*, Oxford: Oxford University Press.

ANDENAS, M. and ANDERSEN, C. (eds) (2012) *Theory and Practice of Harmonisation*, London: Cheltenham: Edward Elgar Publishing.

ANDENAS, M. and ROTH, W.-H. (2002) *Services and Free Movement in EU Law*, Oxford: Oxford University Press.

ARNULL, A. (1999) *The European Union and its Court of Justice*, Oxford: Oxford University Press.

ARNULL, A. (1990) *The General Principles of EEC Law and the Individual*, Leicester: Leicester University Press.

AVGERINOS, Y. (2003) *Regulating and Supervising Investment Services in the European Union*, New York, NY: Palgrave Macmillan.

AYADI, R., ARBAK, E., De GROEN, W. P. and LLEWELLYN, D. T. (2012) *Regulation of European Banks and Business Models: Towards a New Paradigm*, Brussels: CEPS.

AYADI, R., De GROEN, W. P. and LLEWELLYN, D. T. (2011) *Business Models in European Banking: A Pre- and Post-Crisis Screening*, Brussels: CEPS.

AYADI, R. and SCHMIDT, R. (eds) (2009) *Investigating Diversity in the Banking Sector in Europe: The Performance and Role of Saving Banks*, Brussels: CEPS.

BAGEHOT, W. (1873) *Lombard Street*, London: Henry S. King & Co.

BAMFORD, C. (2015) *Principles of International Financial Law*, 2nd edition, Oxford: Oxford University Press.

BANNOCK, G., BAXTER, R. E. and DAVIS, E. (1987) *The Penguin Dictionary of Economics*, New York, NY: Penguin.

BARNARD, C. (2007) *The Substantive Law of the EU – The Four Freedoms*, 2nd edition, Oxford: Oxford University Press.

BEATSON, J. and TRIDIMAS, T. (eds) (1998) *New Directions in European Public Law*, Oxford: Hart Publishing.

BERNITZ, U. and NERGELIUS, J. (eds) (2005) *General Principles of European Community Law*, Lund: Lund University Press.

BIONDI, A. (2010) '*In Praise of Francovich*' in POIARES MADURO, M. and AZOULAI, L. (eds) *The Past and Future of EU Law: Classics of EU Law Revisited on the 50th Anniversary of the Rome Treaty*. Oxford: Hart Publishing, pp. 413–18.

BIONDI, A. and FARLEY, M. (eds) (2009) *The Right to Damages in European Law*, Austin, TX: Wolters Kluwer Law & Business.

BLACK, J. (2010) 'Risk-based regulation: choices, practices and lessons learnt' in OECD *Risk and Regulatory Policy: Improving the Governance of Risk*, Paris: OECD, pp. 185–236.

BLACK, J. (2010) 'The role of risk in regulatory processes' in BALDWIN, R., CAVE, M. and LODGE, M. (eds) *The Oxford Handbook of Regulation*, New York, NY: Oxford University Press, pp. 302–48.

BLAIR, M., MINGHELLA, L., TAYLOR, M., THREIPLAND, M. and WALKER, G. A. (2000) *Blackstone's Guide to the Financial Services and Markets Act 2000*, London: Blackstone.

BLAIR, M., WALKER, G. A. and PURVES, R. (eds) (2009) *Financial Services Law*, 2nd edition, Oxford: Oxford University Press.

BRUNNERMEIER, M., CROCKETT, A., GOODHART, C., PERSAUD, A. D. and SONG SHIN, H. (2009) *The Fundamental Principles of Financial Regulation*, Geneva: International Center for Monetary and Banking Studies.

BUSUIOC, M. (2013) *European Agencies: Law and Practices of Accountability*, Oxford: Oxford University Press.

BUSUIOC, M., GROENLEER, M. and TONDAL, J. (eds) (2012) *The Agency Phenomenon in the European Union: Emergence, Institutionalism and Every-day Decision-making*, Manchester: Manchester University Press.

CHALMERS, D. C. H., MONTI, G. and TOMKINS, A. (2006) *European Union Law*, Cambridge: Cambridge University Press.

CLEAVER, T. (2004) *Economics, the Basics*, London: Routledge.

COOK, H. C. and TREDENNICK, H. (trans.) (2009) *Aristotle: Categories. On interpretation. Prior Analytics*, Loeb Classical Library No. 325, Cambridge, MA: Harvard University Press.

CRAIG, P. (2011) 'Integration, Democracy and Legitimacy' in CRAIG, P. and De BÚRCA, G., *The Evolution of EU Law*, 2nd edition, Oxford: Oxford University Press, p. 13.

CRAIG, P. (2011) 'Institutions, Power, and Institutional Balance' in CRAIG, P. and De BÚRCA, G., *The Evolution of EU Law*, 2nd edition, Oxford: Oxford University Press, pp. 41–84.

CRAIG, P. and De BURCA, G. (eds) (2011) *The Evolution of EU Law*, 2nd edition, Oxford: Oxford University Press.

CRANSTON, R. (1997) *Principles of Banking Law*, Oxford: Clarendon Press.

CURTIN, D. (1992) 'The Decentralised Enforcement of Community Law Rights. Judicial Snakes and Ladders' in CURTIN, D. and O'KEEFE, D. (eds) *Constitutional Adjudication in European Community and National Law*, Oxford: Butterworths.

DASHWOOD, A., DOUGAN, M., RODGER, B., SPAVENTA, E. and WYATT, D. (eds) (2011) *Wyatt and Dashwood's European Union Law*, 6th edition, Oxford: Hart Publishing.

DASSESSE, M., STUART, I. and PENN, G. (1994) *EC Banking Law*, London: Lloyd's of London Press, Ltd.

DAVIES, H. and GREEN, D. (2008) *Global Financial Regulation: The Essential Guide*, Cambridge: Polity Press.

De HAAN, J., OOSTERLOO, S. and SCHOENMAKER, D. (2012) *Financial Markets and Institutions: A European Perspective*, 2nd edition, Cambridge: Cambridge University Press.

DEJOUSSE, R. (1998) *The European Court of Justice*, London: Macmillan.

ELLINGER, E. P., LOMNICKA, E. and HOOLEY, R. J. A. (2002) *Modern Banking Law*, 3rd edition, Oxford: Oxford University Press.

ELLIS, E. and TRIDIMAS, T. (1995) *Public Law of the European Community: Cases, Materials and Commentary*, London: Sweet & Maxwell.

FAIRGRIEVE, D. (2003) *State Liability in Tort – A Comparative Law Study*, Oxford: Oxford University Press.

FERRAN, E., MOLONEY, N. and PAYNE, J. (eds) (2015) *The Oxford Handbook of Financial Regulation*, Oxford: Oxford University Press.

FERRAN, E. (2004) *Building an EU Securities Market*, Cambridge: Cambridge University Press.

FERRAN, E. (1999) *Company Law and Corporate Finance*, Oxford: Oxford University Press.

FERRAN, E. and GREEN, D. (2007) 'Are the Lamfalussy Regulatory Networks Working Successfully?', London: European Policy Forum.

FERRANINI, G. and WYMEERSCH, E. (eds) (2006) *Investor Protection in Europe: Corporate Law Making, The MiFID and Beyond*, Oxford: Oxford University Press.

FRASER, R. and LONG, C. (1992) *The World Financial System*, Harlow: Longman.

GOODE, R. (1995) *Commercial Law*, 2nd edition, London: Penguin Books.

GOODHART, C. (2011) *The Basel Committee on Banking Supervision: A History of the Early Years, 1974–1997*, Cambridge: Cambridge University Press.

GOODHART, C. (2004) 'Some New Directions for Financial Stability?', Zurich: BIS, Per Jacobsson Foundation.

GOODHART, C., HARTMANN, P., LLEWELLYN, D., ROJAS-SUAREZ, L. and WEISBROD, S. (1998) *Financial Regulation: Why, How and Where Now?*, London: Routledge.

GORTSOS, C. (2012) *Fundamentals of Public International Financial Law: International Banking Law within the System of Public International Financial Law*, Baden-Baden: Nomos Verlag.

GROUSSOT, X. (2005) *Creation, Development and Impact of the General Principles of Community Law: Towards a Jus Commune Europaeum*, Lund: Lund University Press.

GRUNEWALD, S. (2014) *The Resolution of Cross-border Banking Crises in the European Union*, The Hague: Kluwer Law International.

HADJIEMANNUIL, C. (1996) *Banking Regulation and the Bank of England*, London/New York, NY/Hong Kong: LLP.

HAENTJENS, M, and De GIOIA-CARABELLESE, P. (2015) *European Banking and Financial Law*, London/New York, NY: Routledge.

HARTLEY, T. C. (1998) *The Foundations of European Community Law*, 4th edition, Oxford: Oxford University Press.

HOOKE, A. (1982) *The International Monetary Fund – Its Evolution, Organisation and Activities*, Washington, D.C.: International Monetary Fund.

HUDSON, A. (2013) *The Law of Finance*, 2nd edition, London: Sweet & Maxwell.

HÜPKES, E. (2000) *The Legal Aspects of Bank Insolvency. A Comparative Analysis of Western Europe, the United States and Canada*, The Hague: Kluwer Law International.

KAHN, A. E. (1989) *The Economics of Regulation – Principles and Institutions*, 2nd edition, New York, NY: John Wiley.

KATTEL, R., KREGEL, J. and TONVERONACHI, M. (2015), *Financial Regulation in the European Union*, Oxford: Routledge, Routledge Critical Studies in Finance and Stability.

KEELEY, B. and LOVE, P. (2010) *From Crisis to Recovery: The Causes, Course and Consequences of the Great Recession*, Paris: OECD Publishing, OECD Insights.

KELSEN, H. (1960) *Pure Theory of Law*, 2nd edition (translation KNIGHT, M. 2009) Clark, New Jersey, NJ: The Lawbook Exchange.

KINGSFORD SMITH, D. and DIXON, O. (2015) 'The Consumer Interest and the Financial Markets' in FERRAN, E., MOLONEY, N. and PAYNE, J. (eds) *The Oxford Handbook of Financial Regulation*, Oxford: Oxford University Press, pp. 695–735.

LASOK, K. P. E. (1984) *The European Court of Justice: Practice and Procedure*, London: Butterworths.

LASTRA, R. M. (2015) *International Financial and Monetary Law*, 2nd edition, Oxford: Oxford University Press.

LASTRA, R. M. (2007) *The Reform of the International Financial Architecture*, The Hague: Kluwer Law International.

LASTRA, R. M. (2006) *Legal Foundations of International Monetary Stability*, Oxford: Oxford University Press.

LASTRA, R. M. (2003) 'Regulating European Securities Markets: Beyond the Lamfalussy Report' in ANDENAS, M. and AVGERINOS, Y. (eds) *Financial Markets in Europe: Towards a Single Regulator?*, The Hague: Kluwer Law International, pp. 211–22.

LASTRA, R. M. (1996) *Central Banking and Banking Regulation*, London: LSE, Financial Markets Group.

LASTRA, R. M. and SCHIFFMAN, H. (eds) (1999) *Bank Failures and Bank Insolvency Law in Economies in Transition*, The Hague: Kluwer International.

LLEWELLYN, D. (1986) *The Regulation and Supervision of Financial Institutions*, London: Institute of Bankers.

LYBECK, J. (2011) *A Global History of the Financial Crash of 2007–2010*, Cambridge: Cambridge University Press.

MOLLE, W. (1997) *The Economics of European Integration – Theory, Practice and Policy*, 3rd edition, London: Ashgate.

MOLONEY, N. (2015) 'Regulating the Retail Markets' in FERRAN, E., MOLONEY, N. and PAYNE, J. (eds) *The Oxford Handbook of Financial Regulation*, Oxford: Oxford University Press, pp. 736–68.

MOLONEY, N. (2014) *EU Securities and Financial Markets Regulation*, 3rd edition, Oxford: Oxford European Union Law Library, Oxford University Press.

MOLONEY, N. (2012) 'Supervision in the wake of the financial crisis: achieving effective "law in action" – a challenge for the EU' in WYMEERSCH, E., HOPT, K. J. and FERRANINI, G. (eds) *Financial Regulation and Supervision: a Post-crisis Analysis*, Oxford: Oxford University Press.

MOLONEY, N. (2012) 'The legacy effects of the financial crisis on regulatory design in the EU' in FERRAN, E., HILL, J., MOLONEY, N. and COFFEE, J. (eds) *The Regulatory Aftermath of the Global Financial Crisis*, Cambridge: Cambridge University Press, pp. 111–202.

MOLONEY, N. (2010) *How to Protect Investors – Lessons from the EC and the UK*, Cambridge: Cambridge University Press.

MOLONEY, N. (2002) *EC Securities Regulation*, Oxford: Oxford University Press.

MOSS, G., FLETCHER, I. and ISAACS, S. (eds) (2009) *The EC Regulation on Insolvency Proceedings – A Commentary and Annotated Guide*, 2nd edition, Oxford: Oxford University Press.

MOSS, G. and WESSELS, B. (2006) *EU Banking and Insurance Insolvency*, Oxford: Oxford University Press.

MUELLER, R. C. (1997) *The Venetian Money Market: Banks, Panics and the Public Debt, 1200–1500*, London: John Hopkins University Press.

PANASAR, R. and BOEKMAN, P. (2010) *European Securities Law*, Oxford: Oxford University Press.

POIARES MADURO, M. (2002) 'Harmony and Dissonance in Free Movement' in ANDENAS, M. and ROTH, W.-H. (eds) *Services and Free Movement in EU Law*, Oxford: Oxford University Press.

POIARES MADURO, M. (1998) *We the Court*, Oxford: Hart Publishing.

PROCTOR, C. (2010) *The Law and Practice of International Banking*, Oxford: Oxford University Press.

SCHAMMO, P. (2011) *EU Prospectus Law*, Cambridge: Cambridge University Press.

SCHÜTZE, R. (2015) *European Union Law*, Cambridge: Cambridge University Press.

SCOTT, H. S. (2010) *International Finance*, 17th edition, New York, NY: Foundation Press.

STEINER, J., WOODS, L. and TWIGG-FLESNER, C. (2006) *EU Law*, 9th edition, Oxford: Oxford University Press.

STIGLER, G. (1975) *The Citizen and the State: Essays on Regulation*, Chicago, IL/London: University of Chicago Press.

STONE SWEET, A. (2011) 'The European Court of Justice' in CRAIG, P. and de BÚRCA, G., *The Evolution of EU Law*, Oxford: Oxford University Press, p. 121.

THEISSEN, R. (2014) *EU Banking Supervision*, The Hague: Eleven Publishers.

THORTON, H. (1802) *An Enquiry into the Nature and Effects of the Paper Credit System of Great Britain*, London: J. Hatchard.

TRIDIMAS, T. (2012) 'Financial Supervision and Agency Power: Reflections on ESMA' in SHUIBHNE, N. and GORMLEY, L. (eds) *From Single Market to Economic Union: essays in memory of John A. Usher*, Oxford: Oxford University Press, p. 55.

TRIDIMAS, T. (2011) 'EU Financial Regulation: Federalization, Crisis Management, and Law Reform' in CRAIG, P. and De BÚRCA, G. *The Evolution of EU Law*, 2nd edition, Oxford: Oxford University Press, pp. 783–804.

TRIDIMAS, T. (2010) 'EU Financial Regulation: From Harmonisation to the Birth of EU Federal Financial Law' in BIRKINSHAW, P. and VARNEY, M. (eds) *The European Union Legal Order after Lisbon*, The Hague: Kluwer International.

TRIDIMAS, T. (2007) *The General Principles of EU Law*, 3rd edition, Oxford: Oxford University Press.

TRIDIMAS, T. (1996) *The European Court of Justice and the EU Constitutional Order: Essays in Judicial Protection*, Oxford: Hart Publishing.

USHER, J. A. (1998) *General Principles of EC Law*, Harlow: Longman.

VALDEZ, S. and MOLYNEUX, P. (2013) *An Introduction to Global Financial Markets*, 7th edition, Basingstoke: Palgrave MacMillan.

Van DAM, C. (2006) *European Tort Law*, Oxford: Oxford University Press.

Van DAM, C. (eds) (2006) *Liability of Regulators*, London: British Institute for International and Comparative Law.

WALKER, G. and PURVES, R. (eds) (2014) *Financial Services Law*, 3rd edition, Oxford: Oxford University Press.

WALKER, G. A. (2007) *European Banking Law – Policy and Programme Construction*, Sir Joseph Gold Memorial Series, International Financial and Economic Law, vol. 6, London: British Institute of International and Comparative Law.

WALKER, G. A. (2007) *Financial Markets and Exchanges Law*, Oxford: Oxford University Press.

WALKER, G. A. (2006) *European Banking Law*, London: British Institute of International and Comparative Law.

WARD, A. (2007) *Judicial Review and the Rights of Private Parties in EU Law*, 2nd edition, Oxford: Oxford University Press.

WEATHERILL, S. and BEAUMONT, P. (1999) *EU Law*, 3rd edition, London: Penguin.

WILLIAMSON, J. (1977) *The Failure of World Monetary Reform 1971 – 1974*, New York, NY: New York University Press.

WOOD, P. R. (2008) *The Law and Practice of International Finance*, London: Sweet & Maxwell.

WOOD, P. R. (2007) *Regulation of International Finance*, London: Sweet & Maxwell.

WYMEERSCH, E. (2015), 'The European Financial Supervisory Authorities or ESAs' in WYMEERSCH, E., HOPT, K. J. and FERRANINI, G. (eds), *Financial Regulation and Supervision: A Post-Crisis Analysis*, Oxford: Oxford University Press.

WYMEERSCH, E., HOPT, K. J. and FERRANINI, G. (eds) (2012) *Financial Regulation and Supervision: a Post-crisis Analysis*, Oxford: Oxford University Press.

Articles in English

ADAMSKI, D. (2014) 'The ESMA Doctrine: A Constitutional Revolution and the Economics of Delegation', *ELRev*, vol. 39, no. 6, pp. 812–34.

ALEXANDER, K. (2015) 'European Banking Union: A Legal and Institutional Analysis of the Single Supervisory Mechanism and the Single Resolution Mechanism, *ELRev*, vol. 40, no. 2, pp. 154–87.

ANAGNOSTARAS, G. (2001) 'The allocation of responsibility in State liability actions for breach of Community law: a modern Gordian knot?', *ELR*, vol. 26, no. 2, pp. 139–58.

ANDENAS, M. (2000) 'Liability for supervisors and depositors' rights – the BCCI and the Bank of England in the House of Lords', *Euredia*, vol. 3, p. 407.

ANDENAS, M. (1995) 'Investment services: Cross border cold calling and the right to provide services', *Company Lawyer*, vol. 8, p. 249.

ANDENAS, M. (1994) 'Rules of conduct and the principle of subsidiarity', *Company Lawyer*, vol. 15, p. 60.

ANDENAS, M. and FAIRGRIEVE, D. (2002) 'Misfeasance in Public Office, Government Liability and European Influences', *International and Comparative Law Quarterly*, vol. 51, p. 757.

ARNULL, A. (2011) 'The Principle of Effective Judicial Protection in EU Law: An Unruly Horse?' *ELRev*, vol. 36, p. 51.

ATHANASSIOU, P. (2014) 'On the Legal and Economic Treatment of Bank Deposits as Investments: Some Reflections', *Journal of International Banking Law and Regulation*, vol. 29, no. 12, pp. 715–20.

ATHANASSIOU, P. (2011) 'Financial Sector Supervisors' Accountability: A European Perspective', *ECB Legal Working Paper Series*, No. 2.

AUBRY, N. and McKEE, M. (2007) 'MiFID: Where did it come from, where is it taking us', *JIBLR*, vol. 22, no. 4, pp. 177–86.

AVGOULEAS, E. (2009) 'The global financial crisis, behavioural finance and financial regulation: in search of a new orthodoxy', *Journal of Corporate Law Studies*, vol. 9, no. 1, April, pp. 23–59.

BAILEY, S. H. and BOWMAN, M. J. (2000) 'Public authority negligence revisited', *CLJ*, vol. 59, no. 1, March, pp. 85–132.

BECKER, F. (2007) 'Application of Community law by Member States' public authorities: between autonomy and effectiveness', *CMLRev*, vol. 44, pp. 1035–56.

BENTLEM, G. (2005) 'Torts, a European ius commune and the private enforcement of Community law', *CLJ*, vol. 64, no. 1, March, pp. 126–48.

BENTLEM, G. (1994) 'Medium hard law – still no horizontal direct effect of European Community directives after Faccini Dori', *CJEL*, vol. 1, p. 469.

BERGSTRÖM, C. F. (2015) 'Shaping the New System of Delegation of Powers to EU Agencies: United Kingdom v European Parliament and Council (Short Selling)', *Common Market Law Review*, vol. 52, no. 1, pp. 219–42.

BEUTLER, B. (2009) 'State liability for breaches of Community law by national courts: is the requirement of a manifest infringement of the applicable law an insurmountable obstacle?', *CMLRev*, vol. 46, pp. 773–804.

BINDER, J.-H. (2004) 'The Advocate-General's Opinion in Paul and Others v. Germany – Cutting back state liability for regulatory negligence?', *EBLR*, vol. 15, no. 3, p. 463.

BLACK, J. (2008) *Forms and Paradoxes of Principles Based Regulation, Capital Markets Law Journal*, p. 425.

BLUNDELL-WIGNALL, A. and ATKINSON, P. (2011) 'Global SIFIs, Derivatives and Financial Stability', *OECD Journal: Financial Market Trends*, vol. 2011/1, pp. 167–200.

BLUNDELL-WIGNALL, A., ATKINSON, P. and ROULET, C. (2014) 'Bank business models and the separation issue', *OECD Journal: Financial Market Trends*, vol. 2013/2, pp. 69–91.

CAPRIGLIONE, F. and SEMERATO, G. (2012) 'Financial Crisis and Sovereign Debt: The European Union between Risks and Opportunities', *Law and Economics Yearly Review*, vol. 1, pt. 1, p. 4.

CHALMERS, D. (1994) 'Repackaging the internal market – the ramifications of the Keck judgment', *ELR*, vol. 19, pp. 380–5.

CHAMON, M. (2014) 'The Empowerment of Agencies under the Meroni Doctrine and Article 114 TFEU: Comment on United Kingdom v Parliament and Council (Short-selling) and the Proposed Single Resolution Mechanism', *ELRev*, vol. 39, no. 3, pp. 380–403.

CHAMON, M. (2010) 'EU Agencies: Does the Meroni Doctrine Make Sense', *Maastricht Journal of European and Comparative Law*, vol. 17, p. 281.

COFFEE, J. (2009) 'What went wrong? An initial inquiry into the causes of the 2008 financial crisis', *Journal of Corporate Law Studies*, vol. 9, no. 1, April, pp. 1–22.

CRAIG, P. (2009) 'The legal effect of Directives: policy, rules and exceptions', *ELR*, vol. 34, no. 3, pp. 349–77.

CRAIG, P. (1997) 'Once more unto the breach: the Community, the State and damages liability', *Law Quarterly Review*, vol. 113, January, pp. 67–94.

CREMONA, M. (1994) 'A European passport for investment services', *JBL*, p. 195.

DASSESSE, M. (1997) 'The European Commission's interpretative communication on freedom of services and the general good in the Second Banking Directive', *Yearbook of International Financial and Economic Law*, p. 45.

DAVIS, R. (2006) 'Liability on damages for a breach of Community law: some reflections on the question of who to sue and the concept of "the State"', *ELR*, vol. 31, no. 1, pp. 69–80.

DAVIS EVANS, A. (2007) 'The Investor Compensation Fund', *The Journal of Corporation Law*, vol. 33, no. 1, pp. 223–96.

DI NOIA, C. and GARGANTINI, M. (2014) 'Unleashing the European Securities and Markets Authority: Governance and Accountability after the ECJ Decision on the Short Selling Regulation (Case C-270/12)', *European Business Organization Law Review*, vol. 15, no. 1, pp. 1–57.

EILMANSBERGER, T. (2004) 'The relationship between rights and remedies in EC law: in search of the missing link', *CMLRev*, vol. 41, pp. 1199–246.

ESTRELLA, A. and SCHICH, S. (2012) 'Sovereign and Banking Sector Debt: Interconnections through Guarantees', *OECD Journal: Financial Market Trends*, vol. 2011/2, pp. 21–45.

FALLON, R. H. (2006) 'The Linkage between Justiciability and Remedies – and their Connections to Substantive Rights', *Virginia Law Review*, vol. 92, pp. 633–705.

FERNANDEZ-BOLLO, E. (2013) 'Structural Reform and Supervision of the Banking Sector in France', *OECD Journal: Financial Market Trends*, vol. 2013/1, pp. 31–8.

FERRAN, E. (2014) 'European Banking Union and the EU Single Financial Market: More Differentiated Integration or Disintegration?' *Cambridge Legal Studies Research Papers*, vol. 29/2014, p. 3.

GORTSOS, C. (2015) 'The Crisis-based EU Financial Regulatory Intervention: are we on the Top of the Prudential Wave?' *ERA Forum Journal of the Academy of European Law*, vol. 16, no. 1, pp. 89–110.

GORTSOS, C. (2013) 'The "single supervisory mechanism": a major building block towards a European Banking Union (the full Europeanisation of the "bank safety net")', *Hrematopistotiko Dikaio*, vol. 1, p. 5., and *ECEFIL Working Paper Series*, no. 2013/8.

GORTSOS, C. (2011) 'The European Banking Authority within the European System of Financial Supervision', *Hrematopistotiko Dikaio*, vol. 1, p. 56, and *ECEFIL Working Paper No. 2011/1.*

GRAY, J. (2008) 'Lessons from BCCI Saga for the Current Accountability Debate Surrounding Northern Rock', *JIBLR*, vol. 23, p. 37.

GRAY, J. (2006) 'Court Castigates BCCI Liquidators' Claim against Bank of England, Legal and Regulatory Commentary', *JFRC*, vol. 4, p. 411.

GRILLER, S. and ORATOR, A. (2010) 'Everything under Control? "The Way Forward" for European Agencies in the Footsteps of the Meroni Doctrine', *ELRev*, 35, p. 3.

GRUNDMAN, S. (2013) 'The Bankinter Case on MiFID Regulation and Contract Law', *European Review of Contract Law*, vol. 9, pp. 267–80.

HAENTJENS, M. (2014) 'Bank Recovery and Resolution: An Overview of International Initiatives', *International Insolvency Law Review*, 2014/3, pp. 255–70.

HARRIS, B. V. (2003) 'Judicial review, justiciability and the prerogative of mercy', *CLJ*, vol. 62, no. 3, November, pp. 631–60.

HATZOPOULOS, V. (1995) 'Case C-384/93 Alpine Investments BV v Minister van Financiën, Judgment of 10 May 1999, NYR (1995)', *CMLRev*, vol. 32, p. 1427.

HOOKE, A. W. (1982) 'The International Monetary Fund – Its Evolution, Organisation and Activities', *IMF Pamphlet Series*, no. 37.

HOWELL, E. (2014) 'The European Court of Justice: Selling us Short?', *European Company and Financial Law Review*, vol. 11, no. 3, pp. 457–77.

JACOBS, F. (2004) 'The evolution of the European legal order', *CMLRev*, vol. 41, pp. 303–16.

KAKOURIS, K. (1997) 'Do the Member States possess judicial procedural autonomy?', *CMLRev*, vol. 34, p. 1389.

LANDSEER, A. and van EMPEL, M. (1998) 'The Directive on deposit-guarantee schemes and the directive on investor compensation schemes in view of Case C-233/94', *European Financial Services Law*, pp. 143–48.

LANNOO, K. (2000) 'Challenges to the structure of financial supervision in the EU', *JIFM*, vol. 2, no. 4, p. 98.

LASTRA, R. M. (2013) 'Banking Union and the Single Market: Conflict or Companionship?', *Fordham International Law Journal*, vol. 36, no. 5, p. 1190.

LASTRA, R. M. and LOUIS, J. V. (2013) 'European Economic and Monetary Union: History, Trends and Prospects', *YEL*, pp. 1–150.

LLEWELLYN, D. (6–7 July 2006) 'Institutional Structure of Financial Regulation and Supervision: The Basic Issues', *World Bank Seminar – Aligning Supervisory Structures with Country Needs*, Washington, D.C.

LLEWELLYN, D. (1999) 'The Economic Rationale for Financial Regulation', *FSA Occasional Papers in Financial Regulation*, no. 1.

LOMNICKA, E. (2000) 'The home country control principle in the financial services Directives and case law', *EBLR*, vol. 11, p. 324.

MALETIC, I. (2014) 'Delegating Harmonization of the Internal Market: The Ruling in Case C-270/12', *Yearbook of European Law*, pp. 501–17.

MOLONEY, N. (2012) 'The investor model underlying the EU's investor protection regime: consumers or investors?', *European Business Organization Law Review*, vol. 13, no. 2, p. 169.

MOLONEY, N. (2011) 'The European Securities and Markets Authority and institutional design for the EU financial market: a tale of two competences: part (1) rule-making', *European Business Organization Law Review*, vol. 12, no. 1, pp. 41–86.

MOLONEY, N. (2011) 'The European Securities and Markets Authority and Institutional Design for the EU Financial Market – A tale of two competences: part (2) rules in action', *European Business Organization Law Review*, vol. 12, no. 2, pp. 177–225.

MOLONEY, N. (2010) 'EU Financial Market Regulation after the Global Financial Crisis: "More Europe" or More Risks?', *Common Market Law Review*, vol. 47, pp. 1317–83.

MOLONEY, N. (2006) 'III. Financial market regulation in the post-financial services action plan era', *ICLQ*, vol. 55, no. 4, pp. 982–92.

MOLONEY, N. (2005) 'Building a retail investment culture through law: the 2004 Markets in Financial Instruments Directive', *European Business Organization Law Review*, vol. 6, no. 3, pp. 341–421.

MOLONEY, N. (2003) 'II. The Lamfalussy legislative model: A new era for the EC securities and investment services regime', *ICLQ*, vol. 52, no. 2, pp. 509–20.

MOLONEY, N. (2003) 'New frontiers in EC capital markets law: from market constructions to market regulation', *CMLRev*, vol. 40, pp. 809–43.

MOLONEY, N. (2002) 'The regulation of investment services in the single market: the emergence of a new regulatory landscape', *European Business Organization Law Review*, vol. 3, no. 2, pp. 293–336.

MOLONEY, N. and FERRANINI, G. (2012) 'Reshaping order execution in the EU and the role of interest groups under MiFID II', *European Business Organization Law Review*, vol. 13, no. 4, pp. 557–97.

OLIVARES-CAMINAL, R. (2012) 'The EU Architecture to Avert a Sovereign Debt Crisis', *OECD Journal: Financial Market Trends*, vol. 2011/2, pp. 167–97.

ORTINO, M. (2007) 'The role and functioning of mutual recognition in the European market of financial services', *ICLQ*, vol. 56, no. 2, p. 309.

OSTERLOO, S. and De HAAN, J. (2004) 'Central Banks and Financial Stability: A Survey', *Journal of Financial Stability*, vol. 1, p. 257.

POSNER, R. A. (1974) 'Theories of Economic Regulation', *Journal of Economics and Management Science*, vol. 5, no. 2, pp. 335–58.

PRECHAL, S. (1998) 'Community Law in National Courts: The Lessons from Van Schijndel', *CMLRev*, vol. 35, pp. 681–706.

PROCTOR, C. (2005) 'Regulatory liability for bank failures: The Peter Paul case', *Euredia*, p. 73.

RUFFET, M. (1997) 'Rights and remedies in European Community law: a comparative view', *CMLRev*, vol. 34, p. 307.

SCHAMMO, P. (2011) 'The European Securities and Markets Authority: Lifting the Veil on the Allocation of Powers', *Common Market Law Review*, vol. 48, pp. 1879–914.

SCHICH, S. and KIM, B.-H. (2013) 'Developments in the value of implicit guarantees for bank debt: The role of resolution regimes and practices', *OECD Journal: Financial Market Trends*, vol. 2012/2, pp. 35–65.

SCHICH, S. and KIM, B.-H. (2011) 'Guarantee Arrangements for Financial Promises: How Widely Should the Safety Net Be Cast?', *OECD Journal: Financial Market Trends*, vol. 2011/1, pp. 201–35.

SZYSZCZAK, E. (1996) 'Making Europe more relevant to its citizens: effective judicial process', *ELR*, vol. 21, p. 351.

TALBERG, J. (2000) 'Supranational influence in EU enforcement: the ECJ and the principle of state liability', *Journal of European Public Policy*, vol. 7, no. 1, March, pp. 104–21.

TISON, M. (2005) 'Do not attack the watchdog! Banking supervisor's liability after Peter Paul', *CMLRev*, vol. 42, pp. 639–75.

TRIDIMAS, T. (2002) 'Black, white, and shades of grey: horizontality of Directives revisited', *YEL*, vol. 21, p. 327.

TRIDIMAS, T. (2001) 'Liability for breach of Community law: growing up and mellowing down?', *CMLRev*, vol. 38, no. 2, pp. 301–32.

TRIDIMAS, T. (1994) 'Horizontal effect of directives: a missed opportunity', *ELR*, vol. 19, no. 6, p. 621.

Van GERVEN, W. (2004) 'Harmonization of private law: do we need it?', *CMLRev*, vol. 41, pp. 505–32.

Van GERVEN, W. (2000) 'Of rights, remedies, and procedures', *CMLRev*, vol. 37, p. 501.

Van GERVEN, W. (1996) 'Bridging the Unbridgeable: Community and National Tort Laws after Francovich and Brasserie', *ICQL*, vol. 45, no.3, pp. 507–44.

Van GESTEL, R. (2014) 'European Regulatory Agencies Adrift?', *Maastricht Journal of European and Comparative Law*, vol. 21, pp. 188–96.

WALKER, G. A. (2009) 'Credit contraction, financial collapse and global recession: pt 1', *BJIBFL*, p. 5.

WALKER, G. A. (2009) 'Credit crisis, Bretton Woods II and a new global response: pt 2', *BJIBFL*, pp. 77–81.

WALKER, G. A. (2007) 'Credit crisis: regulatory and financial systems reform', *BJIBFL*, p. 568.

WALKER, G. A. (2007) 'The deconstruction of financial risk', *JBR*, vol. 9, p. 9.

WALKER, G. A. (1996) 'The law of financial conglomerates – the next generation', *International Lawyer*, vol. 30, p. 57.

WARD, A. (1996) 'Effective sanctions in EC law: a moving judicial process', *ELR*, vol. 1, p. 205.

WOODS, L. and SMITH, F. (1997) 'Causation in Francovich: The Neglected Problem', *ICLQ*, vol. 46, no. 4, pp. 925–41.

WOUTER, W. (1992) 'Concurrent Liability of the Community and a Member State', *ELR*, vol. 17, no. 3, pp. 191–206.

WOUTERS, J. (1993) 'Rules of conduct, foreign investment firms and the ECJ's case-law on services', *Company Lawyer*, vol. 14, p. 194.

Electronic articles in English

BABIS, V. (2013) 'Bank Failures, State Liability, and Protection of Depositors in Foreign Branches: EFTA Surveillance Authority v. Iceland', *University of Cambridge Faculty of Law Research Paper*, vol. 5, http://ssrn.com/abstract=2216847.

BABIS, V. (2012) 'EU Recovery and Resolution Framework: Financial Assistance between Banking Group Members', *University of Cambridge Faculty of Law Research Papers*, vol. 15, June, https://papers.ssrn.com/sol3/papers.cfm?abstract_id=2091194.

BEALE, L. (2010) 'In the Wake of the Financial Crisis', *Wayne State University Law School Research Paper Series*, vol. 10-07, July, https://papers.ssrn.com/sol3/papers.cfm?abstract_id=1681577.

BRAITHWAITE, J. P. (2014) 'Law after Lehmans', *LSE Legal Studies Working Papers*, vol. 11, http://ssrn.com/abstract=2391148.

FERRAN, E. (2012) 'Crisis-driven EU Financial Regulatory Reform' *University of Cambridge Faculty of Law Research Paper*, vol. 6, http://ssrn.com/abstract=2028003.

KARMEL, R. (2012) 'An Orderly Liquidation Authority is Not the Solution to Too-big-to-fail', *Brooklyn Law School, Legal Studies Paper No. 259*, February, http://ssrn.com/abstract=2001619.

KARMEL, R. (2012) 'IOSCO 's Response to the Financial Crisis', *Brooklyn Law School, Legal Studies Paper No. 268*, http://ssrn.com/abstract=2025115.

SCHILLIG, M. (2012) 'Bank Resolution Regimes in Europe I – Recovery and Resolution Planning, Early Intervention', http://ssrn.com/abstract=2136101.

SCHILLIG, M. (2012) 'Bank Resolution Regimes in Europe II – Resolution Tools and Powers', http://ssrn.com/abstract=2136084.

WEBEL, B. (2013) 'Troubled Asset Relief Program (TARP): Implementation and Status', *US Congressional Research Service*, www.fas.org/sgp/crs/misc/R41427.pdf.

Books in French

BOULOUIS, B. J. (1993) *Droit institutionnel des Communautés Européennes*, 4th edition, Paris: Montchrestien.

DRUESNE, G. (1996) *Droit et Politiques de la Communauté et de l' Union européennes*, 5th edition, Paris: Presses Universitaires de France.

PAPADOPOULOU, R. E. (1996) *Principes Généraux du Droit et Droit Communautaire*, Bruxelles: Bruylant.

RIDEAU, J. and PICOD, F. (2002) *Code des Procédures Juridictionnelles de l'Union Européenne*, Paris: Litec.

SIMON, D. (1997) *Le système juridique communautaire*, Paris: Presses Universitaires de France.

Van RAEPENBUSCH, S. (1998) *Droit institutionnel de l' Union et des Communautés européennes*, 2nd edition, Paris: De Boeck Université.

Articles in French

BOUVERESSE, A. (2004) 'Responsabilité des Etats membres', *Europe*, vol. 12, p. 393.

DASSESSE, M. (1998) 'Protection du consommateur: les arrêts Allemagne (garantie des dépôts) et Parodi', *Journal des tribunaux/droit européen*, pp. 9–10.

DENYS, S. (2014) 'Délégation de compétences à l'Autorité européenne des marches financiers', *Europe*, Mars Comm. no. 3, pp. 14–15.

TENENBAUM, A. (2014) 'Les contrats financiers complexes et les obligations d'information: partition d'un dialogue subtil entre la CJUE et les juges nationaux', *Revue des contrats*, pp. 123–6.

Articles in Italian

CARRA, M. (2005) 'La (ir)responsibilità dello Stato per omessa vigilanza bancarisa', *Giornale di diritto amministrativo*, p. 1175.

PISANI, P. (2006) 'Concorso di obbligazioni indennitariè' risarcitorie e gestorie nella disciplina del rapporto tra autorità di vigilanza bancaria e risparmiatore depositante', *Europa e diritto privato*, p. 865.

Uncited Works

Books

AMTENBRINK, F. (1999) *The Democratic Accountability of Central Banks – A Comparative Study of the European Central Bank*, Oxford: Hart Publishing.

BIONDI, A., EECKHOUT, P. and RIPLEY, S. (2012) *EU Law after Lisbon*, Oxford: Oxford University Press.

BLACK, J. (2011) 'The rise (and fall?) of principles based regulation' in ALEXANDER, K. and MOLONEY, N. (eds) *Law Reform and Financial Markets*, Cheltenham: Edward Elgar Publishing, pp. 3–34.

BREYER, S. (1982) *Regulation and its Reform*, Cambridge, MA: Harvard University Press.

BROWN, L. and KENNEDY, T. (2000) *The Court of Justice of the European Communities*, 5th edition, London: Sweet & Maxwell.

DAM, K. W. (1982) *The Rules of the Game: Reformation and Evolution in the International Monetary System*, Chicago, IL/London: University of Chicago Press.

DOUGAN, M. (2004) *National Remedies Before the European Court of Justice*, Oxford: Hart Publishing.

EDWARDS, R. W. (1985) *International Monetary Collaboration*, New York, NY: Transnational Publishers.

FAIRGRIEVE, D., ANDENAS, M. and BELL, J. (eds) (2002) *Tort Liability of Public Authorities in Comparative Perspective*, London: BIICL.

FRANKEL, T. (2012) *The Ponzi Scheme Puzzle: A History and Analysis of Con Artists and Victims*, Oxford: Oxford University Press.

FRIEDMAN, M. (2002) *Capitalism and Freedom*, Chicago, IL: University of Chicago Press.

GALBRAITH, J. K. (1999) *The Affluent Society*, London: Penguin Books.

GALBRAITH, J. K. and SALINGER, N. (1990) *Almost Everyone's Guide to Economics*, London: Penguin Books.

GARDENER, E. (1986) *UK Banking Supervision: Evolution, Practice and Issues*, London: Allen & Unwin.

GOODHART, C. (2011) 'Moral Hazard' in GREEN, C. J., PENTECOST, E. and WEYMAN-JONES, T. (2011) *The Financial Crisis and the Regulation of Finance*, Cheltenham: Edward Elgar Publishing.

GOODHART, C. (2001) 'Regulating the Regulators – Accountability and Control' in FERRAN, E. and GOODHART, C. (eds) *Regulating Financial Services and Markets in the 21st Century*, Oxford: Hart Publishing.

GOODHART, C. (ed) (2000) *Which Lender of Last Resort for Europe?*, London: Central Banking Publications.

GOODHART, C. (1989) *Money, Information and Uncertainty*, London: Macmillan.

GOODHART, C. and ILLING, G. (eds) (2002) *Financial Crises, Contagion and the Lender of Last Resort*, Oxford: Oxford University Press.

HOESCHLER, D. and QINTYN, M. (2003) *Managing Systemic Banking Crises*, Washington, D.C.: International Monetary Fund.

HOPPER, A. and TREVERTON-JONES, T. (eds) (2011) *Outcomes-Focused Regulation*, London: The Law Society.

KEYNES, J. M. (2007) *The General Theory of Employment, Interest and Money*, Basingstoke: Palgrave Macmillan.

LEWIS, C. (1996) *Remedies and the Enforcement of European Community Law*, London: Sweet & Maxwell.

MARSHALL, A. (1997) *Principles of Economics*, New York, NY: Prometheus Books.

MILL, J. S. (2004) *Principles of Political Economy*, New York, NY: Prometheus Books.

RICARDO, D. (2004) *The Principles of Political Economy and Taxation*, New York, NY: Dover Publications.

SINANIOTIS, D. (2006) *Interim Protection of Individuals before the European and National Courts*, Alphen ann den Rijn: Kluwer Law International.

SLOAN, J. and FITZPATRICK, G. (2007) *Financial Markets and Exchange Law*, Oxford: Oxford University Press.
STIGLITZ, J. (2002) *Globalization and its Discontents*, London: Penguin Books.
TISON, M., De WULF, H., Van der ELST, C. and STEENOT, R. (eds) (2009) *Perspectives in Company Law and Financial Regulation*, Cambridge: Cambridge University Press.
TRIDIMAS, T. and NEBBIA, P. (2004) *EU Law for the Twenty-first Century: Rethinking the New Legal Order*, Oxford: Hart Publishing.
TRIDIMAS, T. (2000) 'Enforcing Community Rights in National Courts: Some Recent Developments' in O'KEEFE, D. A. and BAVASSO, A. (eds) *Judicial Review in European Union Law: Liber Amicorum in Honour of Lord Slynn*, The Hague: Kluwer International, pp. 465–79.
USHER, J. A. (2000) *The Law of Money and Financial Services in the EU*, 2nd edition, Oxford: Oxford University Press.
VINALS, J., FIECHTER, J., NARAIN, A., ELLIOT, J., TOWER, I., BOLOGNA, P. and HSU, M. (2010) *The Making of Good Supervision: Learning to Say 'No'*, Washington, D.C.: International Monetary Fund.
WALKER, G. A. (2001) *International Banking Regulation – Law, Policy and Practice*, The Hague: Kluwer International.
WEYMAN-JONES, T. (ed) (2011), *The Financial Crisis and the Regulation of Finance*, Cheltenham: Edward Elgar Publishing.

Articles

ALEXANDER, K. (2009) 'Bank resolution regimes: balancing prudential regulation and shareholders rights', *Journal of Corporate Law Studies*, vol. 9, no. 1, April, pp. 61–93.
ALLEN, W. and WOOD, G. (2006) 'Defining and Achieving Financial Stability', *Journal of Financial Stability*, vol. 2, no. 2, pp. 152–72.
AVGOULEAS, E. (2007) 'EC securities regulation, a single regime for an integrated securities market: harmonised we stand, harmonised we fail? ' Part 1 and Part 2, *JIBLR*, vol. 22, pp. 77–87 and 153–64.
AVGOULEAS, E. (2004) 'The new EC financial markets legislation and the emerging regime for capital markets', *YEL*, vol. 23, p. 321.
BIONDI, A. (1999) 'The European Court of Justice and certain national procedural limitations: Not such a tough relationship', *CMLRev*, vol. 36, p. 1271.
BLAKE, L., POINTING, J. and SINNAMON, T. (2007) 'Over-regulation and Suing the State for Negligent Legislation', *Statute Law Review*, vol. 28, p. 218.
CARIBONI, J., VANDEN BRANDEN, K., DE CESARE, M. and CAMPOLONGO, F. (2008) 'Deposit Protection in the EU: State of Play and Future Prospects', *Journal of Banking Law Regulation*, vol. 9, no. 2, pp. 82–101.
DALE, R. and WOLFE, S. (1998) 'The structure of financial regulation', *Journal of Financial Regulation and Compliance*, vol. 6, no. 4, p. 1358.
EGAN, M. and WOLF, D. (1998) 'Regulation and comitology: the EC committee system in regulatory perspective', *Columbia Journal of European Law*, vol. 4, p. 499.
EISENBEIS, R. and KAUFMAN, G. (2008) 'Cross-border banking and financial stability in the EU', *Journal of Financial Stability*, vol. 4, no. 3, pp. 168–204.
GIESEN, I. (2006) 'Regulating regulators through liability. The case for applying norma tort rules to supervisors', *Utrecht Law Review*, vol. 2, no. 1, pp. 8–31.
GOODHART, C. and SCHOENMAKER, D. (1995) 'Should the Functions of Monetary Policy and Banking Supervision be Separated?', *Oxford Economic Papers*, vol. 47, pp. 539–60.

GORMLEY, L. (2009) 'The consumer acquis and the internal market', *EBLR*, vol. 20, no. 3, pp. 409–22.
GORMLEY, L. (1994) 'Reasoning renounced? The remarkable judgment in Keck & Mithouard', *EBLR*, vol. 5, no. 3, p. 63.
GORTSOS, C. (2012) 'Current developments in European Banking Law', *ECEFIL Working Paper No. 5*.
GORTSOS, C. (2010) 'The supervision of Financial Conglomerates under European Financial Law (Directive 2002/87/EC)', *BFLR*, vol. 25, pp. 295–313.
GRANGER, M.-P. (2007) 'National applications of Francovich and the construction of a European administrative ius commune', *ELR*, vol. 32, no. 2, pp. 157–92.
GRIFFIN, P. (2001) 'The Delaware effect: Keeping the tiger in its cage. The European experience of mutual recognition in financial services', *CJEL*, vol. 7, p. 337.
HADJIEMMANUIL, C. and ANDENAS, M. (1999) 'Banking supervision and European Monetary Union', *JIBL*, vol. 1, no. 2, p. 84.
HERTIG, G. (2000) 'Regulatory competition for EU financial services', *JIEL*, vol. 3, no. 2, p. 349.
HERTIG, G. and LEE, R. (2003) 'Four predictions about the future of EU securities regulation', *Journal of Corporate Law Studies*, vol. 3, no. 2, October, pp. 359–77.
HIMSWORTH, C. (1997) 'Things fall apart: The harmonisation of Community judicial procedural protection revisited', *ELR*, vol. 22, p. 29.
HOSKINS, M. (1996) 'Tilting the balance: supremacy and national procedural rules', *ELR*, vol. 21, pp. 365–77.
INEL, B. (2003) 'Assessing the first two years of the new regulatory framework for financial markets in Europe', *JIBLR*, vol. 18, p. 363.
JOLIET, R. (1995–1996) 'The free circulation of goods: The Keck and Mithouard decision and the new directions in the case law', *CJEL*, vol. 1, p. 436.
KLAMERT, M. (2006) 'Judicial implementation of Directives and anticipatory indirect effect: connecting the dots', *CMLRev*, vol. 43, pp. 1251–75.
LANGEVOORT, D. (2009) 'The SEC, retail investors, and the institutionalization of the securities markets', *Virginia Law Review*, vol. 95, pp. 1025–83.
LANNOO, K. (2002) 'Supervising the European Financial System', *Centre for European Policy Studies Brief No. 21*.
LANNOO, K. (1998) 'Financial Supervision in EMU', *Yearbook of International Financial and Economic Law*, p. 145.
LASTRA, R. M. (2003) 'The governance structure for financial regulation and supervision in Europe', *CJEL*, vol. 10, pp. 49–68.
LASTRA, R. M. (2001) 'How much Accountability for Central Banks and Supervisors?', *Central Banking*, vol. 12, no. 2, pp. 69–75.
LASTRA, R. M. (2000) 'The Division of Responsibilities between the European Central Bank and the National Central Banks within the European System of Centra Banks', *CJEL*, vol. 6, p. 167.
LASTRA, R. M. (2000) 'The International Monetary Fund in Historical Perspective', *JIEL*, vol. 3, no. 3, p. 507.
LENAERTS, K. (2007) 'The rule of law and the coherence of the judicial system of the European Union', *CMLRev*, vol. 44, pp. 1625–59.
MANCINI, G. and KEELING, D. (1994–1995) 'Language, culture and politics in the life of the European Court of Justice', *CJEL*, vol. 1, p. 397.
MOLONEY, N. (2013) 'Resetting the location of regulatory and supervisory control over EU financial markets: lessons from five years on', *ICLQ*, vol. 62, no. 4, pp. 955–65.

NASSIMPIAN, D. (2007) 'And We Keep on Meeting: (De)Fragmenting State Liability', *ELR*, vol. 32, no. 6, pp. 819–38.

NYSTEDT, J. (2004) 'Derivative Market Competition: OTC Markets versus Organized Derivative Exchanges', *IMF Working Paper No. WP/04/61.*

OBSFELD, M. and TAYLOR, A. (2002) 'Globalization and Capital Markets', *National Bureau of Economic Research Working Paper No. 8846.*

OKAMOTO, K. (2009) 'After the bailout: regulating systemic moral hazard ', *UCLA Law Review*, vol. 57, pp. 183–236.

OLIVER, P. and ROTH, W.-H. (2004) 'The internal market and the four freedoms', *CMLRev*, vol. 41, pp. 407–41.

PADOA-SCHIOPPA, T. (1999) 'EMU and banking supervision', *International Finance*, vol. 2, no. 2, p. 295.

ROSS, M. (2006) 'Effectiveness in the European legal order(s): beyond supremacy to constitutional proportionality?', *ELR*, vol. 31, no. 4, pp. 476–98.

SÁINZ DE VICUÑA, A. (2001) 'The legal integration of financial markets of the Euro Area', *EBLR*, p. 223.

SIEMS, M. (2009) 'The foundations of securities law', *EBLR*, vol. 20, no. 1, pp. 141–71.

SINGH, D. and LAMBROSE, J. R. (2010) 'Northern Rock, Deposits and Deposit Insurance Coverage: Some Critical Reflections', *JBL*, vol. 2, pp. 55–84.

SNYDER, F. (1993) 'The effectiveness of European Community law: institutions, processes, tools and techniques', *Modern Law Review*, vol. 56, no. 1, January, pp. 19–54.

STRAETMANS, G. (2009) 'Some thoughts on the future European consumer acquis', *EBLR*, vol. 20, no. 3, pp. 423–42.

THEIL, L. (1992) 'A review of the financial services directives', *JIBL*, vol. 7, no. 12, p. 500.

THOMPSON, S. (2007) 'The globalization of securities markets: effects on investor protection', *The International Lawyer*, vol. 41, no. 4, pp. 1121–44.

TIMMERMANS, C. (2004) 'The European Union's judicial system', *CMLRev*, vol. 41, pp. 393–405.

TRACHTMAN, J. (2000) 'Regulatory competition and regulatory jurisdiction', *JIEL*, vol. 3, no. 2, p. 331.

TRIDIMAS, T. (2001) 'Judicial Review and the Community Judicature: Towards a New European Constitutionalism?', *Turku Law Journal*, vol. 3, pp. 119–29.

TRIDIMAS, T. (1996) 'The Court of Justice and judicial activism', *ELR*, vol. 21, p. 199.

TRIDIMAS, T. (1991) 'Self-regulation and investor protection in the United Kingdom: the take-over panel and the market for corporate control', *Civil Justice Quarterly*, vol. 10, p. 24.

UNBERATH, H. and JOHNSTON, A. (2007) 'The double-headed approach of the ECJ concerning consumer protection', *CMLRev*, vol. 44, pp. 1237–84.

WAGNER, W. (2010) 'Diversification at financial institutions and financial crises', *Journal of Financial Intermediation*, vol. 19, no. 3, pp. 373–86.

WAGNER, G. (2005) 'The project of harmonizing European tort law', *CMLRev*, vol. 42, pp. 1269–312.

WARD, A. (1995) 'Effective sanctions in EC law: a moving boundary in the division of competence', *ELR*, vol. 1, p. 205.

WEATHERILL, S. (1996) 'After Keck: Some thoughts on how to clarify the clarification', *CMLRev*, vol. 33, p. 885.

WEBER, R. (2009) 'Mapping and structuring international financial regulation – a theoretical approach', *EBLR*, vol. 20, no. 5, pp. 651–88.

YOKOI-ARAI, M. (2005) 'The relationship between a single financial regulator and the deposit insurance system: analyzing Japan', *The International Lawyer*, vol. 39, no. 1, pp. 63–86.

Electronic articles

ANDENAS, M. (2008) 'Harmonising and Regulating Financial Markets', http://ssrn.com/abstract=1685971.

AVGOULEAS, E. and ARNER, D. (2013) 'The Eurozone Debt Crisis and the European Banking Union: A Cautionary Tail of Failure and Reform', October, http://ssrn.com/abstract=2347937.

CHEREDNYCHENKO, O. (2010) 'The Regulation of Retail Investment Services in the EU: Towards the Improvement of Investor Rights?', http://ssrn.com/abstract=1702249.

DALVINDER, S. and LABROSSE, J. R. (2012) 'Developing a Framework for Effective Financial Crisis Management', *Warwick School of Law Research Paper No. 2012/05*, February, http://ssrn.com/abstract=2001978.

DJIKSTRA, R. and FAURE, M. (2011) 'Compensating Victims of Bankrupted Financial Institutions: A Law and Economic Analysis', pp. http://ssrn.com/abstract=1968357.

LASTRA, R. M. (2012) 'The Evolution of the European Central Bank', http://ssrn.com/abstract=2020545.

LASTRA, R. M. (2011) 'The Role of the IMF as a Global Financial Authority', www.ssrn/abstract=1617428.

TRIDIMAS, T. (2009) 'Abuse of Right in EU Law: Some Reflections with Particular Reference to Financial Law', http://ssrn.com/abstract=1438577.

Index